TRANSGENDER COMPLETE
A Virtual Handbook

by

Joanne Borden

ISBM 978-0-9914662-7-6

ACKNOWLEDGMENTS

Writing books today is not as simple as when the only possible method of recordation was a pencil or a typewriter. Dealing with computer problems, software, a wealth of new psychological and scientific information is a challenge. Even the standards of formatting and punctuation have a multitude of relatively new rules, since I was in school. Therefore, I want to thank my language expert and editor, Mr. Gregory M. Blair, M.A. Thank you also to Kathi A. Borden, Ph.D., for her psychological consultations, and Mr. Peter R. Borden, M.S. for his editing, software, and other technical assistance.

I also extend my thanks to the Long Island and New York City transgender communities for knowingly or unknowingly providing many of the quotations used.

My thanks also go to Emily Josoin-Roher, M.S.W., my therapist, whose skillful use of near silence guided me to analyze and conclude I needed to come out—needed to expose my true identity, my existence, and enter my happiness into the equation of my life. I have subsequently learned there is no substitute for the freedom of (open) honesty and that honesty helps yield true happiness.

The Long Island LGBTQ Network via Irene Tsikitas and Kerry O'Neil for introducing, supporting, and encouraging me to proceed with advocacy work in an attempt to free LGBTQ people and help others to understand that LGBTQ people are people! Except for LGBTQ people not having a run of the mill romantic preference and/or self-identity, they are just like everyone else.

Thank you to my family for your love and for allowing me to continue loving you. The acceptance of Joanne by Greg, Kathi, Pete, Ro, Brad, Nic, Jake, Blair, and Seth has been Grandpa Joanne's vehicle to complete happiness.

DEDICATION

I dedicate this book to my dear departed wife, Dr. Barbara Cooper Borden. She was an ideal life partner and we were completely compatible. She helped me write better throughout life. Some of her excellence in the command of language and her writing skills rubbed off on me as we jointly edited my business reports and proposals. It has been three decades and I still love and miss you!

TABLE OF CONTENTS

INTRODUCTION

It is hoped this book helps transgender women and transgender men, their families, friends, employers, teachers, therapists, and all others who interface with them to gain an understanding of transgenderism, transgender individuals, and the daily difficulties transgender people face. This book's purpose is also intended to help nontransgender people cope with how a transgender person in their life affects them.

Some situations that are second nature to nontransgender people present a considerable challenge to transgender people. I have endeavored to address their social, medical, ethical, religious, and legal problems.

I did not have any idea I would be writing a book, let alone a virtual handbook. This project started with research regarding the transgender phenomenon, my situation. I needed to learn how and why I became a transgender person and how I could best deal with it. I also needed to explore the possibility that I could learn from others and more easily fit in with "normal" society.

I pursued nearly all of the research I could find on the topic and soon realized I had over 40 pages of notes. Even with all this, I still did not know how I became a transgender person nor did I learn the effect it had on my behavior growing up and becoming an adult.

Surely transgenderism was not a choice. Not one transgender person I know wished for it. From a personal standpoint, I know that being a transgender woman is not simply a chosen lifestyle. I know that because I didn't want to be this way. I never did! I hoped all my life I could be like everyone else. I wanted it to go away! Something or someone, other than me, made me this way. Was it an accident? Was it God? I had to try to find the answer because all I ever wanted was to simply want what I thought other boys wanted.

After concentrating on transgender women, I began to wonder if I could learn how to cope with this basic and core conflict from transgender men—girls and women who are transgender men. Although they seem to go unnoticed in general society, I found they experience nearly the same thing and felt forced to behave similarly. Transgender women may be discussed more than transgender men in parts of this book; however, when that is true it is because early research rarely included transgender men. Even today transgender research predominantly involves transgender women. However, some modern research has found transgender men and women are similar and parallel in experiences.

My 40 pages of notes soon grew to the size of a book. I soon began to wonder how transgender people deal with romance, sports, immigration, and I went on and on to research many other facets of life we might face.

The inquisitive mind never stops. What is it inside each transgender person that always compels her or him to want to be as much a man or a woman as possible, or more like the gender they feel is inside them? What makes them want to put on the clothes of the other sex and do what seemed impossible—walk in public and, in some cases, actually live as a gender different from the sex label written on their birth certificate? Surely it is not some kind of whim or lifestyle. The difficulties, discomforts, and dangers of simply being a gal who never grew out of being a tomboy and tries to look like a guy, or being a "guy in a dress," let alone taking hormones and possibly having a risky and dangerous operation. Without a doubt, no one in her or his right mind would contemplate this unless the feelings were strong, persistent, and indelibly implanted in their mind. I call it a "Biological Imperative" to express one's inner gender.

Mike Penner[1] was a popular sport's beat writer for the Los Angeles Times for 25 years before announcing he would transition (i.e., live as a woman). He said one of his transgender friends put it best.

> The best and simplest explanation I have heard: We are born with this, we fight it as long as we can, and in the end it wins. I gave it as good a fight as I possibly could. I went more than 40 hard rounds with it. Eventually, though, you realize you are only fighting yourself and your happiness and your mental health—a no win situation any way you look at it. When you reach the point when one gender causes heartache and unbearable discomfort, and the other sex brings more joy and fulfillment than you ever imagined possible, it shouldn't take two tons of bricks to fall in order to know what to do. It always wins!

> Penner asked, "How do you go about sharing your most important truth, one you spent a lifetime trying to keep deeply buried, to a world that has grown familiar and comfortable with your facade?"

Mike Penner's 2007 transition had little impact on public opinion compared to Caitlyn Jenner's 2015 transition. Jenner's transition was widely publicized. As a result most people in this country are now aware of transgenderism.

Many of us struggled to drive the need to be the other sex out of our lives all of our lives. We fought with all of our strength, but our struggle always resulted in failure. Most transgender men and transgender women experience that frustration. From the Internet, two transgender women emailed a description describing the difficulty in controlling their need.[2]

> I have tried many times to stop being a crossdresser to no avail. I am what I am and you can't change who you are deep inside.

> I had to find an inner strength to do what I knew I had to do. It is not easy but the woman inside will have her way one way or another. If you do not let her out she will push her [way] out.

The strong, persistent, and indelible feelings are by no means those of the author alone. I have included roughly 180 quotations of transgender individuals who also found the feeling to be ineradicable. They all describe similar incidents such as those quotes immediately above. Most were emailed to me and many are taken from Internet groups, where I usually solicited the responses. Similar emailed quotations are placed throughout the discussions to illustrate and emphasize a point made by me, by a researcher, or by an educator.

Since a great many transgender individuals desire anonymity, credits for these quotations are not cited. Furthermore, I do not correct these quotations. I mostly copy them as received. I only add, in brackets, when I feel something needs clarification. I feel I should not distract from the authenticity and power of the statement, but I do correct punctuation and other details to improve comprehension.

Usually the world recognizes people as either being a woman or a man, period! Only the thinking is binary because we are given no other choice. There is no other choice! However, the real world is not like that. It is not made up of purely feminine and purely masculine people. Most people are not either. They are somewhere in between, some sort of blending of the two sexes, or something else. Furthermore, I dislike the frequently used term "opposite sex" because that indicates the two choices are in opposition to each other and I don't wish to continue the thought that the sexes are opposed to each other. They aren't! They are different. Saying "different sex" or "another sex" describes every blend in between the two extremes. However, I reluctantly use the "other sex" in most places for better understanding, since most people think of sex in binary terms—male or female.

What a dilemma! I found it was simply not possible to rid my mind of the need to express my femininity. It was equally impossible to realize my feminine need, since I thought the ridicule, embarrassment, and subsequent shame would be unbearable. When you think about it, it is amazing that most transgender people maintain any semblance of sanity with such a basic conflict. Some are not as fortunate as I and are self-destructive, even suicidal. An unusually high number of transgender women and men die as a result of violence or suicide by the time they are 30 years old. Some estimates run to 50% and is known as the "50% Rule. However, the number is disputed and no study has been found to verify the "50% Rule." Still, the number of deaths in published studies[3] is very high compared to the occurrence in the general population. A study conducted in 2016 found 41.0 % of transgender people attempted suicide during their life time. This was compared to 1.6% of the general public.

Personally, I found every indication was that I must get rid of the desire to be a woman; however, the need to express my femininity always seemed to return. It is a mystery that has always baffled me. Why was it impossible to put the need out of my mind, permanently? I was able to stop smoking in spite of how much I liked it. I overcame a 30 year nicotine addiction and a long term habit of puffing reinforced 10 million times over several decades. I was able to quit smoking cold turkey. There are many other things that tempt me, but I have little or no trouble resisting them. I was always a self-disciplined person in other situations, but the need to express my femininity was uncontrollable. Why? I have been told that I couldn't resist needing to be feminine because it is part of me. That still doesn't explain why? Why is it "part of me?" Why me?

A year of weekly therapy sessions helped me to accept myself—accept my femininity as a fact and recognize I suffer from a good deal of shame concerning my wanting to be a woman, but my therapy never got close to answering my questions.

It is said the key to success starts with self-knowledge. If you have gender issues, they need to be addressed. It is hard but necessary work. I can testify that the distress will likely only get worse as the years progress. Therefore, I embarked on this research project to try to find the answers. Some of the following is based on this research and some of it is my impression of the transgender people around me. Also included is how other transgender people express their feelings regarding the research issues discussed.

The public seems to be more tolerant of female-to-male transgender people than male-to-female. Lynn Conway[4] is an activist in the transgender community. In an interview conducted by author Joanne Herman,[5] she said,

> While accepting of girls who present as 'tomboys,' our society still has incredibly deep hang-ups about boys presenting in a feminine way. Perhaps that is why there is more information on and opinions from transgender women than from transgender men. Information is plentiful; however, opinion from transgender men is much sparser. I believe there is more than enough bias and violence against transgender men, but the hate for transgender women and the perceived threat is greater.

Lately, we have begun to hear more from and about transgender men and that is a good thing for them and the transgender community as a whole. The more visible we are, the easier it is for people to accept and tolerate us, even if they do not understand us. The experience of Chas Bono has helped the public understand transgenderism is more than a whim. It is the first time many people heard of girls/women who present as boys/men because they assimilate so well. The publicity Bono attracted may have prompted the Boy Scouts of America to accept transgender boys into the Boy Scouts and Cub Scouts in January, 2017.

Aside from that, it is obvious and remarkable to note how similar the male-to-female transgender person is to the female-to-male transgender person. It is also remarkable to note how similar the experiences of the people within each sex group are to each other all through life.

I acknowledge my personal relationship to this topic may create biases in my handling of various topics. Therefore, I explore all alternative thoughts, regardless of how remote they may seem. I do this because I know how easily one can deceive one's self into believing what is thought of as good, proper, and desirable. I am not immune to this human failing, rationalization. The following chapters explore several aspects of being a transgender person. The approach generally traces scientific discovery as well as various researchers' theories regarding, for instance, how and when a transgender person becomes a transgender person. Throughout the book I relate experiences and thoughts of people in the transgender community, including mine. Furthermore, the different situations transgender people face are discussed and ideas are presented regarding how to best deal with them.

Transgender people are thought to be a minuscule population. This is generally based on old hospital records of sexual reassignment operations. I believe the number of transgender people is grossly underestimated because society attaches a high level of shame to transgender individuals resulting in a huge silent population. The controversial size of the transgender population is addressed in Appendix IV, Transgender Population. It is not fully addressed in the body of this book because the number of transgender people does not impact the need for understanding and living with transgenderism.

I have tried to include every source used in the Endnotes. Most of what I have written rests on the shoulders of the many authors, researchers, educators, and others who came before me. I look forward to this book helping transgender women and transgender men understand themselves, accept their transgenderism as a gift rather than a curse, and live happier lives because they are a transgender person. To contact the author with comments or reprint permission, she has a Gmail dot com account under the name of Reach Joanne (one word). It is gratifying to anticipate students, teachers, doctors, and everyone who interacts with a transgender person will gain a better understanding and acceptance of transgenderism and transgender people. Furthermore, it is especially fulfilling to know that after reading this book parents, spouses, children, siblings, friends, and all others who have a relationship or interface with a transgender person may be more prone to accept that person unconditionally. After all, the fact that he or she is a transgender person, comprised of both sexes, frequently is a key reason you became close to that person in the first place.

CHAPTER 1, The Meaning of Sex, Gender, and Transgender

The differences between sex and gender are at the core of the transgender issue. You need to first understand gender as a separate concept from sex, before you can properly understand transgenderism.

Sex Label Given at Birth

In a good deal of literature and lectures we read and hear the phrase, "sex assigned at birth." However, sex is not *assigned* at birth! A sex *label* is assigned at birth. No one can *assign* sex because sex is developed in the mother's womb starting at conception and depends on a chromosome supplied by the father. Gender, on the other hand, is thought to develop somewhere during the gestation process (i.e., discussed more fully later) and discovered by the child after birth.

How we develop into a girl or a boy physically is a complicated process. Experts in the field tell us that determining sex all comes down to our genes. Genes are a part of each chromosome, and chromosomes are in every cell of our body. Genes, influenced by our DNA, carry the code of the things we inherit from our parents. They are an important influence regarding how we will develop and how we will look. They affect how we start life before birth and how we grow afterwards. Genes affect our development as girls or boys. Our sex label is generally determined at birth based on our visible sex organs, is noted on our birth certificate, and later on our driver's license and other documents as either a female or a male. There is no other choice and we have no "say" in it. It just is!

A simplified view of the development of the fertilized egg into a baby is given below to provide a sense of the complexity of the process.

From the start, in the mother's womb, all embryos are physically equipped to develop into either a female or a male. For example, we have both Mullerian ducts and Wolffian ducts. The Mullerian ducts are used by the female and Wolffian ducts by the male. The female's Wolffian ducts and the male's Mullerian ducts are not needed and are allowed to "dissolve" and disappear as the fetus develops.

However, it is genes that determine which sex it will be and genes are controlled (e.g., turned on and off) by the release of chemicals from DNA and other genes. It has been understood for a long time that genes also affect the way our bodies manufacture and use hormones. When female genes are present, they will start the production of estrogen, a female hormone, and eventually a girl will be born. If testosterone, a male hormone, is produced, eventually a boy will be born.

The development of our sex label is a complex process which is ultimately based on our genitals. When the mother's egg is fertilized and during the first 3 weeks, the mother's mRNA and proteins directly control the stages of the embryo's development. After that, the embryo's own DNA takes over.

At 8 weeks, the female starts developing her Mullerian ducts and the male starts developing his Wolffian ducts. However, the fetus is labeled neither male nor female yet. However, a small group of cells called the "indifferent gonads" begin to form and can ultimately develop either way to become ovaries or testicles.

The gonad contains supporting cells that in time will produce hormones, the so-called gonadotropins. Gonadotropins stimulate the growth and activity of the gonads, especially hormones that stimulate the function of the ovaries or testes.

The female fetal development has been studied far less than male development. Until about 30 years ago, every embryo was believed to develop into a female, if not "disturbed" by male influences (hormones).

The male "branched off" from the female and developed differently. At that time, the researchers said Adam evolved from Eve, not the other way around. (Note: according to the Hebrew Bible, the second person created by God was Eve. Her husband was Adam, from whose rib God created her).

Was the easy agreement with this thinking another case of the subjugation of women? Did this imply the female continued along her passive path, while the male branched out and developed to a higher level? Anne Fausto-Sterling, Ph.D.[1] Professor of Biology and Gender Studies at Brown University, criticized the researchers regarding female development as follows:

> The old idea that femaleness is simply the absence of maleness is out of date. If there are two X chromosomes, then a specific process takes place in producing a girl.

As Rose, Lewontin, and Kamin[2] point out, there is a specific feminization process, the development of the embryo into a girl or a boy is a different, but a parallel process.

At 6 weeks of gestation, the girl's Wolffian ducts, that only the male needs, degenerates and the Mullerian ducts develop toward the Fallopian tubes, uterus and vagina. There is also a rise in estrogens at about 6 weeks. By the 12th week, the indifferent gonad begins to develop into an ovary. Meanwhile, the supporting cells form the cells that will surround the ova (i.e., granulosa cells). The chromosomes in the gamete cells begin to separate, but they cease their activity until puberty.

Much more is known about male development. At 6 weeks, the sex determining region "Y" gene (SRY gene) promotes a protein (i.e., H-Y antigen), which binds to the DNA molecule, causing it to bend and affect 19 different genes. The actual sequence of events is still largely unknown, but the hormone-producing cells of the indifferent gonad become the primitive testes (i.e., Leydig cells), while the supporting cells eventually become the sperm producers (i.e., Sertoli cells). There is a rise in androgens (male hormones) paralleling the female rise in estrogens and a hormone is produced that degenerate the Mullerian ducts (i.e., Mullerian inhibiting factor) that only the female needs.

At 8 weeks, the embryo is referred to as a fetus and most of the features of the adult are visible.

Until the 8th week, the external genitalia grow identically for both sexes, but by the 12th week, a difference can be noted. For a female, the genital tubule develops into a clitoris, while the urogenital membrane develops towards forming the labia. For the male, an enzyme, "5-alpha reductase," converts testosterone to dihydrotestosterone and the genital tubule, that became the clitoris in the female, becomes a penis in the male. At this time, the urogenital membrane that became the female's labia becomes the male's scrotum.

DNA is an important part of this process. It is known that one's DNA shapes many distinctive human qualities. Its sequence of chemicals turns gene switches on and off. A slight change in the DNA can cause major changes. For example, a "slight" DNA change can even result in the production of a completely different species (i.e., the production of a chicken or a panther). It can also cause changes that are far less dramatic. For example, for the male, the DNA chemicals signal the sex determining region Y gene (i.e., the SRY gene) to turn "on," which in turn triggers the release of testosterone. This and the interactions of the SRY gene with other genes determine the development of the male sex.

Somewhere in this process, a baby's brain is "wired" to be either a boy or a girl.

The above may sound complicated; however, it has been grossly oversimplified here. Besides imparting basic information regarding fetal sexual development, it is here to indicate the complexity of fetal development. This complexity, compounded by the role of DNA, its processes, its timing, and other factors provides abundant opportunities for variations. Is a transgender child produced by a variation in this process? Is it a small change in the DNA, a slight change in the composition of the DNA chemicals, a difference from the ideal sequence of DNA chemical signals that are sent to the genes? Is it the hormone "strength" itself, the timing of the hormone release, or is it another variation in this process that causes a trace of maleness in some females' brains and femaleness in some males' brains, thus resulting in a transgender child? Perhaps it is all of the above, some of the above, or none of the above and something else. Although some researchers believe in an answer, no one has a proven the answer, yet.

Gender Identity

The sex label assigned at birth is based on one's genitals. On the other hand, gender identity is the sex with which you identify. When a child first becomes aware that there are boy children and girl children, he or she knows which it is. Children don't choose a gender—they know their gender intuitively. it is a feeling "inside." That is, what you feel you are or should be. gender is even defined differently in different cultures. Native Americans[3] had several tribes that dealt with gender in ways we are just beginning to appreciate.

Native American tribes of Southwestern United States (Pueblos) included Mujaderos[4] (in Spanish, "mujer" is a woman and "eros" is the ending for male words, such as caballeros), so named by the Spanish conquistadors. The Spaniards, observed young bucks who were made to ride horses bare back continually and masturbate excessively. The genital irritation from riding bare back plus the weakening of their genitals from overuse, caused them to trade some of their male secondary sex characteristics (e.g., a beard) for feminine ones (e.g., breasts). They lived and worked among the women.

They were totally accepted as women in that society and filled the feminine role in all aspects of life. (Note to aspiring transgender girls: Don't rush out and buy a horse, yet!).

The Navajos of the southwestern United States recognized three sexes. Nadles (i.e., Intersex people, formerly called hermaphrodites) a third classification, which was sometimes considered both male and female and at other times neither. Their approach to something in addition to female and male is considered an enlightened and humanistic approach. The Nadles had a special status, specific tasks, and clothing styles. They were often consulted for their wisdom and skills.

If you were a Sioux, you could choose whether you lived as a woman or a man. Women could fight alongside the men and have wives. Other physical males lived their lives as women. Most people have heard such people referred to as "two spirited." This term, previously used only by some tribes, was adopted at the Intertribal Conference of 1990, to be used to describe the sexual variants in all Native American tribes.

Shamen among the Cheyenne, Navajo, Pawnee, Lacota, Ute, and many other less known tribes, exhibited a two spirit identity. That is, they assumed the dress, attributes, role, or function of the sex other than the one they were labeled with at birth. It is believed the Two Spirited Shamen were so widespread in the tribes of the Americas, and indeed in the world, that it is believed to have been recognized in ancient times. Such two spirit Shamen were thought to be especially powerful. They were highly respected and sought out in their tribes. Africa and other parts of the world had Shamen also.

In these cultures, what we now call a transgender person had a recognized place in society. However, after the Spaniards came, many tribes imported transphobia and homophobia from contact with the Europeans. Early records of the Spanish conquerors reflected such acculturation of Native American tribes.

Some other cultures included a "third" sex. They included the Sekrata of Madagascar, the Mahu of Tahiti, the Sererr of Kenya.[4] Ancient India had several names for the third sex.[5] The Spaniards, English, other European countries, and Islamic nations introduced transphobia and homophobia in India, the Pacific Islands, Africa as well as the Americas through their invasions.

In our culture, we recently separated the meanings of gender and sex and developed the concept of gender identity to deal with the fact that some people identify with a sex different from the label given to them at birth. Gender describes what you feel you are, should be, or want to be. Sex describes the sex organs with which you were born.

The definition favored by some feminists is that gender is the result of social conditioning. However, that has been shown to be false and the feminist theory is changing with the rest of the culture. The key to gender identity is in genetics and the workings of the brain. In the new conventional wisdom, we are all prewired for many things, including gender, previously thought to be in the realm of upbringing, choice, or experience.

Transgender researchers insist transgenderism is biologically implanted in the brain during the development of the fetus. The idea that gender identity is solely constructed by social experience is considered outmoded, although some laymen cling to that idea.

I feel both the biological and socialization theories are compatible. Our brains are wired to be predisposed toward one sex or the other and this has a major effect on our sex specific behaviors by the time we are born. Our behavior is later modified after we are born by interaction with others, which can modify our neurons and general brain wiring through repetition.

As an example of how this modification occurs can be seen in how you learn to touch type on a computer. Each time you think of a specific letter, it becomes associated with a specific hand, then a specific finger on that hand, and finally, the appropriate position of the hand before striking the proper key. As you repeat this over and over, your brain assigns more neurons to that activity, until you have laid new circuits between these neurons. Now, when you sit at a keyboard and type the correct letters, you bypass the process of thinking about the proper hand, finger, and position of the hand. It becomes "second nature" to the typist. It is automatic, so to speak.

A similar thing happens with our behavior, which is dictated by our gender. Even before learning to speak, parental facial expressions and tone of voice can reinforce or discourage aspects of an infant's behavior. Homo sapiens (that's us) were the first to have this ability. Boys are expected to be more daring. Parents allow and thus signal approval. They only discourage the behavior if the boy will injure himself. On the other hand, girls are reinforced with the behavior expected of girls. It is called "girl behavior." Even before verbal communication is established, a parent signals approval or disapproval and reinforces or discourages certain behavior. In this sense, socialization plays a part in ultimate gender development. However, this conditioning does not and cannot change the basic "wiring" of the brain toward gender. In the case of transgender children, socialization does not "rewire" their brain variation either. It can, however, reinforce or moderate it.

As described in her book, *The Female Brain,* Louann Brizendine, MD,[6] said,

> There is no unisex brain. . . . Girls arrive already wired as girls, and boys arrive already wired as boys. Their brains are different by the time they're born, and their brains are what drive their impulses, values, and their very reality.
>
> The brain's first organizing principle is clearly genes plus hormones, but we can't ignore the further sculpting of the brain resulting from our interactions with other people and with our environment. A parent's or caregiver's tone of voice, touch, and words help organize an infant's brain. . . . Scientists still don't know exactly how much reshaping can occur to the brain nature gave us. We know enough to see that the fundamentally misconceived nature versus nurture debate should be abandoned: child development is inextricably both.

Most people use sex and gender interchangeably. They consider them to mean the same thing. However, they're not the same any longer. Commonly, gender is considered a psychological concept. The personal thought of one's self as a male, female, both, or neither. It should not be thought of as synonymous with the term "sex," since gender is only within the mind and does not have to be the same as ones label assigned at birth based one's genitals. Simply put, gender is solely what's going on in your head and sex is a nonneurological thing. However, they weren't always thought of separately.

In 1955, John Money, Ph.D.,[7] first used the term "gender" to discuss sexual roles. One's sexual role was considered one of two discrete, nonoverlapping congenital attributes—male or female. This is visually determined by one's primary sex characteristics. These two mutually exclusive categories allowed for no variation. You were either one or the other—a girl or a boy.

Later, we began to see one's gender not as either male or female, but as a blending, analogous to a "gray scale." But gender still basically consisted of either male or female for almost all people. There was thought that a tiny minority of the population is somewhere between—in the gray area. Most usually the in-between people were like the Nadels of the Navajos. Actually, they were Intersex people, which were previously referred to as hermaphrodites.

However, after a review of current research and more experience with both gender variant and traditional individuals, researchers have been led to see gender not as either/or, male or female, but as a mix of male and female development within the same individual. Females who identify as males and males who identify as females exist. Each is a combination of both a male and a female to varying degrees. So, with that in mind, a person's gender and sex may not be the same. This is where we get into the transgender realm.

Transgender

When a female (physically) identifies to a degree as a man, he is referred to as a transgender man, or a trans man. When a male (physically) identifies himself as a woman, she is referred to as a transgender woman or a trans woman. The general rule is both should take the pronouns appropriate to their inner gender (i.e., their gender identity, not their sex). Some people feel they are neither male nor female and prefer "gender neutral" pronouns that they create, such as "ze" and "hir." Furthermore, there are some who believe people will be less sexist if sex specific pronouns were not used (i.e., this is based on Relativism,[8] which states our perception and our thinking are determined by our language). However, that is a poor argument, since Chinese, and several other languages, are genderless, while their societies are even more patriarchal than in the western world. My feeling is sex-differentiating pronouns are really unnecessary; however, they do not contribute to a society's prejudice based on sex. I feel the only criteria for the use of pronouns that are proper are the ones the individual prefers.

The word transgender is also a relatively new term. Its use started in the 1960s and 1970s. Its present use as an umbrella term to describe all gender variant people evolved in about 1990. At that time, it was adopted to bring the many small groups of gender variant people together under a single banner. It was thought that by establishing a single large group they would have more political and social leverage. The word transgender is used basically for political alliances.

If you moved any distance away from your physical sex organs you fit under the transgender banner. The gender variant groups include male-to-female (MtF) and female-to-male (FtM) transsexuals, female and male crossdressers, drag queens/kings, and all people with an unconventional gender expression including nontransgender and nonhomosexual people.

Aside from the political and social need, I believe the development of the term transgender was much needed because it will eventually be found it describes a single phenomenon (this is explained in more detail later).

The transgender phenomenon varies from slight to intense due to completely variable congenital factors plus completely variable sociological factors. The line separating the subcategories is not precise and thus somewhat subjective; however, they do have value in describing the general mix of nature and nurture. The sociologic factor may change during the lifetime of a transgender person, but not the fact that nature and nurture are both present.

The congenital transgender "intensity" is reinforced and/or moderated by other congenital factors, just as the sociological factors are influenced both ways by the interaction of many factors, resulting in individual differences.

In the final analysis, I am certain researchers will prove we are all different, but the result of the same highly variable factors.

Sometimes bias is voiced by one subgroup against another subgroups. This is inappropriate and self-destructive, since they are all products of the same phenomenon.

At one time, all sex and gender variants were lumped together. They were considered one category and simply a variation from the "normal." Magnus Hirschfeld[9] coined the word "Transvestite" in 1910. He separated homosexuals from transvestites and properly recognized the two involved different manifestations of the sex/gender spectrum. Homosexuals involve same-sex intimacy, whereas transvestites cannot be defined by sexual preference. That is, they are composed of individuals who prefer same sex intimacy, different sex intimacy, both, or neither.

Harry Benjamin,[10] a doctor who was influenced by Magnus Hirschfeld's work, studied transvestites in the 1950s. He is famous for establishing criteria specifying who is eligible for a sex reassignment operation and what that person must do prior to being granted an operation. He felt a doctor needs to be as sure as possible that changing a person's sex is appropriate for that specific individual. A doctor's prime duty is premium non nocere (first, do no harm).

Keeping do no harm foremost in his mind, Benjamin categorized males into seven groups. The main purpose of his 17 year study was to establish criteria for who should properly have a genital operation. He established a separate category for each "type" of gender variant individual. Three of the seven categories he established were for what he called transsexuals, three for transvestites, and a seventh category for the average man.

Benjamin described each category in detail. The 3 transvestite types are: Transvestite Pseudo—Type I, Transvestite Fetishistic—Type II, and Transvestite True—Type III. The 3 transsexual categories are: Nonsurgical—Type IV, True Transsexual Moderate Intensity—Type V, and another True Transsexual High Intensity—Type VI. His Type VI described the genital operation candidates. Currently, the use of the term transsexual is starting to be used to indicate only Type VI individuals, and in some cases, Type V.

I couldn't fit myself in any one category or even between two adjacent categories. I was mostly in category V, but some part in most other categories and so were other people I know quite well. On the surface, Benjamin's categories may seem contrived, even though they are used widely. He recognized this when he added, "It must be emphasized again that the remaining six types are not and never can be sharply separated."

However, he accomplished his main purpose, which was to distinguish between transsexuals who need and sought a genital (and/or breast surgery) from all other people. Benjamin also developed a procedure surgical candidates must follow for 1 year before being allowed genital or breast surgery (e.g., being on hormone therapy plus living and working full time as a woman (for genital surgery). These standards of care were relaxed in 2012, when Revision 7 to The Standards of Care was issued.

Now, lengthy psychotherapy is not required for hormone therapy. The prescribing doctor can make that determination. Furthermore, living full-time as a woman or man for a year is no longer required a for genital or breast removal operation, but recommended.

Some people Benjamin called "transsexual" reject that label and refer to themselves as a "transgender person," since they feel their transgenderism has to do with gender and has nothing to do with sex. Christine Jorgenson, the first transsexual person to publicly announce her genital operation, insisted on being called a transgender person and gave the same reason. Others reject the term transgender because "trans" implies a crossing from one gender to another, when they feel they were always the gender in their mind. Some object to the term "male to female" or "female-to-male" for the same reason and prefer the term "affirmed females" or "affirmed males."

There is nothing wrong with viewing yourself any way you prefer or even accepting the terms of others, if you wish, but to debate this is simply a waste of energy.

Some people still believe transgenderism is caused by how a child is raised. This has been disproved. Intersex children were frequently altered just after birth to be female because a vagina was surgically easier to construct successfully than male genitalia. In some cases, their true gender was not known and, at the time, it was further believed gender identity is societally based. They were subsequently raised as girls. Later in life, those who should have remained boys generally behaved like a female-to-male transgender persons and sought their true male identity.

The most famous case was written about by Dr. John Money, who wrote a 1955 paper titled, "Sexual Behavior and Orientation as Male or Female Does Not Have an Innate, Instinctive Basis." He believed we learn whether we are male or female "in the course of the various experiences of growing up."

In 1967, Money launched a famous experiment, the Reimer Case. The parents of an infant, whose penis was damaged beyond repair during a circumcision, consulted him. He advised them to have the baby castrated and later have surgeons construct a vagina and give him feminizing hormones. He further advised they never tell "her" of the accident at birth and raise the child as a girl.

Money followed the case and wrote several articles, since the child seemed to adapt to the female role by playing with dolls, liking dresses, etc., thus proving his theory. Money's book *Sexual Signatures* expounded on the success of his theory. Time Magazine even wrote that this case made a strong argument for the belief that sex differences are "immutably set by the genes at conception" is questionable. However, a Rolling Stone reporter, John Colapinto,[11] reported the true facts in his popular book, *As Nature Made Him.*

He showed that David Reimer never adjusted to being a girl. He wanted to play with his brother's toys and exhibited other characteristics of a young boy. At school, he was a discipline problem. He fought with and beat up other kids. David, at 14, became seriously isolated and depressed. His parents finally told him the truth about his accident at birth. He said knowing the truth gave him a measure of relief. He later had phalloplasty performed and married a woman. However, he died at the age of 38. He shot himself.

In 1934, a group of medical reseachers[12] cited another case of a genetic male born with hypospadias (i.e., the urethra did not travel inside the penis). He was both dressed and treated in every way as a girl from birth. At the age of 14, he started to doubt his sex label. He started to show all the signs of a boy's interests as was possible for his situation. In spite of pressure from his parents, he insisted his sex was male. After assuming the male role, he adjusted easily without the need for any psychotherapy.

More cases are cited in the literature that clearly show there is an inborn predisposition to being male or female regardless of sexual assignment, rearing or any other influence. In addition, the transition to one's true gender from another is generally made smoothly and without psychological problems.

The experience with Reimer, other cases, and intersex children prove the way you are raised does not determine your gender. You are not born neutral and you do not learn your gender identity after birth.

Lipsitt and Levy[13] and several other researchers in several locations found a marked difference between girls and boys during the first few days of life. Boys had greater strength than girls and girls had a lower threshold to stimuli than boys. These and similar differences in early exposure to life are thought to continue throughout life and also influence us regarding our gender roles.

Dr. Milton Diamond,[14] an expert on human sexuality at the John A. Burns School of Medicine, University of Hawaii, encapsulated this view in an interview on the BBC in 1980,

> Maybe we really have to think . . . that we don't come to this world neutral, that we come to this world with some degree of maleness and femaleness which will transcend whatever society wants to put into [us].

Dr. William Reiner[15] is an urologist who also practices Psychiatry. He devoted his career to treating children born with irregular genitals such as a scrotum along with a phallus that resembled a clitoris, micropenis, genetic males without a penis, and cloacal exstrophy (children born without genitalia and a pelvic opening where the genitals should be). He followed up a group of male children, who could not function sexually as such. Being males, they developed as males everywhere except in the pelvic region. In the womb, they were subject to the usual male androgen exposure and thus were males. Such babies were usually treated socially, legally, and surgically with bilateral castration and feminizing genitoplasty. They were raised as girls. Sometimes even the parents didn't know of their birth condition.

Doctor Reiner followed a group of 24 children who were born male, but raised as girls. Later in life, he found thirteen declared themselves to be boys, seven declared themselves girls, two refused to declare any gender identity, one seven year old wanted to live as a boy, and one child died. In total, 60% of these children, raised as girls without a penis or any knowledge of their genital condition at birth, identified as males. Even though they did not have a clue regarding their having atypical genitalia at birth, apparently the in-utero exposure to testosterone was stronger than all their feminine education and all their conditioning by being treated as girls from birth to the time of the follow up. No one denies "learning" influences gender development; however, no amount of such exposure can change the brain's wiring.

People might wonder why only 60% of the children changed to male. This result challenges the premise of the superiority of exposure to testosterone over socialization because they all did not change to be male.

Milton Diamond explains that social pressures are different for each individual. There is an infinite number of ways individuals respond to the interaction of hereditary and social factors. There are a number of individuals who rightly feel they would not change genders, since the social, emotional, and other costs to them are too high. Diamond continued with,

> We can only repeat that there is a great deal of varying response to the interaction of nature and nurture.

To dramatize the inherent quality of gender, the case of one of the children in the Reiner study, Kayla, at seven years of age, exhibited all the characteristic behavior of a boy. Kayla, as part of the study, had been castrated and was being raised as a girl. "She" was not a happy child, was aggressive, and would fight. "She" played with cars and trucks, not the dolls "she" was given. Furthermore, "she" chose a boy's name and insisted "her" schoolmates call "her" that. Finally, "she" would not go to school at all.

Reiner gave Kayla a battery of psychological tests and found "she" overwhelmingly measured as a male. When he told Kayla's parents the results, they decided to tell Kayla "she" was born a boy. They asked Reiner to tell "her." Reiner explained to Kayla that when "she" was born, "she" did not have a penis; therefore "her" doctors and parents had decided to raise "her" as a girl, since as a boy she would be either teased by other boys or never be able to undress before another person. From the John Hopkins Magazine article, Reiner recalled,

> His eyes opened about as wide as eyes could open. He climbed into my lap and wrapped his arms around me and stayed like that for half an hour.

This convinced Reiner that you are born either a boy or a girl, and, regardless of surgery or rearing, you remain that way. He added,

> When you work with these kids, you see that they're not making a decision, they have always known. The sense of what you are (boy or girl) is a crucial existential aspect of humanity. It is powerful and inborn. . . . The absence or presence of a penis is incidental. The most important sex organ is the brain.

Transgenderism is probably the most stigmatized of the Lesbian, Gay, Bisexual, Transgender, and Queer (LGBTQ) groups because it is rarely understood. Transgender individuals rarely understand it themselves, so how can they possibly explain it to others and obtain more widespread acceptance. Since it is rarely understood, it allows many false beliefs to contribute to the group's problems.

After reading and studying a good deal of transgender material, I conclude that when a baby first recognizes that there are boys and girls, he or she identifies with one or the other. The child does not select a gender. The child knows the gender he or she is intuitively—it's automatic!

The myth that anyone who is a transgender person is mentally ill has no basis in fact. The transgender population has been found to be different, but sane (as described in the American

Psychiatric Association's Diagnostic and Statistical Manual Number V). Although disputed in some quarters, as a group, transgender people have been found to have a superior intellect (Jennifer Diane Reitz, Money, et al., Collaer, et al.[16]), which frequently leads them to occupy responsible positions requiring a stable personality. The American Psychological Association defines a mental illness as a condition causing distress or disability. Few of the great number of transgender women and men I have been in contact with would fit this criterion.

Furthermore, there are some people who believe transgender people are sex fiends and pedophiles. There may be sex criminals who are mistaken for transgender people because they sometimes pose as women to put their prey off guard; however, it is rare, if ever, that there are reports of cases of transgender individuals committing sexual crimes against anyone, especially children. Transgender women like genetic women tend to be nurturing and are rarely child abusers. Police and human rights organizations reports indicate there has been no incidents of assault on women or children either before or after transgender human rights laws were passed from the first 1993 law to the present day (see Appendix VI-Survey—No Assaults Due To Transgender Nondiscrimination Laws).

The most prevalent misconception is that if you are a transgender person, you are gay/lesbian because you want same sex intimacy to appear to be heterosexual. This misconception grew from the fact that at one time you had to be gay to qualify for a genital operation. As a result, many transgender people pretended to be gay in order to get the desired operation. Furthermore to this, at one time homosexuality and transgenderism were thought to be the same thing. But that was over 100 years ago.

There is no doubt that the transgender population includes some members who are gay/lesbian, some mentally ill, some sex offenders, and, I suspect, even some are pedophiles. However, I believe you will find the same thing, in roughly the same proportion, in the general population. Transgender individuals are exactly the same as anyone else in the general population, except for the mismatch of their sex organs and their gender identity. That is, they feel their gender is different from the physical indications of their gender.

Comparison of Gender and Sex

Some differentiate the sex label assigned at birth and gender (identity) in simplistic fashion: gender is between your ears and sex is between your legs. We all know what sex is indicated by the baby's genitals. If modern technology did not reveal it before birth, when a baby is born the doctor takes one look at the baby's genitals and knows, with certainty, the child's sex. Your genitals are a good indication of gender. Genitals can be surgically altered to indicate a different sex, but your chromosomes and a good deal of your body remains your original sex indicator. Since the custom is to keep ones genitals covered, in general society it is possible to assume a life as a different sex without an operation. It is not always easy, but it can be done if all outward appearances—such as hair, makeup, clothes, gestures, and voice—are trained to be like the other sex. In reality, outward appearances are unimportant only for other people. Aside from other people, your true gender is solely the gender you feel inside.

Gender is real but it is not as visible as gender indicators (e.g., genitals, clothing, etc.) are. Therefore, it is more difficult for some people to understand. Gender is how you identify yourself. The way you feel about yourself. Gender identity, as distinguished from physical sex, is often described as one's subjective sense of one's own sex. You have no way of demonstrating or proving this "feeling." It is just there! Dr. Carl W. Bushong,[18] a psychologist, compared this subjective sense of gender to pain. He said,

> Pain is unambiguously felt but one is unable to prove it or display it to others.

With some "girls" who are wired to be males, their gender identity started with believing that they are boys. They believe they will develop just as boys do. When they are disappointed that they do not grow a penis and grow breasts instead, they realize that they may think and feel they are boys, but the boy is only on the inside and is invisible to the rest of the world. Transgender girls experience the same conflict. They are sure something is wrong with them when they don't get breasts like their sister. Jenifer Rietz, in her life story said,

> Early in the morning, the teacher asked the class to line up, boys on one side and girls on the other, for some sort of game. I stood with the girls, of course. When this caused the predictable problem, I threw quite a tantrum, and the

teacher, at a loss, had me stand in the Venetian slatted closet until she said otherwise. I stood there, crying, seeing the classroom through thin wooden slats, for most of the day.

Transgender men wrote,

I recall as a very small child, maybe three years old, looking in the mirror at my butt length hair and thinking about why none of the other boys had long hair like me.

[At] about 12 years old, my body started to change . . . to look more and more like a girl. [I] didn't like it at all.

Several transgender women also wrote the following about their youth. Some experiences exactly paralleled the experienced of transgender boys:

In kindergarten the teacher had the girls curtsey and stand to one side of the room. The boys were instructed to bow and stand on the other side of the room. I naturally curtsied and stood with the girls. When the teacher corrected me, all the boys laughed. At that moment I knew I had a secret.

I know I thought that [I] would be getting breast as all the girls around me were. How devastated I was when I did not. What was wrong? Why did they get them and I did not? From that moment I wondered why them but not me, even up till I found out that I was trans.

I wondered why I was not allowed to wear female things. I feel as I am a woman so why? Just because I [am] not in the right body. That is not fair.

The major early difference between transgender girls and boys is that many transgender boys are allowed to be tomboys. When they don't grow out of it, they often think they are lesbians and only later learn they are a transgender man, as these transgender boys said,

I was in middle school [and] you could say, "I came out of the closet!" I told my friends I was a Lesbian. Some friends said they already knew, some friends were a little shocked but ok with it, others were not ok with it. . . . I lived as a "Lesbian" for a good 3 years and I was still feeling that I didn't fit in. I wasn't "with" myself, what I was identifying as didn't make me happy. I still felt as if I was hiding behind a mask but [I] just didn't know what to do. When I was about 15, friends online [to whom] I had been talking . . . finally [helped me] to realize why . . . I felt so wrong in the body I had. I finally figured out what was wrong with me. . . . [I] felt I had found my golden ticket to happiness.

I was never comfortable saying I was a girl or a Lesbian. I was never comfortable wearing girl clothes or acting like a girl. I was never comfortable with my girl name or my girl body. I . . . started identifying as a FtM transgender or for a shorter phrase a Tranny Boi [transgender boy]. Just with that first step a great weight was lifted from my shoulders.

I came out as transgender when I was nineteen. I didn't know that I was transgender from a very young age, but I had always thought that I should look like a man. That is how I imagined myself in my head. I didn't find anything unusual about that. I didn't explore my identity further until college when I was introduced to the LGBTQ community. When I started to meet other transgender people something clicked. I was amazed. Wow, you can really change how you look/sound/are.

A study this author conducted found a correlation between the age of first memory of transgenderism and whether you thought you were a girl or wanted to be a girl. Those who remember believing they were a girl remember back to roughly 4, 5, and 6 years old. Those who felt they wanted to be a girl, remember no further back than the ages of 8, 9, and 10 (see the study in Appendix V, Category Versus Age of Transgender Realization).

How did we learn we weren't the other sex or shouldn't want to be the other sex with such certainty? Did someone we believed who was an authority tell us in definite terms we are a girl or a boy? Did our mother, father, or older siblings convince us of that? Were we realists and once we knew the difference, a simple look at our own body revealed the basis of our birth assigned label. Are we now only acting the part of a woman or a man for some reason we can't identify? Is there something hidden in our psyche, something that makes us disregard the knowledge that we actually (i.e., physically) are women or men, and makes us want to act accordingly?

I remember that I had a desire to be a girl at an early age. I have no memories I ever felt I actually was a girl. If I ever felt I actually was a girl, it had to predate the reach of my memory because my first memory of wanting to be a girl was accompanied by the knowledge that it had to be kept a secret. Knowing it had to be a secret indicates there was a previous encounter in wanting to be or believing I was a girl. I may have been told I am not a girl and it is bad to want to be a girl. Somehow I was convinced I was or had to be a boy. My belief was thus changed from I was a girl to wanting to be a girl. Simultaneously, with that change, I gave birth to a secret to avoid further disagreements or shame. I hear this phenomenon from many other transgender women.

Given these facts, transgender children bury their true sex inside themselves. I felt forced to bury the girl inside me, just as many boys like me feel forced to do. She was carefully hidden and had to be a closely guarded secret. It doesn't take too much intelligence to understand that this secret would be safe if you can act like all the "other" boys. That was the only way many transgender girls could figure out to protect their secret so no one would know. A similar reaction was found in transgender boys. They had to stay with the girls, try to fit in and be like all the other girls.

It is interesting to note the different reaction girls and boys have to their gender conflict dilemma with the outside world. Children labeled girls escape to the tomboy label. Later, if they do not know there is such a thing as transgenderism, they think they are lesbians and find they don't fit in there either. The only difference between transgender boys and girls is girls can be Tomboys for a while but boys can never be sissies. Today transgenderism is more widely known so boys and girls know they are or should be the other sex.

One transgender woman tells how when as a preschooler she put on her sister's school clothes. She was told in no uncertain terms that those were girl's clothes and it is bad to put them on. Although she wanted to dress in her sister's clothes all the time, she knew immediately this had to be her best kept secret. She learned boys don't do that! After that reprimand, she never violated the boy-girl restrictions, publicly.

Does that incident describe the type of situation that changes the thinking from you are the other sex into you want to be the other sex? Does it also teach us we have a secret?

In their own words, some transgender women relate their stories,

> When I heard about Renée Richards, people in my class laughed at that, so getting up in front of the class and saying "that['s] what I want to be when I grow up" was not going to happen.

> In the 3rd grade I had a very fem boy in my class. Used to color his finger nails in red crayon. Yeah, this did not go over well with the other boys in the class. I learned from that point on, never tell anyone.

> I started dressing like a girl at an early age, 5-ish. I remember finding an old dress of my sisters. (Loved that dress.). It was her old Halloween costume when she dressed as a princess. I used to wear it when I could. Wore it in front of my friends once, and they laughed (I think with me). Since I was always funny, I think they thought I was being cute and a smart ass. I was like "no this is who I really am." Then I think mom told me that boys don't wear this. So that might have started it. I got caught a lot more by mom /sister/ granddad, and even dad growing up. Dad told me when he caught [me] that if I did it again, he would put me outside for all to see. Well I knew I did not want that, so [I] made dam[n] sure dad never caught me again.

> After getting caught with some red nail polish on my nails, I confessed my deed in embarrassment and I was told by my dad that if he ever caught me doing that again, he would send me to school dressed as a girl. As I think back, I wonder why I didn't slip on a skirt that night. I was such a stupid kid; my one chance and I blew it.

> I must have been about 5 or 6 when I played around with nail polish. I thought I could put it on and later wash it off with soap and water. Mom found out and took it off. She was understanding. That is my earliest recollection. We have some pictures in the family album where my sister

dressed me up in her recital costume. I must have been 3 or 4. Like everyone else, I continually salvaged my sister "toss-aways" from the trash, and dressed when I could—in the night, alone, and afraid of discovery.

I learned quickly that there is no such thing as coed patty cake.

The numbers of these stories are endless. Everyone has her or his individual personal story and they usually result in a secret. All the stories are a version of learning that "boys don't do that" or "tomboys will grow out of it." Students of this phenomenon tell us most transgender women are a severely "closeted" group, due to similar experiences. Boys simply cannot wear a single feminine garment. Girls can and do wear pants all the time. The pain they experience is when they are forced to wear a dress.

In the past, I sometimes projected my gender difference onto others because I suspected they felt similar to the way I felt. If a guy admired the outfit a girl was wearing, he was suspect. If a guy pointed out a general advantage that a girl had over a guy, he was also a suspect. I thought everyone must have similar feelings to mine, but either to a lesser extent or he was able to control those feelings better than I did. This projection of my feelings onto others may have been my desire to have everyone be like me, so I would be like everyone else. I now have strong doubts that everyone has a similar desire. Logically, if everyone were like me, or even a little like me, the world would have accepted transgenderism centuries ago.

The divide between men and women is rarely breached. The most ironclad and enduring rule to be "normal" and accepted is that your gender identity absolutely must conform to conventional concepts. That is, you must be the same sex and gender, either totally female or totally male. If you are recognized as being even slightly outside the "norm," you become the subject of ridicule and isolation. You must conform to current social expectations, or else!

CHAPTER 2, The Stages of Transgenderism

Transgenderism is not an individual's choice or life style. Before the Internet, transgender people didn't even know their "conflict" has a name. They sort of have to learn it for themselves, as they "grow" along.

A decade ago few people had heard of transgenderism. I feel the creation of the word transgender as a banner to include many groups has helped make the phenomenon more widely known. Although changes are now occurring rapidly and more people know of it, hardly anyone really understands the subject in any detail.

Some researchers believe there are distinct stages a transgender person goes through. After childhood, the stages that researchers cite are The Realization, Resigned to the Fact, and The Final Stage. I add two more, "Discovering a Transgender Community;" and "The Final, Final Stage."

In the Beginning—a Childhood Dilemma

In the minds of most transgender children, they either think they are the other sex or they want to be the other sex. In either case, transgender children are faced with a difficult problem. They learned fairly early in life people reject their feelings regarding their gender and want them to be like the indications of their sex. People want and even demand they dress and do the things "appropriate" for the sex they were labeled with at birth. That includes their appearance, actions, clothing, toys, playmates—everything. Nearly every person and object seems to have a sex—male or female. No one wants to see a person doing things reserved for the other sex or having anything that indicates the other sex. It is okay for tomboys to be like a boy, but only until it is time for them to grow out of it. However, no one likes a sissy, a boy who is girly, at any age. From the transgender child's view, you conform or you will be ridiculed and abused.

Most people know there are people who dress as the other sex. They have no idea why they do it and, in most cases, they don't know who those people are. So it is with those who dress as the other sex. They don't know why they do it. They don't know why they are different from other people. Most don't know there are others like them. They do know, at some point in life, no one wants them to be the other sex even though that is what they feel inside.

Most transgender girls and boys learn they shouldn't express their inner gender, but they must! Something they don't understand drives them to dress as the other sex and be like the other sex. As an infant, they may seize any article and transform it to represent the other sex's clothes. Later, they turn to borrowing their mother's, father's, sister's, or brother's clothes and soon learn people think that is bad. For the most part, they eventually translate "don't do it" to "don't do if there is any chance of someone seeing you do it." In some children, the drive to discard their sex label and be the other sex is so strong and the child so insistent, that the parents are obliged to recognize a serious problem.

Regardless of how the parents react, the child finds he or she can't discard his or her inner gender. In the worst case, the child is evicted from the home and driven to suicide or must find a life on the streets. In most cases, parents drive the need for their child to be the other sex underground. What could be more of a dilemma? If you decide to hide your identity, you live in the closet and pay the penalty of isolating an important part of your identity. You experience guilt that hiding engenders and shame that you must do something others frown upon. If you can't hide your transgenderism, you pay a different kind of penalty and frequently end up isolated in some sort of a closet anyhow.

Most transgender children eventually conform as well as they can, adopt a persona expected of them, and hide his or her true gender. Consciously or not, his or her loved ones, who are their only authority, are denying the child's true existence. The child's world insists the gender must match the body. In effect they are saying the child's true existence is not legitimate, which adversely affects the child's happiness and mental health.

For the last few decades, there has been a growing recognition of transgenderism. Transgenderism has been found to involve more individuals than previously believed. Due to current knowledge, transgenderism is also being recognized earlier in a child's life. Dr. Peggy Cohen-Kettenis,[1] who runs a major gender clinic in the Netherlands, has seen the average age of her patients plummet since 2002.

Catherine Tuerk,[2] who since 1998 has been in charge of a support network for parents of children with gender variant behavior at the Children's National Medical Center in Washington, D.C. said,

We used to get calls mostly from parents who were concerned about their children being gay. Now about 90 percent of our calls are from parents with some concern that their child may be transgender.

Attendance has increased steadily at the Trans-Health Conference in Philadelphia, which many parents of transgender children attend. In 2002, the first conference's attendance was 150. In 2012 the attendance grew to 2,400, a 20% increase over the previous year.

Parents of transgender children are faced with a difficult situation. They realize that even in today's climate, a nontransgender life is easier and they would like their child to have the best life possible. To do that, their child needs to be like everyone else. The temptation to hope their child will grow out of it is strong. The child may grow out of it, but the parent action or inaction will not play a role in that eventuality. The child may grow out of it if the child's Effective Transgenderism is weak enough for it to be "buried" by the need to be like everyone else. Perhaps an easier outlet such as living as a gay person is found.

The most frequent result is parental disapproval, which drives their child underground into the closet and the closet is not conducive to a good life. Children have been known to grow out of it, but it was never anything a parent did. It occurs on its own. Parents sometimes turn to a therapist who claims to be able to change the child. If a therapist says there is a cure, run for the nearest exit! Those practices border on torture and involve unethical treatment (this is discussed later in this chapter). The success stories of therapists who claim to change the child sometimes appear to succeed because the child conforms only to end the discomfort of the treatment and simply goes underground.

Some children insist on the gender they seem to intuitively perceive. Many doctors have learned transgenderism is to be taken serious. In some children transgenderism is so strong that life becomes unbearable if they are forced to live according to the sex label assigned at birth. In this case, your choice is either to have a dead child or a live transgender one. A recent study found 41% of transgender people attempt suicide in their lifetime. The number of successful attempts was not reported. Although I haven't seen any specific study, I have personally heard a doctor say one in five transgender children commit suicide.

In 2005, physicians in the U.S. started treating children diagnosed to be a truly transgender child with puberty blockers, drugs originally intended to halt precocious puberty. The blockers put transgender teens in a state of suspended sexual development until it is determined that the child is old enough to make a serious medical decision. The blockers prevent boys from growing facial hair, body hair, an Adam's apple, developing a deep voice, or any of the other physical characteristics that a male-to-female transsexual would later spend tens of thousands of dollars and countless hours to reverse. They allow girls to grow taller and prevent them from getting breasts.

Hormone treatment—introducing estrogen or testosterone—is delayed because the treatment has some irreversible affects. Since some children seem to change their mind and want to continue as their birth sex label, the proper plan is to delay the sexual development decision until the child is old enough to make a responsible decision.

The Realization

The exposure of transgender people has increased since the advent of the Internet. Television, radio, newspapers, and magazines run stories regarding transgenderism more frequently. Transgender individuals are appearing more and more in public. It is a self-feeding phenomenon. The more transgenderism becomes known and subsequently accepted or even tolerated by the general population, the more likely transgender people will emerge from the closet. Still, the need to hide one's transgenderism continues for most individuals and that hiding even continues to the grave for some. Unfortunately, real understanding and general acceptance is still far off.

Frequently, you learn no one will accept your true gender. You can't tell anyone. If you do, they may verbally or physically hurt you. Even your parents and siblings say you are mistaken. They say you cannot be the person you know you are and you must be what the physical indications of your gender says you are. By denying your identity, without realizing it, they are destroying your self-worth and inducing feelings of shame.

Basically, the realization is that the conflict between your physical indications of sex and your gender identity is not accepted by anyone, even those who are closest to you and you love. You must do as good a job as possible to hide your true self, with no exceptions.

As long as your secret is maintained, you must lie to your loved ones. You can never tell the whole truth.

Resigned to the Fact

Soon after you realize the physical indications of your gender and the gender you know you are or aspire to be are different, you learn there is nothing you can do to change your feelings. You learn it does not matter how much or how conscientiously you try to fight it, you never win the battle.

You hope to bury all thoughts of wanting to be the other sex (i.e., your true self) because you learn no one will accept your true gender. You can't tell anyone because you are sure to be criticized and cause people to laugh at you. Your loved ones say you cannot be the person you know you are and you must be what the physical indications of your gender says you are. Your feelings do not count! You must be what other people say you are.

Tomboys experience a degree of permissiveness early in life because everyone believes tomboys are cute and will grow out of it. On the other hand, there is zero tolerance for even a slight expression of femininity by boys. Boys learn early in life that exhibiting any feminine behavior must be corrected immediately.

On the surface, girls seem to have an easier time for a while; however, this later puts them at a disadvantage. On average, they typically struggle longer before they learn, later in life, about transgenderism and its unacceptability to others.

Parents hope their children will grow out of it, and some do or seem to grow out of it. Many go underground and understand their gender feelings are a secret. Some cannot do that. They cannot hide their gender identity and pay the terrible price of being tormented by others throughout their lives.

Many transgender people never discover the word transgender or know that they are something called transgender. They simply know they are the other sex or want to be the other sex. After fighting it and praying for it to go away, they eventually give up and realize that's the way it is and that's the way it is going to remain. Simply put, you become resigned to what nature, God, or whoever and whatever made you this way. You may still hope to be rid of the feeling and be cured, but a cure never happens! There is no such thing as a cure because there is no sickness!

Every time you stop to analyze what you are doing, you think, everyone can't be wrong. Dressing in the clothes of the other sex is something you should not be doing. It is wrong and it is bad. You are disgusted with yourself. As a result, you try to force a cure by purging (i.e., throwing away any items of the other sex that you have acquired). You vow you will never put such garments on again, ever! You sincerely mean what you tell yourself but it is just a matter of time before you violate your vow and do it again. You can't get away from your true self. Try as you may, there is no escape! You are stuck with it! You are you!

Whether you are labeled a girl or a boy, you have no idea there is any chance of changing your body and appearance enough to be recognized and accepted as the other sex. You never consider the possibility of transitioning and actually becoming a woman or a man because you never even heard the word transition in this context. Sure, you heard of Christine Jorgenson and Renée Richards, but thought they were not ordinary people. What they did was impossible for an ordinary person. If you are born a girl, the problem is worse. You never hear of a girl being made into a man. Even if you could become a woman or a man, what kind of life would you have? Who would love you? There is no place for that kind of person. Where can you ever fit in? There is no life available to you except a conforming one.

After decades of hoping for a cure and trying to hide your true feelings from yourself, you give up and you are resigned to the fact that your feelings are "for keeps." You know you can appear to fit in, but you will never really fit in and be like everyone else. One transgender girl discovered that you are not accepted by anyone:

> I'd expected to be teased mercilessly by the boys but was crushed when the girls ridiculed me.

You feel unique and very alone. You feel you are the only person in the world trapped like this. You know you must cope with it in the best way you can. You will always be alone in this. It is bad enough to have to control and cope with it, but the distress is even greater, since you must do it by yourself, alone, all alone. Transgender men said,

After I enrolled in college, I did not go home for four years. I didn't go home for holidays. I didn't send birthday cards. I didn't talk to my parents. At that time in my life I thought it was best to sever ties with my family. They couldn't accept me. They just made me feel bad about myself. Imagine that the people you love the most make you feel like you are nothing. I wasn't allowed to go home unless I was a fake person, a fantasy that my parents had of me.

I was convinced that I was going to spend the rest of my life alone [be]cause no man would want to be with someone like me.

I cried this morning, just now, but only for a minute or so. I guess I was crying about being alone. But this is how it is.

Gianna Israel's Gender Library[3] labels it "aloneness." Someone in distress said,

I know we wish to be able to talk to the people closest to us, but they will [be] the ones that will hurt us the most. It is very lonely, but [I] keep my mouth shut. They will never have the decency to respect someone. I hope that there is someone in the TS [transsexual] community that a girl can talk to and share things with. I am so tired of being alone.

The Researchers' Final Stage

Some researchers consider the final stage as actually becoming, as much as possible, the other gender. They say you slowly "peal away" your birth sex label, piece by piece. This can be simply a mental process or it may involve taking hormones and even undergoing surgery. The process allows you to be the other sex as much as you wish to be, as much as you can be, or as much as you think you can be.

I can identify with the stages outlined above; however, at best the timing and clarity of each stage is hazy for me. The stages are not as clear cut in my mind as the writers seem able to describe. The reason it is not clear may be because there were many major conflicts in my mind all along the way.

Discovering a Transgender Community

In addition to the above stages, I feel there are 2 other important stages that should be mentioned. The most important and meaningful one is, if and when you discover there are others that feel as you do—a great number of others. You learn that what you read in transvestite literature was not all fiction, as you thought. You can determine what is real by consulting the Internet. That knowledge is a relief in itself. It is a great emotional relief to know that after all you are not all alone. There are others who can understand and accept you because they feel just as you do. You are not completely alone anymore.

I always felt like an outsider. But looking back, in high school and college I was actually fairly popular and busy with extracurricular activities. Other people sought my company. People seemed to like me. Why wouldn't they? They didn't know my secret. I felt I would not be liked if people knew my secret. That alone isolated me in my mind.

It was my shortcoming that I did not recognize I was liked. I put myself on the outside because my mind knew I was different and I couldn't be on the "inside" (i.e., close to the other kids). I had too much to hide.

Finding a large group of others like me opened new vistas. Eventually, I had a best friend for the first time in my life. Everyone had a best friend at one time or another, but as a guy I never did. The most wonderful thing that ever happened to me was to hear her refer to me as her best friend. That never happened before in my whole life. Tears welled up in my eyes. What a euphoric feeling! For once I felt like an insider and looking out at everyone who wasn't her best friend. I wanted them to wish they had a best friend like I had. I actually hoped they wanted to be her best friend and an insiders like me. How juvenile was that? Perhaps it was, but I felt that way. The warmth I felt to be "inside," with my best friend, was worth the long trip to visit her (how sad is that?).

Not having a best friend is not uncommon among the transgender population. I asked an Internet group of transgender women if they had a similar experience and never had a best friend. The answers I received were as follows:

I was exactly the same.

I had friends but not really a best friend in the sense you mean it. I don't even have any friends now but I know [a] million people. I cannot share everything even with my "friends" that I am closest to. . . .I know whereof you speak.

As I was growing up I only had two friends which I knew from school. Other than that I mostly stayed to myself, never going out or to dances, not even the senior dance. Basically I was like that my whole life, not talking to anyone.

For the longest time, I too lacked a best friend, but coming out to my office mate whom I admired and respected dearly, enabled me to find in her a best friend. She accepted [me] completely and with total empathy.

I too never had a best friend, someone to confide in, and share my deepest thoughts and desires with. . . . I guess being transsexual did cause me to be lonely and introverted.

Actually I have to agree with you about the low level of socialization as a youth.

I never had a best friend either. But I do now.

Furthermore, you feel good that your deception and dishonesty is no longer universal. No one likes the dishonesty, the deception, and especially the hiding we feel society forces us to adopt. I personally hated even more the fact that I stopped thinking I was a liar. It all became a second nature game of deception. This deception, sneaking, and hiding is depressing and self-destructive. I guess making it a game helped me avoid depression. Not everyone is that lucky.

These are feelings similar to those felt by nearly all transgender people. As an example, a girl wrote,

I went to see my doctor last Thursday, and told her all about [my transgenderism]. She asked me many questions, and I answered her. It was such a relief to have someone to talk to. . . . I walk[ed] out of the doctor's office so happy I felt like I was floating. I got an early Christmas present. I feel like a new person.

There is a close alliance among transgender people, since we are glad for the mere knowledge that others like us exist and we are grateful for their companionship. Finally, you find a community of people where you can be yourself. One transgender woman put it this way:

> In any event, I am trying to say we are all sisters, and we are family, and we are all different in our own ways.

From other transgender people, you learn of organizations, groups, and functions devoted to the transgender community. In their company you can be honest and open about your inner feelings and actually have fun while openly being a girl. It is similar for transgender boys who find others who feel like a guy. They never really fit-in with the girls, the boys, or with lesbians. It feels good to find a place where you can freely participate in conversations and express your feelings to someone. You don't have to guard your words when participating in a conversation. Ralph Waldo Emerson said of a friend, "Before him you can think aloud."

I am not alone in this. I find most transgender individuals have kept these feelings a secret for as long as they can remember and they are eager to tell their story. I also find all their stories are unbelievably similar, almost identical.

It is like being stranded on a strange and isolated island and finding the natives, dressed in loin cloths, living primitive lives, and with strange customs speak exactly the same language as you, with the same dialect and fluency as you do. A transgender man wrote,

> I listen to these trans people tell about their experiences and I'd realize that what they said could have come out of my mouth.

I am angry with myself for not discovering there are other people like me sooner. I have had a computer since the late 1970s, long before IBM made the personal computer a household "appliance." I thought I was unique. It never occurred to me to use it to find out if there were others like me.

The Final, Final Stage

There is another stage, and I believe it is the true final one—the Final, Final Stage. At least it was the final one for me. It is when you have no secrets from anyone in your world, even those you care most about. At that time, you can begin to freely express your inner feelings. You no longer need to be guarded when you speak of your feelings and experiences.

I recently arrived at that final stage—my final step to complete liberation from deception and hiding. I never thought I could or would do it. My spouse died 22 years earlier, but telling my grown children was the most difficult and emotional experience I initiated in my life.

I tried to figure out how and when I could do the least harm to them and myself. You cannot avoid doing some damage to those you love, but at some point you feel your happiness should enter the equation. I needed to be able to be myself without hiding and restricting my life to the transgender community. Who said "boys" don't do that?

Most transgender women want to be recognized as a female (i.e., "pass") and so did I; however, now that I do pass, I feel it doesn't matter. I freely declare what I am. I don't go around with a sign on my forehead saying, "transgender below;" however, although most people believe that I am a genetic woman, I declare my transgenderism whenever appropriate.

Just after declaring myself to my children, I was feeling free and wanted to demonstrate it, plus sometimes my sense of humor rules:

> I was in a theater seated next to a woman. She was obviously alone as I was. We spoke to each other as women tend to do while waiting for the curtain to go up. After a while, a man occupied the seat on the other side of the woman. He was seriously invading her territory—her seat. I couldn't hear the exact words, but she properly complained to him and he was not very gracious about it. Unlike most stories, this one ends when the curtain goes up. The woman then turned to me and said in a low voice, "Men aren't very nice! Women are much nicer." I replied, "I agree, that is why I became one."

After a drawn out "Oh," she added, "That is very interesting!" The reply was a typical older feminine noncommittal first reaction to a shock. At any rate, the curtain went up soon after that, so I couldn't see how she reacted. I am curious to know if she would have continued to talk to me as just another woman or not after the initial shock.

Of course when I said I *became* a woman, it was a quick, shocking, and humorous way of making my point. It is important to demonstrate to the public that we are like everyone else in every way other than having a birth sex label and gender identity that do not agree. This is part of my efforts to integrate, which I feel is the only way to help transgender people come out of the closet now and in the future. No one should have to experience the agony of needing to express their inner feelings and simultaneously fear the shame and embarrassment of exposing that fact. No one should feel they must stay "in the closet" in spite of their strong desire to open the door.

There are many transgender people who contribute to that belief. They try to change the world and made it better for others. They try to tell the world transgenderism is simply like any other birth variation and people should be more tolerant of different people, people that vary from the usual and the expected. Bigotry may die hard and frequently only when the bearer dies with it. However, it is important to at least try to make things less evil. It may seem to be rare; however, if you succeed only once in a long while, the effort becomes worthwhile.

The Cure

The Hebrew Bible's Book of Deuteronomy prohibits the wearing of the clothes of the other sex. Also, transgender people were thought to be the same as gay/lesbian people, the prohibitions against same sex intimacy in the Book of Leviticus also applied to *all* transgender people. In the Bible's English translation, homosexuality and transgenderism are both an abomination. Therefore, all transgender people were an abomination and gay or lesbian transgender people were an abomination twice. These prohibitions were adopted by Christianity and Islam and through their invasions spread to many other lands and cultures.

For 2000 years a cure has been sought for transgender and gay/lesbian people. In the late nineteenth century, even though transgenderism and homosexuality were recognized as separate phenomenon, a cure was still sought However, a cure for both or either was never found. So in Biblical times they were stoned to death. Later they were burned to death. Death was the only cure; however, there seemed to be a mysterious inner drive that forced transgender people to assume the other sex in some way in spite of the dangers. (The force for gay and lesbian people was a primary drive for a romantic relationship, not necessarily for sex.)

The more modern cure was lobotomy, drugs, imprisonment, and reparative therapy. To this day, a cure was never found. Medical scientists have learned through various research procedures that there can't be a cure because there is no sickness. Any "cure" noted was on the surface to stop the treatment.

The defense transgender people used through the ages was the invention of a special kind of closet. Their closet was not to store things. It was a secret place, physical or mental, where they could be the other sex or simply imagine they were the other sex.

In 2011, reparative therapy was determinedly to be unethical by a large group of doctors experienced in transgender health issues.[4] Since then some states have outlawed reparative therapy and some states have eliminated it through Executive Order. It was determined decades ago that it is impossible to make the mind conform to the body's sex. The only treatment is to change the body to conform to a transgender person's mind.

On October 1, 2012, California Governor Jerry Brown signed the first law prohibiting reparative therapy. Soon after that New York governor Andrew Cuomo issued an Executive Order that eliminated reparative therapy in New York. Hopefully, all other states will follow with laws prohibiting the practice of reparative therapy. I have often referred to reparative therapy as the modern name for torture.

All this is no longer a concern to me. All that stuff became purely academic ever since I cured myself. With the strength God gave me, I was able to overcome the shame and guilt and openly declare my womanhood. I now conform to the Biblical words. I now dress as a woman all the time and stopped wearing the clothes "*that pertaineth unto a man.*"

CHAPTER 3. Transgender Research

Gender dysphoria (dysphoria—a state of dissatisfaction) is becoming widely understood in scientific and medical circles as having a biological basis with a congenital origin. Up until March, 2013, the American Psychiatric Association classified transgenderism as a mental disorder called Gender Identity Disorder. Many people objected to the characterization of transgenderism as a mental disease.

Transgenderism is strongly believed to be associated with a fetus' atypical neurodevelopment of the brain. Although I subscribe to that, we need to be aware that a biological cause of transgenderism is politically correct and it is what some researchers (and I) want to be true.

The belief that transgenderism has a biological cause goes as far back as the Vedic Society (early Hindu) recorded in 1500 B.C.E. In 1869, Karl-Heinrich Ulrich[1] coined the name Urning for it. Also in 1869, Karl-Maria Kertbeny's[2] transgender research verified transgenderism is separate from homosexuality. Kertbeny's research involved mostly male to female people. Perhaps that is because male to female individuals are more visible and do not blend into society as well as female-to-male transgender people do. Also, women were once totally controlled by men, who would not think of allowing women to express anything other than femininity. This gives the false impression that male-to-female people are much more prevalent than female-to-male individuals.

Researcher Georg S. Kanz of the University Clinic for Psychiatry and Psychotherapy of the MedUni Vienna conducted a study (Medical University of Vienna, 2015) that suggests that there is a strong genetic role in gender identity and it resides in identifiable configurations in the human brain. Diffusion-based Magnetic Resonance Tomography (MRT) was used. The examination revealed significant differences in the microstructure of the brain's connections between male and female control subjects. Transgender persons took up a middle position between both genders.

Throughout history research is entirely of Western origin. On April 1, 2002, Sam Winter,[3] professor at the University of Hong Kong, published a report after examining 235 key publications on transgenderism published between 1992 and 2002. He found about 41% were from European countries and 48% from North American countries, for a total of 89%. These two parts of the world account for only about 20% of the world's population; however, almost all research stems from there. Only 7% were from Asian countries which have a much larger population and a more permissive culture regarding transgender people.

Recently, efforts have been launched to correct the lack of studies originating in Asia. There is a good deal of organization and research now done in Asia (described later in this chapter and CHAPTER 9, Transphobia—Transgender Discrimination).

Hormonal Influence on Gender Identity

The genes that will develop a male baby are programmed to induce the manufacture and release of hormones by sending out enzymatic signals to produce androgens, such as testosterone, and Mullerian inhibiting hormones. If the genes are programmed to produce a girl, enzymatic signals induce the production of estrogen, Mullerian hormones, and Wolferian inhibitors.

A hormone "flood" needs to be released to get the desired result. The hormone "flood" occurs twice. The first determines the physical characteristics of the embryo (This gives the baby the label of girl or boy). The second hormone "flood" affects the development of the brain (This gives the baby it's gender identity).

One theory regarding the development of a transgender baby is that the second "flood" of hormones is weak or insufficient, is timed poorly, there is a lack of the fetus' ability to utilize (i.e., absorb) sufficient hormones, or possibly some female hormones in the boy or male hormones in the girl get into the mix. Some step in the developmental process (described in Chapter 2) may also cause a variation. Any one or combination of possible causes described above, could develop differently than in the typical baby and those parts develop somewhat like the other sex (i.e., a girl has some part of her brain develop like a boy's and a boy baby has some parts of his brain develop like a girl's).

This has been found to be essentially true in the 2008 researcher at the Prince Henry's Institute in Melbourne, Australia. Lauren Hare[4] and Vincent Harley[5] performed tests on three specific genes involved in sexual development. They found the transgender women's population generally has a longer version of an androgen receptor gene. It is known that longer versions of the androgen receptor gene are associated with less efficient testosterone signaling.

Some researchers concluded there is a biological cause of transgenderism. That is, they believe inefficient testosterone results from the reduced androgen and/or poor androgen signaling. These differences might reduce testosterone action and under-masculinize the brain during fetal development. This has an effect on gender development in the womb.

Harley added,

> There is a social stigma that transsexualism is simply a lifestyle choice; however, our findings support a biological basis of how gender identity develops.

Terry Reed,[6] a founding member of the Gender Identity Research and Education Society, said she was convinced of a biological basis of transsexualism. She added,

> This study appears to reinforce earlier studies which have indicated that, in some transgender people, there may be a genetic trigger to the development of an atypical gender identity.

Her belief suggests there may be several other routes to transgenderism; however, a biological element will always be in the etiology of transsexualism.

Although nearly all research has involved transgender women, labeled boys at birth, it is believed that the same applies to transgender boys labeled girls at birth.

Hopefully, future studies will prove, beyond a shadow of a doubt, the phenomenon these researchers believe is a natural occurrence. That occurrence will lead to greater social acceptance of transgender people.

The male and female gonadal development has always been considered independent and the determinant of an individual's sex. Opposing signals regulate this development. The maleness signal arises from the XY chromosomes and the presence of the SRY, the trigger that starts the release of testosterone. This is similar to the female's R-Spondin 1.[7] R-Spondin 1, which is also essential in sex determination.

The Prince Henry's Institute is conducting research to understand the mechanisms of these two diverging pathways by using the techniques of cell and molecular biology.[8] This research may help to explain the development of transgenderism.

The work at Prince Henry's Institute takes a giant step forward from the conclusions reached by Magnus Hirschfeld in the early twentieth century. In any case, it seems there is more than one possible cause of gender differences.

One possible cause is similar to the belief at the Prince Henry's Institute that an atypical relation with testosterone, or an exposure to estrogen, results in a particle of the female in the male fetus. The atypical hormonal influence does this by affecting parts of the brain so the outwardly male person has some part of the brain develop as a female's would. Furthermore, one can infer a labeled girl transgender baby was atypically exposed to estrogen or had some exposure to male hormones that implanted some with the feelings of maleness in their brain.

Although all the research points to a genetic basis for transgenderism, there are some researchers who believe there is also a possibility transgenderism itself causes these brain differences. Animal experiments tend to discount that belief. Roger Gorski,[9] at the University of California at Los Angeles, manipulated the hormone levels of newborn rats and he was able to produce male rats that demonstrate feminine behavior. Others, working with mice, have noted that female fetuses that were positioned between two male fetuses, during development, were to some degree masculine in appearance and behavior indicating an influence of a male hormone.

Researchers simplify this phenomenon by explaining the exposure to both male and female hormones in the mother's womb causes some fetuses' body to develop along one path and the brain to develop along another path.

In spite of all the research into brain differences, the findings are more likely a symptom than a cause.

The Effect of Foreign Substances

A second possible cause of transgenderism is that estrogenic and androgenic foreign substances, present in the mother, influence the development of the fetus. This came to light from a study also performed in the Netherlands. This study found that relatively large amounts of certain foreign chemicals accumulated in the mother and were passed on to the fetus. This resulted in more feminine play in boys and more masculine play by girls. Additionally, different chemicals resulted in feminine play by both boys and girls. This occurs because certain chemicals cross the mother's placenta and are thus passed on to the fetus where they accumulate.

The fact that a large majority of these chemicals are feminizing supports the belief that there are a larger percentage of male-to-female individuals than female-to-male transgender people. Others feel the numbers are similar; however, female-to-male transgender individuals pass as men more easily than those labeled men do as women. This helps the perception that male-to-female transgender people far outnumber the female-to-male population.

It has been established that most polluting substances are biased toward feminizing (this is discussed later in this chapter regarding polluting chemicals in more detail).

The entire story of the mechanisms that cause a variation are mostly unknown. We are not sure whether they are caused individually or in combination by genetic errors, susceptibility, environmental toxins, maternal stress, malnutrition, drugs, radiation, or possibly a wide variety of things that have not yet been discovered. Whatever the true reason(s), whether it is one of the above causes, some of them, all of the possible causes, or something else, brain development regarding the usual female/male development, apparently is influenced in the mother's womb.

The reduced hormone signaling along with all the other possible factors must be variables in the fetus' brain development. This would account for the high variability of transgender people (i.e., the variability of a transgender person's specific identity as an occasional closet crossdresser and every variation up to seeking an operation). Something parallel occurs in both a male identity and a female identity.

An Infinite Variation of Gender

All this has led to the fairly recent thinking that there are more than simply two sexes—male and female. Transgenderism is quite variable. In my mind, if you were to draw a graph depicting maleness and femaleness, with each starting at opposite ends of the horizontal axis, with the greatest intensity high at each end on the vertical axis and the strength of each tendency descending toward the opposite end (i.e., the other gender), an "X" would be formed somewhere at the middle (see Figure A below). That is, I believe there is an infinite variation of femaleness and maleness in individuals, regardless of the physical indication of their gender. The strength, intensity, purity, or homogeneousness of one's belief of belonging to a specific gender is derived from birth (i.e., genetically).

However, outwardly gender identity is either tempered or reinforced by sociological factors. For the physical indicated female, gender self-identity varies from the ultrafeminine to the transsexual man. In the physical indicated male, it varies from the macho guy to the transsexual woman.

Pioneering researchers in the transgenderism field originally thought transgender women far outnumber transgender men. Now they believe their numbers are approximately equal.

In the past, researchers have depicted the variability of maleness and femaleness as a bimodal graph—one male and the other female "hump," with a connection between them. I feel this outdated "picture" only maintained the old concept of two genders with varying intensities (i.e., two normal curves). My feeling is that gender identity is a continuum of femaleness and maleness that intersect at the middle.

The recognition of the Intersex and the transgender population has also changed the thinking from the existence of two sexes to an infinite variety of sexes. The fact that genetically there are many variations of the typically female XX and typically male XY chromosomes has helped reinforce the thought that there are more than two distinct sexes (e.g., XXY and XYY).

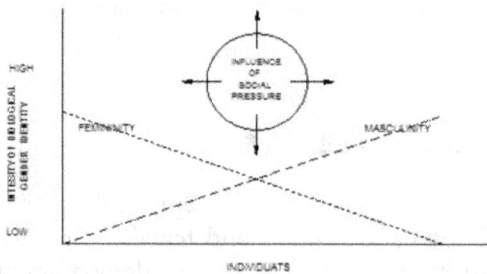

Figure A - The Infinite Variety of Masculine and Feminine Feeling Persons.

Figure A: The above section and readings on the subject, help demonstrate what I have come to believe; there is an infinite variety of femaleness/maleness in the general population. Furthermore, I feel this is also true of the transgender population, since that population is part of the graph in Figure A and fits somewhere between the two extremes.

The variation helps explain the different categories of transgenderism (i.e., transsexuals, crossdressers, etc.). Now, one can conclude that although the various transgender categories are all cut from the same cloth, they are also individuals and are unique individuals (due to the effect of varying genetic and varying sociological factors). Thus, variability applied to another variable yields an even more variable population.

For example, a large number of transsexual individuals, perhaps most of them, are placed somewhere in the middle of the extremes. They feel content and very much a woman without surgically altering parts of their body. However, I know transgender women elsewhere on the scale who are unrelentingly driven to alter their genitals and other parts of their body to feel "complete" (i.e., like a complete woman). They feel they can only be happy, if they are "complete." Transgender men have a more difficult path. Gender operations are generally unsuccessful causing most to avoid that path and satisfy themselves surgically with mastectomies and hysterectomies.

I know others at the other extreme of transgenderism, who are content with dressing as a woman and going out once a month. They are usually, but not always, married "men." Still others dress and never venture out of their home, mostly out of shame, embarrassment, and fear of looking like a guy in a dress, losing their family, losing their friends, losing their job, or some combination of these issues. I feel that in addition to their varied genetic component, all of them are feeling the effects of social pressure, each to a different degree, which intensifies or moderates their strength of transgenderism. Just as social pressures "forced" many of us to keep our transgenderism a secret, social pressures enables some of us to keep our feelings in check.

One other situation should be mentioned. Some transgender people only think about being the other sex. They would love to see themselves dressed, but want to avoid the possibility of looking ridiculous to themselves and others. They are content with fantasy alone. That way, they visualize themselves as a perfectly fine looking woman or man.

At one time, I felt this pressure and restricted my dressing to "the closet." However, I was never satisfied with secretly dressing as a woman whenever I was alone at home or at night in a hotel room when I was away on business. I needed more than that. I had to find feminine garments I could wear and still appear dressed completely masculine. A woman's slip-on shoes (i.e., loafers);

trouser socks; women's jeans or pants; women's workout suits; women's tee shirts; a double breasted jacket that could be buttoned the man's way with the addition of a single inside button; an outer jacket with a zipper, so it didn't button the "wrong" way; and anything from a woman's department, as long as the color and style was not obviously feminine, would help me cope with my dilemma. That is, the dilemma caused by my pressing need to express my femininity by dressing as a woman and still conform to society's insistence that I appear as a man. Simply put, I found ways to dress as a woman and appear as a man at the same time. That helped ease the distress and frustration of containing my true gender. I am not certain whether it was the fact I was wearing women's clothes or my preoccupation with outsmarting the world regarding my gender identity.

There were limits to this deception. Some transgender women I know wear pantyhose under their trousers and socks. I only did that at work once. I found they interfered with concentration on my work—another instance of social pressure altering feminine expression (i.e., my inner need to excel in my work).

Even a cursory observation of transgender women indicates there is a wide variation in how transgender women react to their situation. Dr. Sam Winter performed a study titled, "Heterogeneity in Transgender: A Cluster Analysis of a Thai Sample." He reported, in the International Journal of Transgenderism (2006, Volume 9, Number2), on the traits selected by the participants (i.e., those that they identified with and also those traits they aspired to).

The vast majority, almost 70%, of transgender women identified with characteristics indicative of being androgynous, 21.4%, identified with traits considered undifferentiated (i.e., neither female nor male), and 6.6% of the sample identified with characteristics overwhelmingly feminine.

The fact that the majority chose androgynous characteristics to identify themselves surprised me, since I hear so much female identification from the transgender people I know and with whom I correspond. This result is said to be similar to American society.

Upon further reflection, my explanation changed to feel that the tendency to lean toward the androgynous identification might have occurred because transgender women reflect both worlds. That is, the effects of spending so much time in the male persona, while actually feeling like a female, or wanting to be one, resulted in the androgynous responses.

Regarding research in general, I have difficulty with some terms that are often used to define the diagnosis of transgenderism. Terms like "intense" and "strong" [desire to be the other sex] are meaningless. I find these are subjective and relative terms and should not have a place in any scientific endeavor. For example, a nagging pain to one person may be an unbearable pain to another. We need to see researchers use positive and objective terms only.

Polluting Chemicals and Gender Changes

Several studies conducted in various countries have shown chemical pollutants contribute to the occurrence of transgenderism. These chemicals are said to be responsible for the increasing number of transgender people in recent years. The use of diethylstilbestrol (DES) for pregnant women several years ago, the presence of DDTs, PCBs, and many other pollutants in the air, water, and food crops have all been shown to be "endocrine disruptors" (the term endocrine disruptors have been more recently and properly described by the U. S. National Academy of Sciences as "hormonally active agents"). As the former name implies, an "endocrine disruptor" disrupts the normal function of the endocrine system. These hormonally active agents may be found in many everyday products—including plastic bottles, metal food cans, detergents, flame retardants, food, toys, cosmetics, and pesticides.

In this country, the National Institute of Environmental Health Sciences, an arm of the National Institute of Health, supports studies to determine whether exposure to hormonally active agents may result in human health effects including lowered fertility, an increased incidence of endometriosis, and some cancers. Research shows hormonally active agents may pose the greatest risk during prenatal and early postnatal development, when organ and neural systems are forming. It is the effects on prenatal and early postnatal development that are of primary interest here.

In particular, most of the hormonally active agents (i.e., chemicals) contribute to feminization and only a few contribute to increasing masculinity, since the majority of pollutants are strongly estrogenic and/or antiandrogenic (male hormone suppressing). The introduction of a factor that increases female estrogen like hormones and the antiandrogen substances tend to feminize the male fetus and/or babies shortly after birth. They have little effect on females for the obvious reason that normally estrogen levels are high and testosterone levels quite low naturally in females. That obviously is what makes females female.

Since there are fewer polluting chemicals that suppress estrogen and are androgenic (promote the male hormones), chemicals seem to have less of an effect on the female population because they both occur infrequently and because of the nature of the usual female hormonal make up. This may account for the fact that male-to-female transgender people reportedly outnumber the occurrence of female-to-male transgender people, even though historically and sociologically being a man was thought to be superior to being a woman.

Additionally, the comparison of the number of male-to-female and female-to-male transgender people may be biased, since genital changes from female-to-male (FtM) are not visibly as successful as those from male-to-female (MtF); therefore, female-to-male operations are infrequently sought and in most cases avoided. This results in a biased statistic because few transgender men seek a genital operation and statistics are generally drawn from hospital records of gender operations.

From country to country, the reported number of transsexuals and ratio of MtF to FtM transsexuals also varies. It is believed that is due to environmental factors and in some cases due to sociological factors. The ratio varies from 2.3 in Germany to 6.1 in Australia. The ratio in the United States was found to be 4 physically male transsexuals to each physically female transsexual (1:100,000 MtF and 1:400,000 FtM).

The Singapore statistics showed the highest incidence of transsexuals of any country (1:2900 MtF and 1:8300 FtM). Some of this was attributed to large concentrations of pollutants that were found in the shoals around the island. The concentration of pollutants is likely an accumulation of pollutants before environmental precautions were taken and originally caused by the great amount of shipping in and out of the island. These statistics showed Singapore had 3 MtF to 1 FtM as opposed to the US's 4:1. I wonder if a list of pollutants for each location would simply reflect the different concentration of pollutants or show a significantly different concentration of female producing chemical pollutants to explain the difference. This research did not make such a comparison.

Another reason proposed for the relatively high incidence of transsexuals in Singapore may be sociological. There are strict laws and high penalties for gay behavior and many gay/lesbians pretend to be transsexual, since the police do not harass transsexuals. However, there are 2 factors involved. Pollutants were observed to be extremely high and sex reassignment surgery has always been well established in Singapore. Both factors are at play: more transsexuals occur and a greater number of them present themselves for surgery.

Some researchers predict the attention to environmental issues in this country, as well as the international efforts to clean up the water and air and limit the use of agricultural pesticides, may reduce the comparative incidence of MtF transsexuality in the future.

Although pollution might be a secondary cause or a contributing factor to the occurrence of transgenderism, it is unlikely it is the sole cause, since transgender girls like me were born and raised before DDT, PCBs, and other extensively used agricultural pesticides existed. Certainly, pollution was far less evident back then.

Please note that the statistics above refer to postoperation transsexuals, which are used because hospital surgical records are the only statistics available. Preoperation and nonoperation transsexuals and other transgender people are not counted in these statistics.

CHAPTER 4, Transgender Sexual Characteristics

Since wanting to be the other sex was recognized before puberty for many of us, I feel that being a transgender person does not involve sexual preference. Even those who became aware of a desire to be the other sex later in life knew something was different that set them apart from the rest of the world. I derive some measure of comfort from this thought because I would prefer my reason for wanting to be female wasn't due to some sexual fantasy.

There is a good deal written about the sex habits and practices of transgender individuals. However, sexual preference regarding FtM and MtF transgender people is personal and specific to each person.

Transgender individuals can be heterosexual, gay/lesbian, bisexual, asexual, or any other sexual preference or no preference at all. Being a transgender person has nothing at all to do with sexual preference. They are two separate and distinct issues. Transgenderism is an identity. Sexual orientation is a behavior.

The transgender population, however, is divided among the various sexual orientations a bit differently than the general population. One reason is due to the confusion of having different reference points (i.e., "physical indications of sex" different from a "brain sex"). You can interpret sex with anyone as either different-sex or same-sex, depending on whether your point of reference is the physical indications of sex or the "brain sex."

Many transgender people married in their youth because there was no other acceptable life. Most people conformed to heterosexuality and did not violate the prevalent homosexual taboo. If you were labeled a girl, you married a man. If you were labeled a boy, you married a girl.

Confusing Sexual Orientation

Transgender individuals can present a confusing situation regarding sexual orientation. Although bisexuality is common in the transgender community, the majority of the total population is monosexual, either heterosexual or homosexual. When dealing with a transgender person, there are two different reference points with which to make the sexual orientation determination—the sex-label assigned at birth or the sex with which they identify.

Thus, given a particular situation, sexual preference can be heterosexual or homosexual. If you were labeled a male at birth, but really were a woman inside, you would be heterosexually attracted to and desire intimacy with a man. However, society generally ignores what they cannot see and determines sexual orientation by one's birth label. Sexual orientation is a mixed bag in the transgender community.

Responding to the question of a suitable partner, transgender men (i.e., labeled a female at birth) indicated that a nonlesbian nontransgender woman would be the choice:

> I'll give that a "Hell no." Lesbian women who want me aren't the women I want.

> If a trans guy wants to date a Lesbian that is fine by me. [It] doesn't hurt me at all. Bravo to him for going after what he wants! I wouldn't dare criticize him for his desires or identity.

> My bottom line is that I'm not attracted to men.

> Personally, [I] do not go for bodies or genitals or looks. But I do enjoy women more most of the time.

Many transgender men seem to not want to be with a lesbian because that implies they are female. This seems to be the prevalent thinking. They would rather be with a woman who prefers men. That validates their manhood. On the other hand, some transgender women (i.e., labeled a male at birth) said they prefer men and a great number prefer women. Could there be a homophobic component that affects born males more than it affects born females? Transgender women said,

> Rather than being romantic with a man, or another of us girls, my dream is to have a gg [genetic girl] as a lover.

> Why do all cd [crossdressers] want to be with a gg? I have done that and realize I am not a Lesbian, I am a wom[an] and wom[en] like to be with men with their strong arms. When you do that you are truly a normal womyn [woman].

Well, not all want to be with a "G/G." Some would prefer to be with one, others might be attracted to men or need the validation that being with male brings. I think that partnering with a cis woman [nontransgender woman] is an aesthetic preference for many of us: they're softer, smell nicer, and are generally easier on the eye than many male specimens. A lot of us here started off life as male, but we got past that. Why not surround ourselves with the creatures that we admire?

Depends on your life philosophy . . . there are those of us who adopt a submissive persona, and those of us that are independent individuals. If you need the submissive role, depending on men to satisfy your needs, then more power to you. Some of us prefer the strong 'storm the barricades' [and] build your own business role in ourselves.

I love to be accepted as a woman and treated as a woman in all respects. For me, those all respects include sex. . . .I want to be wined and dined and then made love to. I want to be swept off my feet and kissed long, hard, and deep right in the middle of the dance floor. I want that physical contact. I don't know how the other girls feel about this. Do they perceive it as being gay or are they so totally committed to being a girl that they also want to be taken to bed? And when I say taken to bed, that means by a man.

I love the date I have just started, I love the prep of the bath, the shaving, and picking out my clothes, my makeup, and shoes. I love the dominance. Not all men are romantic. It verifies my womanhood to answer the door dressed. I love the feel of the warm kiss. I have to admit I have also been a slut and find it hard waiting for the 3rd date to have sex. All my friends are girls so now they love to hear about my adventures.

The above illustrates that being a transgender woman or man has little to do with sexual orientation. I once told myself that if I am really a woman, I should want to be intimate with a man. Well, I hear some of my friends describe their excitement by a man's muscles and similar stories. I never felt that way. The validity of being a woman on a date with a man does sound appealing, but the payoff, sex, is not worth it for me. However, the greatest validation of my femininity came when a lesbian "hit" on me.

Am I a lesbian? As most transgender people, I seem to always have a new question stirring self-doubt. Researchers tell us that self-doubt is a common characteristic among transgender people, especially transgender women. Why shouldn't there be self-doubt? We are being and doing something that is unacceptable to society.

Since I do not seem to be sexually attracted to either men or women, I question my motives regarding a lack of an attraction to men, which should come naturally to a woman. Am I feeling the lifelong effects of homophobia? Below are some of the possibilities transgender women and transgender men consider:

1. I am not really the other sex.
2. Something else wants me to behave like the other sex.
3. I have been sociologically imprinted with a taboo of what would be gay, given my physical sex.
4. I am not only a transgender person and thus different from other people labeled my sex at birth, but I am also different from most people of the other sex, regarding the usual sexual preferences (i.e., preferring intimacy with the other sex, considering my physical sex.).

A transgender man said,

I'm pansexual. That means I'm attracted to all gender identities and sexes.

Regarding the sexual orientation issue, an interesting situation exists. A transgender man is physically a female. To be heterosexual as defined by general society, "she" would have to be attracted to men. However, according to "his" brain gender, that would be same sex attraction. When applying the same person's attraction to a woman, his brain says heterosexual and society believes it is homosexual. This same contradiction exists for transgender women.

Generally, when labeling a transsexual's sexual orientation, one should properly consider the sex of the individual's identity. Therefore, a transgender woman would be heterosexual with a man. Just as the proper use of pronouns is generally determined by the person's presentation, sexual orientation is determined from the same reference point, usually the one being transitioned to.

All in all, transgender relationships can be confusing until you realize that when it comes to relationships, labels really are immaterial. As one transgender woman said,

> I am viewing it as someone that needs to feel connected with the person with whom they have sexual relations. . . .It shouldn't be labeled a "heterosexual" relationship or a "homosexual" relationship but a "loving" relationship.

Regardless of labels, the ideal relationship needs to be a loving one.

People with sexual attraction to neither women nor men are sometimes described as asexual; however, the term does not always fit exactly since asexual implies a lack of all erotic interests. Magnus Hirschfeld described a person who is not attracted to men or woman outside themselves, but to the woman (or man) inside themselves, as automonosexual (see Chapter 1, Endnote 9). Ray Blanchard[1] coined a word for this condition, autogynephilic ("love of one's self as a woman").

John Money referred to this phenomenon as analloerotic (see Chapter 1, Endnote 7). The word comes from the Greek "an" or "lacking" and "alloerotic" sexual desire or attraction to another person of any gender (i.e., analloerotic refers to lacking in sexual attraction to people of any gender, but not necessarily to one's self).

The above manipulation of terms can be confusing; however, asexual, automonosexual, analloerotic, and autogynephilic are similar since they all describe a person who has no erotic feeling toward another woman or man. The difference is their erotic feeling may be for sex itself or for the person within. Although the terms were originally used to describe transgender women as all older studies, they are equally valid for transgender men.

There is no descriptive word for someone who is not sexually aroused by either a man a woman or one's self, but the thought and/or the orgasm itself. I wonder, in that case, would sexually goal-oriented or orgasmic goal-oriented be an appropriate description?

As related in the literature there is a relatively high incidence of asexual women and of women who are disinterested in sex. If this is true, it might have a direct connection to their low level of testosterone.

Personally, I believe—regardless of testosterone level—I have never lusted for either men or women the way I observed other people did. I recognize transgender women should heterosexually be attracted to men; however, a larger percentage of transgender people than in the general population are lesbians. That is, they are attracted to women, which according to their brain sex is homosexual. I believe the homosexual taboo prevalent as they grew up has brain washed them, even in their female state, to avoid intimacy with a man. Perhaps this explains the higher percentage of lesbian and bisexual transgender women than in the general population. The brainwashed homophobic mind may also explain why transgender people never had the urge to have sex as a woman or to have sex as a man with a man.

Some transgender women say they fantasize they are in the feminine role with a woman or imagine their female partner is a man. Is this also an expression of homophobia?

Regarding women, in my younger years, I did not aggressively pursue sex with the girls I dated, like the other guys did. One girlfriend from my past that I met after fifty years said, "I always liked you because you never tried to talk me into having sex." (If I knew I was supposed to, I would have tried simply to maintain my male persona).

While out in the street, my male friends would call my attention to a pretty pair of legs as they walked down the street, the "boobs" a girl had, or mention the sexy body, etc. I never initiated such appreciation, although my male persona looked without adding a remark. It just wasn't me. After I married, I rationalized that joining in the lust for women on the street would be unfaithful to my spouse. Although it would be macho and good for my assumed persona, I never did that. I do admire a pretty woman, but not in the lustful way my friends did. This, I have learned, is another typical trait of transgender women, although I feel asexuality and a good deal of nurtured homophobia was involved.

The study of transgender people's sexual characteristics was enlightening for me. It taught me that sexual orientation might mean more than the direction you are facing when you do it.

The Bisexual Connection

Bisexuality is a valid transgender subject, since a disproportionate number of transgender women and men are bisexual compared to the general population,. Marshall Miller,[2] founder of the BiHealth Program, estimates there are twice as many bisexual women as there are lesbians, yet little is publicized about bisexual people compared to lesbian people.

The dictionary defines the term bisexual as an individual's capacity for emotional, romantic, and/or physical attraction to more than one gender. This capacity for attraction does, or does not, have to involve sexual interaction.

According the Merriam-Webster dictionary, bisexuality means relating to, or characterized by, a tendency to direct sexual desire toward both sexes. Bisexuality is a behavior or an orientation involving physical and/or romantic attraction to both males and females. It is one of the three main classifications of sexual orientation, along with heterosexual and a homosexual orientation.

Bisexuality does not require a person be attracted equally to both sexes. People who have a distinct, but not an exclusive preference for one sex over the other may still identify themselves as bisexual.

People used to think of bisexuality as a stage between heterosexual and same-sex intimacy. However, bisexuality is a valid sexual orientation along with heterosexual and other orientations. Furthermore, some people mistakenly believe a person who has a same-sex experience is gay/lesbian, when they may be bisexual or even heterosexual.

In 1995, Lisa Diamond[4] studied 79 women, who identified themselves as lesbian, bisexual, or unlabeled. Those identified as heterosexual were not included in the study. At that time, their ages were between 18 and 25. She followed up with her participants for several years and found they never wavered from their attraction to both sexes. The study found the participants were more consistent with the model of bisexuality as a stable identity, rather than a transitional stage.

Dr. Diamond further found bisexual women were more likely than lesbians to switch between a self-description as bisexual and unlabeled, rather than as lesbian or heterosexual. This indicated they identified as bisexual and not any monosexual classification. In fact, a good definition of bisexuality might be "not monosexual."

We find comments throughout history about bisexual individuals. Krafft-Ebing,[5] in the eighteen hundreds, suggested bisexuality is how we all start out. It is the original state of human sexuality. He felt sociological factors steered bisexuals away from bisexual behavior or self-identification as a bisexual.

Sigmund Freud[6] agreed. He felt all human beings are bisexual and their libido is distributed between objects of both sexes.

It is distributed in a manifest or latent form. Based on his clinical observations, he believed people remain bisexual all their lives and repress their nonheterosexual behavior.

Alfred Kinsey,[7] a zoologist, studied this idea in the 1940s. Kinsey developed a "scale" regarding sexual orientation. His scale went from heterosexuality at one end to homosexuality at the other. Kinsey originally used bisexual to mean intersex people, since he preferred to use bisexual in the biological sense of the term.

I believe bisexuality, like transgenderism, is simply not understood by the general public, in spite of the fact that they both have been studied for well over a hundred years. Perhaps bisexuality has been difficult to comprehend because it is a challenge to the binary thinking regarding sexual orientation.

Biphobic people conclude if someone is bisexual, she or he must have a tendency toward infidelity since she or he must have a lover in each of the two sexes. Other biphobic thoughts include: bisexuals are indecisive, they can't make up their mind; they are over sexed and always on the prowl; or bisexuals are in between a heterosexual and a homosexual person on their way to homosexuality.

Different cultures vary widely when considering the likelihood of a bisexual population. Some cultures appear to have a complete absence of bisexual individuals and others recognize it as a widespread sexuality. For example, bisexuality is wide spread among the Sambia of New Guinea and in similar Melanesian cultures.

There have been several studies comparing bisexual individuals' sexual habits with others. Many are demeaning and all simply are rubbish. Bisexuals are no different than people who identify themselves as having other or same sexual preferences.

The transgender community contains a high number of bisexual people. That is probably due the fact that a high percentage conform to societal demands and are married in what is considered a heterosexual relationship. Frequently, they follow their brain sex with outside sexual encounters. So, a transgender woman is married to a woman but seeks the attention of men. Similarly, a transgender man is married to a man but would prefer to lure a woman.

In this regard, one transgender woman said,

Many of my TG [transgender] friends tell me that they desire a man when dressed but not when they are in drab [men's clothes].

Perhaps Freud was right. We are all bisexual. But many identify as heterosexual due to societal pressures and a need to conform to those societal "norms." Those who hide any feelings toward the same physical sex become suspect when they protest their preference is not for the same physical sex. They protest (too much) to avoid drawing questions from observers.

In 1995, Harvard professor Marjorie Garber[8] made the academic case for bisexuality in *Vice Versa: Bisexuality and the Eroticism of Everyday Life*. She felt as Sigmund Freud, that if not for repression, religion, repugnance, denial, laziness, shyness, lack of opportunity, premature specialization, a failure of imagination, or a life already full with erotic experiences with only one person or gender, everyone would identify as bisexual.

The Homosexual Connection

Until the early twentieth century, homosexuality and transgenderism were thought to be the same thing. Even today, people automatically assume a transgender person is homosexual. It is true transgender individuals can be homosexual; however, they are not exclusively homosexual. Most are heterosexual and others, more often than in the general population, are bisexual.

It is recognized by nearly all authorities that transgender individuals can be heterosexual, homosexual, bisexual, asexual, or whatever. Any authority can tell you that sexual orientation, such as being a gay or transgender person are, without question, two distinctly different phenomena, or are they?

Whether or not homosexuality and transgenderism are completely different is questionable. Two different investigations demonstrate there is a transgender-homosexual connection. Simon LeVey's[9] investigation (1991) found that a part of the brain's hypothalamus (i.e., a nuclei named interstitial nucleus of the anterior hypothalamus 3, for short called the INAH3) is about twice as large in men as it is in women. Furthermore, the size of homosexual men's INAH3 was similar to heterosexual women. In another investigation, Alicia Garcia-Falgueras and Dick F. Swaab[10] found the same INAH3 relationship regarding transgender women and nontransgender women.

It seems there is a physiological connection between homosexual men and transgender women regarding the INAH3's size. However, investigations of the BSTc region of the brain found homosexual men and transgender women to be different in both volume and neuron number (see Chapter 5).

Regarding the INAH3, the Garcia-Falgueras and Swaab's studies dealt with the two factors usually considered in research of the brain: the volume of the area studied (i.e., its size) and the number of neurons (i.e., nerve endings) in that area. It was found male-to-female transsexuals had femalelike characteristics in both attributes.

Gay men, on the other hand, departed from both attributes being femalelike. They had a femininelike volume and a masculinelike neuron count. This, plus the fact that transgender women were feminine in both characteristics, allowed researchers to conclude INAH3 volume may be related to sexual orientation and neuron number may be related to gender identity.

Because of the similarity of the volume of the INAH3 between transgender women and gay men in the research, I interviewed a gay man I knew because he presented as a man, but self-identified as a woman. He said he dressed as a girl "all the time" in his younger years. I asked why he stopped "dressing" and he replied he stopped dressing as a woman when he discovered sex. His self-identification as a woman and presentation as a man made me question more about him. Was he saying he was a woman because of his passive sexual role? However, since he dressed as a woman regularly in his younger years (i.e., before puberty), was he a transgender woman who could identify as a woman, but didn't have a need to dress as one?

Was he a transgender person, a homosexual person, or some combination I haven't encountered yet? It doesn't seem likely that he dressed in girls' clothes to facilitate sex with men because he indicated most of the time he dressed in feminine clothes, he wasn't sexually aware and was too young for sexual activity. He claimed he really was a woman, but perhaps when he "found" sex, he found enough womanhood to satisfy himself. There is a possibility that he dressed as a woman because he saw himself in a woman's role regarding future relationships with men. Another possibility is that when he found sex he was old enough to recognize the difficult social problem associated with a man dressing as a woman and was able to avoid that complication. Perhaps living as a gay man presented more easily found opportunities to have sex as a woman. Is he a transgender woman following his brain sex and not homosexual at all?

Determining one's (subconscious) classification—motive—is a complication transgender people have. If a transgender man is partnered with a man; therefore, if he is a transgender person, according to his physical sex he is in a homosexual relationship. However, if his brain sex says he is a woman, she is in a heterosexual relationship.

Dr. Richard Green,[11] retired Director of the Adult Gender Identity Clinic in England, found a connection between homosexual and transsexual youths. He observed 44 feminine boys, apparent transsexual youths, as they grew up. They were naturally expected to grow up as transsexuals; however, most grew up to be homosexual. He concluded, "We can't tell a pregay from a pretranssexual at 8 [years old]."

The Head teacher, Sitisak Sumontha, said in his 35 years of working in the Thailand Education System, he has come across "many boys like this [between 10% and 20%] who want to grow to be women. Many go on to have sex change surgery, while others will live as gay men."[12]

It is observed some transgender women never act on becoming a woman. At the other extreme, some transgender women seek every surgical procedure and socialization training available to be as much like a woman as is possible. Of course, transgender women exist everywhere between the two extremes. Individual differences are alive and well in the transgender community, just as everywhere else. There are no two people and no two transgender people exactly alike.

The inquiry into an individual's sexual orientation usually stops once it was agreed they are a transgender, homosexual, bisexual, or heterosexual person. The individual and no one else seems to asked the important question of why. Why homosexual? Why bisexual? Why heterosexual? .

The discussion with the gay man above prompted a closer examination of the possibility of a homosexual-transgender connection. Also, society says—and it sounds logical in that context—if a transgender woman really is and thinks like a woman, she heterosexually should want any intimacy to be with a man. This inquiry's need was reinforced by the fact that the volume of the INAH3 was the same in homosexual men and transgender women, and they both were similar to heterosexual women. Furthermore, if there is a transgender-homosexual connection, how often does homosexuality occur in transgender women and how often are homosexual men transgender women?

An interview with several self-described homosexual men was undertaken to explore "the transgender-homosexual connection." The major questions put to the participants were, "Did you ever want to be a girl or a woman? Did you ever wear girl or women's clothes?" The interviewees were also asked questions designed to prompt them to talk about the subject and hopefully stimulate their memory regarding the initial questions. "Did you ever fantasize being a girl or a woman?" "After a shower, did you wrap the towel around your waist and feel it looked like a skirt?"

I interviewed 88 gay men and I found it practical to divide them into three basic groups as follows:[13]

Group 1 (56.8%) were those who definitely show no trace of transgender behavior or thinking;

Group 2 (14.8%) consisted of those you might describe as "maybe," but the behavior and feelings could not be placed in either of the "definite" categories; and

Group 3 (28.4%) showed definite transgender like behavior at one time.

The questions were asked at two LGBTQ Centers on Long Island, New York; however, most of the participants questioned attended a National Services and Advocacies for GLBT Elders (SAGE) conference in New York City and were from all parts of the United States.

Each of the three groups had an expected within-group variation. The within-group variation was not recorded or scored. However, the answers indicated there were definitely a variation within all three groups.

It is felt if the results were to be scored according to the intensity of transgenderism in the nonrandom sample, it would fit the graph in Figure A (CHAPTER 3—Transgender Research, An Infinite Variation of Gender). That is, a completely variable sample with a descending degree of transgender intensity.

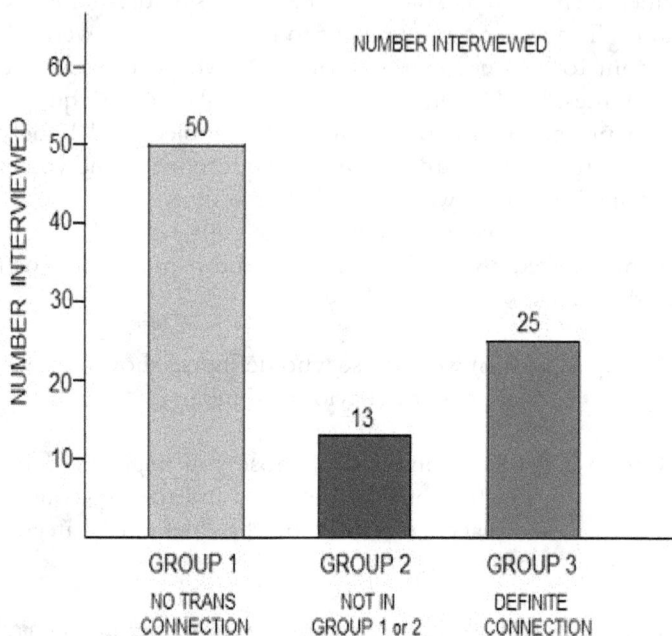

FIGURE B - Gay Men's Inclination Toward Transgenderism - Groups

The interviews with lesbians to determine if there is a connection between lesbians and transgender men were unsuccessful. In interviews with several self-described lesbians, it was found those that thought they once wanted to be a boy/man always mentioned the fact that boys and men had advantages they envied. Wanting to be the other sex for personal gain excludes a person from being classified as a transgender person.

Did the interviewed lesbians want to be a boy/man because their brains were "wired" that way (i.e., transgender) and justified their feeling by saying that boys had advantages, or was the desires to be a boy/man primarily for the advantages men have?

Since it was not possible to separate wanting to be a man for personal gain from using men's advantages as a justification for an inner feeling, the study was confined to gay men. However, in discussions with several lesbians, it was apparent there is also a connection between lesbians and transgender men.

The LeVey, et al. studies indicated a physiological similarity between gay men and heterosexual women. The Zhou, et al. study found a similarity between transgender women and nontransgender heterosexual women. Those two studies demonstrated a connection between homosexual men and transgender women (i.e., If "a" = "c" and "b" = "c", then "a" must = "b"). Furthermore, the above interview found 28% of the gay population questioned showed, a strong tendency toward being transgender women.

Taken together, the results of the study reinforce the belief there is a transgender-homosexual connection. I feel additional studies should be done to establish a gay man's scale from no transgender inclination to strong transgender inclination.

In any case, it is interesting to note Dr. Kenneth Zucker's[14] reparative therapy's "cure" for transgenderism "successfully" resulted in homosexual individuals. This study indicates the result of no therapy or action may produce a similar result. Furthermore, the Thai school experience plus Dr. Greene's study indicate Dr. Zucker's cure is likely to be "time" rather than "therapy." It should be noted here that WPATH, the World Professional Association for Transgender Health, has stated Reparative Therapy (sometimes referred to as Aversion Therapy) is unethical.

The Asexual Connection

Asexuality is sort of like bisexuality in reverse. Whereas bisexual people are sexually attracted to females and males, asexual people are attracted to neither. Engaging in sexual activity is not the determinant of being asexual or not. Asexual people have engaged in sexual activity, but their objective may be the only route to a romantic relationship.

Asexual people are frequently thought of as the opposite of hypersexual, which includes an excessive inclination toward sexual activity. Asexual individuals are those who do not experience sexual attraction. It should not be confused, however, with someone who avoids sexual activity for religious or other reasons. Asexuality is a purely internal orientation without outside influences.

Although sexual activity is not the goal of asexual individuals, romantic involvement is sought.

The Asexual Visibility and Education Network (AVEN) was originated to create understanding and acceptance by the general public, gather a community of asexual individuals, and promote discussion. AVEN was founded by David Jay[15] in 2001. It now serves as an informational resource for asexual people, their family, friends, and other interested parties.

Unlike other nonheterosexual sexual orientations, asexuality was never persecuted and most people would know what the name implies, without actually understanding or ever knowing an asexual person.

Asexual individuals are fairly common in the transgender population. The reason is not clear. However, it seems there are a larger percentage of asexual transgender people than in the general population. If I were to speculate, I would say that comes about due to two factors.

First, older transgender people married for various reasons. They, of course, married someone of the other sex, which was the only possibility at the time. Some may not have been sexually attracted to the other sex, but filled the role expected of them. The second factor was the strong homosexual taboo that existed for their whole life.

Thus, they had no sexual attraction for their husband/wife and a strong taboo kept them from allowing themselves to be attracted to their same sex. They may have been romantically involved with their spouse, but their sexual excitement was not directed to their spouse or someone of either sex.

Men Who Like Transgender Women

Men who seek the company of and intimacy with transgender women are frequently referred to as "admirers." Most men are not admirers. I tested this statement out on a dance floor. A man I never met before asked me to dance at a hotel restaurant/bar. After dancing a while and wanting to see if he asked me to dance because I was a woman or because I was thought of as a novelty, I leaned forward and whispered in his ear, "You know you are dancing with a transsexual." He immediately took a step backward, waved bye, bye with his hand and quickly retired to the other end of the room and subsequently disappeared from sight.

Furthermore, violence toward transgender women points to the fact that at least some men hate transgender women or more likely are threatened by the fear that any attraction to them would make them a homosexual. Yet it is known other men are attracted to transgender women. A quick look at a transgender web site demonstrates this. I wondered what kind of person seeks the company of and intimacy with transgender women?

Heterosexual men want a woman who wants to be a woman. Heterosexual women want a man who wants to be a man. A homosexual woman, a lesbian, wants a woman who wants to be a woman and was always a woman. A homosexual man, a gay man, wants a man who wants to be a man and was always a man. What does that leave for a transgender woman or a transgender man?

Of course, some think there are exceptions to the above. For example, I know some gay men who partner with a feminine gay guy. Generally, neither the feminine gay guy nor his partner wants him to be a woman. Furthermore, this question does not refer to a man solely seeking an orgasm. Some men will have sex with a totem pole because they want an orgasm. I am referring to a woman wanting a relationship with a transgender man and a man wanting a relationship with a transgender woman. I previously thought a lesbian in denial would want a transgender man and a gay man in denial would want a transgender woman. They could satisfy their desire for intimacy with a same sex physical body and avoid the homosexual stigma by having their sex partner look like the other sex. Some literature suggests several other possibilities that are less than flattering and this may be true in some cases. However, I have come to the conclusion a mentally sound admirer would best be described as a bisexual man, just as a bisexual woman could be interested in a transgender man. They would be a perfect fit.

I suggested admirers could best be described as bisexual in a posting on a transgender woman's web site. Admirers responded to how they "classify" themselves:

Yes, bisexuality is a good answer for us admirers!

I would have to say bisexual.

Many times I have wondered about that question myself. This is what it is for me. I love the illusion that a passable, petite lady has for me. At that time, I am with a WOMAN. I know that person is male, but yet do not care for the male person until she starts to be femme. . . . I know what is in those panties, yet will never check out or have any interest in a male's anatomy. The hottest thing that can make me crazy hot are the real ts galz [transsexual woman] that have that huge appendage and breasts. My answer in a nutshell is this

. . . yes bisexual would be a classification I will tell you here, although I have never told another soul of this.

Some of us men are right here waiting for a woman who wants a relationship with ONE guy. Of course, chemistry is important. A pic is a pic and a heart is a heart? What do you want? Both? Hard to find sometimes for us all.

I consider myself Bi, but whenever I am around a transgender woman I always treat her [as] a real woman that she truly is inside, and always feel that I am with a real woman, so I should not thin[k] of myself as Bi but as Straight. But as you must know most men are VERY homophobic and do not feel the same way as me, to them it's not about the person, but about the pinas [penis] in their pants, and god forbid your girl's is going to be bigger than yours, lol. So because of them I consider myself Bi. But I have never bin [been] with men and not attracted to them at all.

But I am only 35, so I will see, lol. I try to keep an opened [open] mind about everything in my life.

A bisexual man would not have an objection to a transgender woman's physically male body nor to her feminine appearance and demeanor. A bisexual man could certainly feel both comfortable and satisfied on both levels by being intimate with a transgender woman.

As always, transgender research is far more extensive regarding transgender women than transgender men. However, as in most characteristics, many parallels exist between the two. Research has found genetic women and transgender women have a similarity regarding the size and the number of neurons in a part of the brain's hypothalamus. Furthermore, women's size and neuron count are different from men. It is also known transgender men have that part of the hypothalamus similar to genetic men. Science has previously shown that these same small areas of the brain's hypothalamus are programmed to experience a strong predisposition toward feeling like a girl or like a boy.

CHAPTER 5, Similarities—Transgender and the Other Sexes

The Brain Sex Theory

In 1995, the journal Nature reported findings in The Netherlands, by Doctors Zhou, Hofman, Gooren, and Swaab,[1] that involved a region of the brain that may hold an explanation for gender identity dysphoria. This region of the brain, called the bed nucleus of the stria terminalis, central (BSTc), had been known for a long time to influence sexual behavior. It had also been known to be much larger in males than in females. In fact, a man's BSTc was found to be about 44% greater in size than the BSTc region in genetic women.

Zhou, et al. looked for a brain similarity between genetic women and postoperative transsexual women. (Note: postoperative transsexuals are frequently used in studies of this kind because a simple postmortem physical examination of the body distinguishes a postoperative transsexual woman from a genetic woman or a man, with absolute certainty). They examined the BSTc region, since it was known to influence sexual behavior.

They found male-to-female transgender women have a smaller BSTc region than men, and its size is comparable to the size of a genetic woman's BSTc. It has been reported elsewhere that female-to-male transgender men have a BSTc the size of males. Homosexual men also have a heterosexual man's BSTc region's size.

Where homosexual women fit, in this regard, is not known, since it was not explored in this study.

In 2000, Kruijver, Pool, Hofman, Gooren and Swaab[2] reinforced the Zhou group's findings. They examined the number of neuron endings in the BSTc region. The differences between men and both women and transgender women were even more divergent. Men had 71% more nerve endings in the BSTc than both genetic and transgender women.

The sample size involved in these investigations was criticized because it was small and small sample sizes are prone to error. The small sample size was partly because the part of the brain studied is so small that it can only be studies post mortem. It was suggested a larger sample size should be examined. However, the measurements were so close to each other that the results were said to be strikingly positive and therefore the conclusions were statistically sound.

The BSTc size grouping's $p = < .005$ resulted in a far closer relationship than generally accepted by statisticians to show the relationship was not the result of a biased sample (i.e., $< .05$ would have been a "strong" enough result to assure that there was a 99.5% chance that the sample findings were not biased). The measurement of the number of neurons had a $p < .04$ and was also credible.

This similarity between a transgender woman's brain and a genetic woman's brain was simply attributed to the fact that the postoperative transsexual baby was born with a small BSTc region or, more likely, the BSTc region was programmed from birth to grow to a smaller size, just as a genetic female's does.

The critics entertained the idea that some other factor in the life of a postoperative transsexual woman caused the BSTc to become, and/or stay smaller. This possibility had to be explored because it is known some life experiences can cause changes to parts of the human brain.

The brain seems to be designed to change under some conditions. Scientists refer to this ability to change, the plasticity of parts of the brain, as neuroplasticity. They believe the brain is designed to allow such a change. However, neuroplasticity was found by the Kruijver, et al. researchers not to be a factor in the study sample.

Based on the participants in the sample, the research showed neither the addition of female hormones nor the deprivation of male hormones caused a change in the size of the BSTc region of the transgender women's brains. Neither did other life-related factors affect the size. The evidence strongly suggests the transgender baby was born with a small BSTc region, in the same way women's are born. Furthermore, the BSTc similarities may account for the early inner feelings of femininity of transgender girls and genetic girls.

I believe the similarity of part of transgender men's brains to that of genetic men's accounts for the feeling of masculinity in both transgender boys and genetic boys.

The Kruijver study also showed sexual preference was not a factor in the study, also based on the sample utilized.

In considering this research, the remaining question is which came first, the chicken or the egg? Were the children born programmed to have a BSTc the size of the other sex, which caused them to become a transgender person, or they first become a transgender person and that resulted in them having a BSTc region comparable to that of the other sex? Could the two possibilities have occurred simultaneously?

Brain Sex Theory Controversy

The research of the BSTc has become known as the Brain-Sex Theory of Transsexualism. It suggests a possible neuroanatomical marker for transsexualism in the brain. Some research scientists have questioned both the Zhou and Kruijver conclusions.

Chung, et al.[3] in 2002 issued what some called the most serious challenge to Zhou's and Kruijver's conclusion. They found that significant BSTc volume and neuron number does not develop in humans until adulthood. Most transgender people, however, report their feelings of gender dysphoria began in early childhood.

I don't understand why this is a challenge. Is the development of the BSTc any different than many other things that develop later in life? What Chung found was perhaps there is something, yet undiscovered, that determines the BSTc size. That is, perhaps the BSTc size is a symptom and not the cause. It is quite possible there is something different that triggers the development of the BSTc region later in life.

There are physiological changes triggered to become active later in life. This varies from the release of hormones in the fetus to the onset of puberty in the child. Chung actually agreed, using other words, that this could be an explanation that makes his findings compatible with both Zhou's and Kruijver's conclusions.

An additional criticism by Chung, et al. was a suggestion that the sample included only heterosexual transsexuals whereas Zhou, reinforced by Kruijver's investigation, claimed the study sample contained both heterosexual and homosexual transgender participants.

The small sample size has also been criticized, but the statistical tests say the conclusions were valid. Volume's $p = < .005$ and neuron count's $p = < .04$ were both statistically indicative of an unbiased sample.

Another study[4], performed in 2002, confirmed that the concentration of neurons in physical males who are transsexual women is essentially the same as that of genetic females. It was also confirmed that homosexual and heterosexual males, as well as female-to-male transgender men, all had more a more numerous neuron count in the BSTc region. This further reinforced the previous finding that this region is unaffected by postnatal hormone levels.

The Hulshoff Pol, Schnack, et al[5] study, in 2006, suggested cross sex hormone therapy might have been responsible for the Zhou/Kruijver findings. However, both the Zhou and the Kruijver investigations concluded that hormone regimens were not a factor in their sample. This newer study did not invalidate the explanations but it said they were irrelevant, since the simplest and most plausible explanation of the Zhou/Kruijver findings is they are attributable, at least largely, to the effects of "cross" hormone therapy administered during adulthood.

Many other studies were performed since and the Zhou and Kruijver studies and the original results have repeatedly been reinforced.

The Journal of Clinical Endocrinology and Metabolism, in 2000, reported a study with 42 participants. Male-to-female transsexuals have femalelike neuron numbers in a limbic nucleus. Other factors clearly support the belief that transsexuals' differentiation between the brain and genitals and feel they can develop in different gender directions. That pointed to a neurobiological basis of Gender Identity Dysphoria.

In 2000, Kruijver, et al.[6] found the circulation of androgens had to do with reproduction, cognition, and neuroprotection. The circulation of androgens did not affect sexual orientation or transgenderism.

In 2008, Alicia Garcia-Falgueras and Dick F. Swaab also studied the hypothalamic uncinate nucleus[7] to learn if there is a brain similarity between transsexuals and genetic women. They found the volume and nerve count were similar to the results of previous studies of this nucleus. However, their study showed the similarity of transgender women and genetic women in this nucleus was not due to estrogen treatment, since premenopausal women and postmenopausal women were the also the same. The investigators concluded their observations indicate this is, at least partly, a marker of an early atypical sexual differentiation of the brain. Furthermore, they said, the changes observed in the $INAH_3$ and the BSTc may belong to a complex network that may structurally and functionally be related to gender identity. This seems to be the most plausible conclusion.

The original Zhou, et al. conclusions seem to endure in spite of repeated criticism of every aspect of the study. The transgender community, and that includes this author, are biased because we would like to believe there is an anatomic reason for the way we feel about our own gender. The search for a positive, unquestionable, nontheoretical answer, including the mechanism through which gender conflict occurs, continues.

If there really is an anatomic reason for transgenderism, is it that simple? Is that it? Does the size and neuron number and what triggers those characteristics explain the mystery of why some people are transgender inclined and some are not? The one disappointment with this theory is that the region of the brain under discussion is so tiny, it is best measured after the person dies. It would be productive to find a way of measuring these nuclei on participants that are alive, so a diagnosis can be made and treated early in life, when a diagnosis would be most useful.

The regions involved in these studies are part of the hypothalamus, sometimes called the "primitive brain." It has long been known to be the regulator of the autonomic system (i.e., the heartbeat and other involuntary or autonomic physiological activity). Hormone production and sexual behavior are controlled here. I feel there is likely to be far more involved in this issue.

The more recent research conducted at UCLA, led by Dr. Eric Vilain,[8] involved pediatric genetics and how the effect of hormones impact prenatal development. Working with his team, he discovered 54 genes are linked to gender. Before this discovery, it was thought hormones were completely and solely responsible for the distinction between the male and the female in an individual. However, these genes are activated before the switch of the SRY gene is turned on (the SRY gene is responsible for releasing the testosterone that makes the fetus a boy). Eighteen of the 54 genes were produced at noticeably higher levels in males. Thirty-six genes, the balance of these 54 genes, were produced at higher levels in females. In the future, the continuation of this research could determine where the transgender feeling of being born in the wrong body originates. However, as of now, the research continues and we must wait for the results. Eventually, we may have the answer.

This research at UCLA suggests transgenderism may result from a mutation of a gene that protects against sex reversal or other interference with the usual sexual development and functional integration of a number of different genes that contribute to sex determination, sexual differentiation, and sexual behavior.

The UCLA research could suggest transgenderism may be caused by the opposite of a gene mutation that causes a particular sexual development. It may also be the opposite—a genetic mutation of the gene that prevents a mutation from happening.

Transgender Sexual Orientation

It is a fact transgender individuals are like the general public regarding variation in their sexual orientation. They can be heterosexual, homosexual, bisexual, or anything else, just as is the case for nontransgender individuals. The only unique thing about transgender sexual orientation is that the same transgender person can be considered heterosexual or homosexual with a specific individual at the same moment. Your sexual orientation depends on whether you are considering the brain sex or the physical sex. The general public seems to cling to the physical sex when defining sexual orientation. However, the proper base line is the brain sex. When some transgender men prefer a female partner, they are being heterosexual because their brain sex is making a choice; however, some people refuse to accept the brain sex theory and consider them lesbians, using their physical sex as the basis for determining sexual orientation.

My personal observation is that a disproportionate number of transgender women are attracted to women (i.e., they are brain sex lesbians). I feel at least part of the reason for this is that older transgender women spent a substantial part of their life recognizing they are physically men and thus look upon an attraction to women as heterosexual behavior. They avoid intimacy with men, which they have always been taught was homosexuality and a serious taboo.

However, some may simply be expressing their male side, sexually, while expressing their feminine side in other ways. No one ever said a transgender people can't be both a woman and a man at the same time.

Researchers have found older transgender women are attracted to women and most of the younger transgender women are attracted to men. I feel this is logical. Older transgender women have been exposed to a strong homosexual taboo for a relatively long period of time. Therefore, such relationships are avoided. As a result, they seek the acceptable route and gravitate toward intimacy with women.

On the other hand, younger transgender women experienced a more permissive society and:

1. Did not experience the social implanting of homophobia over a long time that older transgender woman felt.
2. Being a woman allowed them to never fully accept their manhood.
3. Are sociologically more like a woman and live in a world that accepts homosexuality more readily.

Important questions I have not found in all the research and studies is why some transgender individuals feel they are a woman (in the wrong body) and others feel they simply want to be the other sex? The study in Appendix V, Category Versus Age of Transgender Realization, indicates those that want to be a woman have shorter memories that do not go back to an early enough age? Those whose memory goes back to ages 3 through 6 always believed they were female. In spite of this study, could there really be two or more different kinds of transgenderism?" Are we also dealing with something else?

CHAPTER 6, What Makes A Transgender?

One's gender identity is a subjective sense of one's own gender. The subjective gender is real to the individual and recognized long before they are conscious of their physical gender. One's gender and sex are usually aligned with each other and that is the way society says it is supposed to be. However, some people know, at an early age, there is a disagreement between the two. They frequently discover their conflict at about 6 years of age, when the school separates the boys from the girls. Sometimes it occurs before that.

The conflict is not perceived as "normal." That is, it is not what you are supposed to feel or what the usual or average person feels about their gender. Professionals in the field suggest that after a transgender person learns the sex their genitals describe, she or he quickly learns people insist their gender must fall in line with their genitals. Transgender people try to conform and be what everyone expects them to be. This is true because no alternative is known to them. They need to be like everyone else and fit in to avoid ridicule and even isolation. In the effort to be like everyone else and gain general acceptance, most create the persona that conforms to what the rest of the world insists they are.

Adopting an Acceptable Persona

Most transgender children are good at creating a female or male persona, the one everyone wants them to have. Outwardly, they seem to be just like everyone else. Some even convince themselves that they are their physical gender. Transgender boys are generally faced with this later in life, since a tomboy persona experiences a certain amount of permissiveness that is not given to transgender girls. Nevertheless, most transgender children know they are different from their peers early in life.

A small number of transgender children insist on the gender they feel they are and pay dearly for it. Transgender boys, who are not good at creating a female persona, pay a price of being isolated, ostracized, called names, taunted, teased, ridiculed, and sometimes beaten by their playmates because they are too masculine. Some transgender girls similarly do not adopt a male persona well and display feminine characteristics. As a result, they are isolated, ostracized, called names, taunted, teased, ridiculed, and sometimes beaten because they are too feminine.

Some women and men who cannot adopt an "appropriate" persona wrote the following:

> I was beat up regularly at school because they didn't like that I didn't want to do boy things.

> When I was in junior high school (those are times I wish had never happened), I was shunned and snickered at. I got my ass kicked so many times it isn't even funny. I defended myself, but there are only so many battles you can fight at age 12. My classmates used to call me 'Beth the Boy.' It was very hurtful and embarrassing to know that before I even told anyone, people knew I was different from them.

> I was called a sissy in school, but confused everyone by having girlfriends.

The sexes are basically separated socially in elementary school. Usually transgender boys are considered butch or lesbians and many actually believe it until they find out there is a thing called transgenderism. Similarly, transgender girls are isolated from boys because they are too feminine. Transgender girls are often beaten and overtly harassed, whereas transgender boys are beaten less frequently, but more often overtly ostracized by both girls and boys.

The female and male personas are constructed early. The persona of the birth labeled sex is definitely established between the ages of 8 to 15. After all, every child wants to fit in and be like everyone else. It is a deception they become aware of when they eventually feel they must express their "true self" somehow, in some way. One transgender girl wrote how she found a measure of successful feminine expression:

> I'd buy lollipops that made my lips red.

Many of us have experienced the same thing. I also once had a lollipop that made my lips red. I liked having my lips red. It was like wearing lipstick "legally." I unsuccessfully looked for similar lollipops for a long time, but never could find another one. That simply describes a single example of the frustration we feel frequently. A transgender child's life is filled with similar frustrations.

I don't remember thinking I was a woman trapped in a man's body, as others insist they are feeling. Like many transgender women I know, I was sure I always wanted to be a girl; however, I have no memory of feeling I was in the wrong body.

I always wondered if the fact that some transgender girls actually believed they were a girl and others knew they wanted to be a girl indicated 2 different phenomena or was it the intensity of their inborn transgenderism. Perhaps it is being a realist and you recognize your body says you are not a girl or could it be something else? My research (see Chapter 1 and Appendix V, Category Versus Age of Transgender Realization) indicates the difference is how far back we remember. Those who remember back to ages 3, 4, 5 or 6 believe they are a girl and those who do not remember that far back do not. They only recall always wanting to be a girl.

In any case, revealing my transgenderism was the best thing I could have done. I now live as a woman and only think about my being a transgender woman when I am "forced" to. Regarding mental health, the benefit of transitioning was converting gender dysphoria to a sense of euphoria.

Since with a simple glance I knew I couldn't be a female, I used to believe my male persona was real and my wanting to be a woman was a perversion or at best a sickness. Even so, I felt my nagging need to express femininity had to be accommodated in some way. It is a frustrating and tense life.

The obvious way to pacify your need to express your femininity or masculinity was to be as much like your gender identity as possible. That is the basic reason for dressing as a woman or as a man. Wearing the clothes of the other sex is the only way we can feel like our true sex. The simple act of "dressing" results in an euphoric feeling. Medical scientists describe this almost all consuming need to express our inner sex, our true sex, as a Biological Imperative.

For example, I prayed to walk in the street dressed as a woman once, just once, before I died. I really meant it. I prayed for it for years. After I took that first walk, I needed to do it again and again. I wanted to be a woman as much as possible, go where they go and do what they do. I used to joke with a friend that we earned a new merit badge[1] with each new womanly thing we did or each new place we went to that women go to. Wanting to appear "en-femme" more and more is like being freed from a lifelong prison. A prison constructed with bars made of shame. The pleasure of expressing femininity is reinforced by your knowledge that you can express your femininity—yield to your invisible biological demands—without consequences.

It is a self-reinforcing need. The ultimate objective is to live as a woman 24/7.[2] Some individuals continue expressing themselves more and more; others panic at some point and discard their other sex's garments. However, there is absolutely no permanent escape, and 99.9% of those who purge are sure to start again at a later date.

The Double Life

Many of us were not lucky enough to be born in a permissive society and had to carry our transgenderism as a secret for our entire life. We lived with an enormous burden we could not share with anyone. Cultural and social pressures act against our biological predisposition. If you have a compelling need to be the other sex, then you must do what you must do. However, it would be far better to be able to avoid the guilt and shame, the hiding and sneaking. That stuff is harmful. Society may become permissive in the future, but it was long before that, when many of us were born and matured feeling compelled to hide our gender and only express it secretly.

Society compels us to live a double life. A transgender man expressed for all of us this way:

> I know that some people I'm friends with now wouldn't be friends with me if they knew I was a transsexual.

Living a double life takes its toll. It is not a happy situation when you must hide your compelling need to dress as the other sex to escape detection. The hiding is accomplished often and over such a long period of time that it becomes automatic. In some cases, when you are "out" and no longer hiding, it requires a conscious effort to overcome the habit and stop hiding.

No one is happy to live a deceptive life because the lie must be perpetuated in your everyday life. It is not constructive to deceive others even though your fear of embarrassment and the subsequent shame of exposure seems to justify it.

For transgender men, the double life is just as harmful. It may seem transgender guys have a little easier time, since dressing like a man can be stylish and cute; however, dressing as a man all the time is definitely not acceptable and makes others label you with names that are derogatory and hurtful.

I believe one's transgender classification (e.g., crossdresser, transgenderist, transsexual, etc.) is due to how each individual adjusts to the conflict between their inner gender and their need to be so called "normal"—the gender everyone insists you are and everyone expects you to be. Later, the conflict becomes how and to what extent a transgender person resolves the gender issue. Aside from exposing your secret, there is not a generally best solution to this conflict, only a subjective and personal best solution.

Best solutions are usually arrived at as a compromise. Most often the compromise is temporary and frequently changes over time. The changes are due to a growing need that seems more pressing each year. More often, learning you can be accepted in public as your true self is a frequent occurrence. This is true even if you are only secure enough to go to transgender parties or bars that have a "Trans Night."

Self-Doubt

I have a habit of questioning myself regarding the motive of my actions. Being a woman is one of the feelings that I question. I started therapy because I wanted help in determining if I am really a woman (inside). In our first meeting, I told my therapist I wanted help in determining if I am really a woman or simply being a good student of Stanislovsky[4] (i.e., a good methods actor). Although therapy was beneficial, it did not answer my question, so I turned to research. I tell this personal story because it is typical of many transgender people's story.

As discussed, some researchers suggest most children want to be like everyone else—to fit in. Transgender children are no exception. They also want to fit in, be like everyone else, and consequently they act the part expected of them. They need to do this in order to survive, peacefully.

This is an important complication for me. Now my basic question has changed to: Am I acting the part of a woman now, or was I acting before, when I was being a man? This latter question has a strong possibility of being synchronized with my general approach to life. I believe I was always a realist. In navigating through life, I did what was possible. It was not possible to be a woman. It was only possible for me to be what my physical state said I was—a man. Although I may have wished otherwise, I knew there was no magician who could wave a magic wand and change me into the girl I wanted to be, so I felt compelled to be the default sex—a boy. I think I did a fairly good job of it. As my approach to life's challenges has always dictated that I do the best job I possibly could regardless of what it was, even if that job was being a man.

I can't be sure of the answer to my revised question. I really don't know if I am acting as a woman now, was I acting before when I was being a man, or something else. I can't be sure because I know it is human nature to rationalize thoughts and adjust things to make them the way we want them to be or think they should be.

This is not unusual. Many transgender people question themselves. What we want is contrary to what is thought of as the expected or the usual. There is good reason to question what we do. People that insist we are the sex we were labeled with at birth have anatomical evidence, tangible evidence, of our sex—our genitals. What do we have? We have nothing to prove our true and inner sex. It is impossible to show our feelings or our intuitive knowledge of what we are.

There are positive signs that say I am acting now as a transgender woman. I have the mind typically associated with masculine aptitudes like fixing things, numbers, mathematics, and science. However, I have just as many typical feminine attributes that tend to say I am a woman and that I was previously acting the part of a man.

It has been suggested that there are other possibilities. Maybe I was acting as a man before and I am also acting now, only this time as a woman. Kathi Borden, Ph.D., a Clinical Psychologist and my daughter, has suggested that maybe I was not acting before nor am I acting now. Perhaps I am both a man and a woman. My long life as a man must leave some measure of masculinity inside me.

I guess everyone grows up acting. That is how we learn many things. Boys use their father, an uncle, and an older brother as role models and mimic how other boys talk, walk, etc. Girls have their mother, an aunt, or an older sister as role models and learn to act the way other girls talk, walk, etc. We all learn to act our gender part mostly by listening and observing. We even learn from listening to parental telephone conversations.

It is possible that, to some degree, I was acting as a man and am also now acting as a woman. However, this is not what I mean when I question was I acting before or am I acting now. The question boils down to when was I not acting or acting the least? What is my true gender? If I remove the acting from all my "roles," would what I am left with be my "true gender." Since that is not possible, I don't think I will ever know the answer with certainty. Oh, if only transgender research regarding how we get this way would advance faster!

Are the mentioned aptitudes rationalizations? Many women have a mathematical and scientific aptitude thought to be typically masculine.[5] In Britain, girls have been outperforming boys in scholastic aptitude tests. Only since 1988 have boys regained the lead in math.[6]

I also have some attributes that are typical of women, but I am not the only man to have them. I was always more nurturing than most men. I diapered my babies (1956) before most men would do it. I enjoyed the interaction and my ability to play an active part in raising my children. I can sew. My mother selected me, the youngest of three children, to serve my father dinner when she could not be home to do it herself. She knew me best and saw something she thought made me more qualified to temporarily take her place.

When I was young, I always avoided fights. To this day I tend to express agreement with a friend's suggestions. Avoiding controversy is said to be found more in women than men. Also, creativity is more common among women and was a substantial part of my success in the branch of my profession. Furthermore, from reading this, you can see I possess a woman's facility for expressing herself.

Curiously, I hated writing book reports in school. To avoid doing a report, I used the same report for years until a teacher shamed me out of reporting on Jack London's *The Call of the Wild* because it was "too juvenile" for me. I think that might have had more to do with my slow reading habits. However, I was on the staff of my high school newspaper, wrote a regular column for my college newspaper. I single-handedly wrote an engineering society's newsletter for seven years, and for a few decades wrote effective sales letters.

I could go on and on describing both masculine and feminine virtues, so that is really not much help. I know I always wanted to be a girl/woman. I still wish I could have been a girl and now want to be a woman. I don't want to be a man, but in a sense why should I? I did that! I was actually being a man for most of my life, but wanted to be a woman at the same time. Now, I want to be a woman for the rest of my life. I don't yearn to be a man as I once yearned to be a woman.

Reflecting upon the last few paragraphs has led me to more readily accept the possibility that either I was not acting in both my genders or I acted in both of them. On the other hand, wanting something to be has nothing to do with what you truly are. Many transgender women I know also question themselves on this topic. Even those headed for a genital operation have doubts about what they are doing and afterwards, why they did it. Furthermore, I see a direct correlation between intelligence and a self-questioning attitude. Self-doubt is said to be a transgender trait.

Revealed By Your Actions

Another phenomena transgender women share is people they tell their secret to say they suspected it all along. Some people who knew me as a guy and now know I am a gal, say they are not entirely surprised at my being a transgender person. They say, "You gave hints by your actions and words." Different friends had different things they pointed out: I always dressed well and looked nicely "put together;" I took long baths; I like sleeping on satin sheets and pillow slips; I favored wearing silk underwear; and I talked on the telephone to a friend every night for almost an hour. A friend said, "Guys don't do that!" I gave other "hints" typical of a female. I feel these people were, in fact, surprised at my revelation of being a transgender woman and only thought of these "hints" in retrospect.

Of course, some transgender people can't help presenting their inner gender. Transgender women wrote the following regarding this topic:

> Everyone important to me knows about me. Come out of the closet. I have had feminine feelings all my life, so when I took the big step, and admitted who I really am, I was told "we know." My actions have always been feminine.

> I finally came to terms, with who I truly am, I am a woman on the inside. I told my ex-wife, who knew all the time, and then we had our daughter come over, and I told her. I had an appointment with my doctor and I told her about [me], how I have felt all of my life, and that I have come to terms [with] who I am. I am not embarrassed [about] who I am.

She has been inside of me every day. My doctor told me that she could see it the first time we met, and has seen me at a shopping mall, and she always smiled and wished that I would talk about it. Well the glorious day finally did come. My doctor told me she is going to recommend me for hormone therapy. I was so filled with joy.

Psychologists would say my hints expressed a deep desire to tell others I am a woman. I feel I was always simply being myself, in a masculine way. The honest truth is I was not actually the typical male. I was different in many ways from most of the men I observed. I was not interested in sports or cars. Any interest in sports was part of my male persona. Most men know a lot about car models. I only recognized the car models I owned and knew little about their attributes. I didn't do things the other men did. I never wanted a guys' night out. I favored the company of (other) women and my family. I was interested in and always carefully matched or coordinated my clothing in a nearly compulsive manner. I almost never went without covering my chest even on hot summer days, except for a few occasions, mostly on the beach where my male persona dictated I had to uncover part of the time, regardless of the discomfort that brought. I never thought the reason was to be like a woman. I just felt a need to be covered. As a child, I remember liking to play house with my cousins, but lost my interest when they wanted me to play the father's part, "because I was a boy." Of course, I was conscious that I was different, but I didn't think anyone noticed. At the time, doing these womanlike things was not conscious or deliberate. It simply was being myself.

CHAPTER 7, Transitioning—Becoming Who You Are

Transitioning

In the transgender world, the process of "transitioning" is simply when a transgender person is in the process of changing his or her gender presentation; however, it is not always simple to make that change when we consider the effects it has on others. In terms of affirming one's gender, to what degree and precisely what form one's transition will take is an individual and personal decision. There is no requirement that transitioning result in a person who is totally female as is possible or totally male as is possible. The purpose of transitioning should not be to become a woman or a man in one's presentation; it should be directed toward becoming yourself—your personal need to be comfortable with yourself.

Your transition needs to be no more than enough of a change to be what or who you are. It can be as simple as wearing or having a symbol on your person that helps you feel more like your inner self—the gender you want to affirm or feel you really are. At the other extreme, it means changing your body to look like the sex you are or desire to be. That can include altering your primary sex organs, facial features, voice, and deportment to be able to "pass" as your true gender. It may also mean to function sexually—even with an appliance. It is a completely personal thing and can be anything in between the two extremes.

The politically correct term for "gender transition" that transgender men favor is their "desired metamorphosis." Some transgender women frequently describe it as their "affirmed gender."

Changes in body appearance seems to be an issue most nontransgender people think of. A transgender man wants to get rid of his breast and add a penis. A transgender woman wants to add breasts and get rid of her penis.

The expense of these changes are frequently beyond a person's ability to pay and therefore they suffer without the procedure(s). Most insurance companies did not pay for transgender medical expenses. They claimed such medical procedures were cosmetic. The Internal Revenue Service (IRS) did not allow a medical deduction for transgender treatments for the same reason. The Affordable Care Act has changed I.R.S. rulings and reversed that.

Another important issue with many transgender men is urinating. It is a nonissue and relatively simple for a transgender woman. She merely sits down as other women do; however, standing like a man while urinating is a difficult and frequently an important issue for some transgender men. There are some methods and several devices that are described and sold on the Internet to make this possible. This urinating issue is discussed later.

Whatever you seek should be what you actually need or what you perceive you need to function comfortably and happily. Happiness is the key word!

Some people are satisfied with primarily a mental transition and others need to exhaust every possibility of physical change because that is what it takes for them to feel feminine or masculine, as the case may be. If a person is to be true to one's self, she or he must follow a personal need and transition as far as they need to achieve their own comfort level, at their own pace, and not what anyone else might think or say. Furthermore, the form of transition one takes does not have to be permanent.

Lately, I see a "new" tendency in a number of transgender youngsters. Generally, they are satisfied without surgical intervention. From the kids at LIGALY, a Long Island young LGBTQ group, many seem to prefer a more androgynous look. It is difficult to determine if this approach to transitioning is being adopted by a transgender population that would have sought surgery in a previous generation. Some students of this phenomenon believe a continuous blurring of the feminine and masculine roles is the cause. I feel the androgynous look adopted by many in this younger generation is an expression of a more permissive society. Past generations' were shamed into "the Closet" and dressed there as close to a woman as they could get. The older transgender generation envied women in heels and skirts and tend to dress that way. Younger transgender women observed women in pants and flat heeled shoes. Therefore, they tend to dress more androgynously as women frequently do.

Many transgender individuals seek hormone therapy. They do this because the expense is affordable, especially since many medical insurance companies cover the cost and under the Affordable Care Act (ACA) hormone therapy is covered. The repeal of the ACA is currently under discussion and its replacement may not cover hormone therapy. In any case, hormone therapy prepares transgender people for a genital altering operation, if that is what is ultimately being sought. Hormones alter bodies so they are "chemically" like a woman or a man. For transgender women, hormones make you feel more feminine and effectively give you the mind of a female, except for the social conditioning woman get as they grow up. Furthermore, hormones result in the hemoglobin count in the female range, the soft skin of a woman, the shrinking of the testicles, and physical features of a woman (e.g., breasts and feminine distribution of body fat). Although the addition of estrogen is beneficial to feminization, the reduction of testosterone is probably the most influential factor in being womanlike.

A transgender man taking testosterone (testosterone is referred to as "T") experiences more changes than the transgender woman does from lowering testosterone and increasing estrogen because testosterone is such a powerful chemical. It dominates estrogen rather quickly. Most transgender guys taking testosterone have an increase in hemoglobin count; grow face and body hair; have a lower pitched voice; redistribute some body fat to masculine proportions; experience an enlarged clitoris; have an increase in libido; experience a cessation of ovulation; and develop a coarser feeling skin. However, aggression similar to a male does not seem to increase substantially. Generally, a transgender man feels more like a labeled at birth man feels. Simply put, hormone therapy is what causes the most dramatic changes in ether a transgender woman or a man.

Some MtF transgender individuals hate their genitals just as transgender men hate their breasts and feel they need to get rid of them. The genital operation serves transgender women well by allowing them to feel that their body looks more like a woman. The removal of their breasts does a similar thing for transgender men. Breast removal also relieves transgender men of binding or layering clothes to hide their breasts. Genital and breast operations simply have little other effect than altering body appearance. Hormones are what really do the job physically and mentally.

After the testes are removed (orchiectomy), the patient ceases to manufacture testosterone, so blocking its production is not an issue. However, a transgender man is at a disadvantage in this area since he will not experience a parallel change in natural hormone production (i.e., estrogen) unless a hysterectomy is performed, which is far more dangerous. However, a transgender man can overpower his estrogen by taking testosterone.

Aside from hormones, a genital operation is aesthetic and supports the individual's piece of mind and happiness. Sexually, a gender operation to form a penis is far more difficult than forming a vagina. It is unlikely to result in the ability to penetrate their partner. In addition, phalloplasty is a long operation involving eight to ten hours and can yield complications mostly due to urinary system alterations. Another surgical option for transgender men is metoidioplasty, which is a simpler procedure. It takes two to three hours. Testosterone enlarges the clitoris and metoidioplasty repositions it more like a penis. There is less possibility of complications with a metoidioplasty operation.

On the other hand, the MtF can "perform" sexually as-a-women, by permitting penetration. Orgasms are not always preserved.

Surgery seems simple on the surface. You start on a gurney, get wheeled into an operating room, and take a deep breath from a mask. You don't have to do anything. The surgeon does all the work. Simple! nothing to it! That is, until you are conscious again in your hospital room. At that time, the "fun" begins with intense pain and discomfort, but that passes eventually and the healing process begins. You can now "see" your brain sex and your physical sex look aligned. For some, there is an advantage in having your sex legally changed—female or male. It verifies your gender is now what you always felt you were or wanted.

Gender operations generally serve the transgender person's personal preference. A transgender woman said,

> The [genital] surgery helped me. It didn't do anything for society. Society doesn't look between my legs. They don't pay any attention to what genitals I have. If I'd spent the money on hair removal or breast implants . . . things like that . . . [it] would have helped me survive in society better.

The complications from surgery for the FtM can be harrowing. I know of a case that had top surgery (i.e., breast removal) and three additional operations to correct things that went wrong. Even with the so-called simpler metoidioplasty operation, one transgender guy reported five post operations to correct problems that developed. That is why many transgender men do not seek bottom surgery. The MtF people generally have fewer complications from the surgery.

Passing

Operation or no operation, hormones or no hormones, a large percentage of the population of transgender women and men look to "passing" as an important objective. That is, they strive to achieve the appearance, actions, and speech of their inner gender so they will be accepted as the gender they are or wish to become. Some say the need to "pass" is simply a desire to visually achieve the gender that is in your head. I feel the desire to "pass" is not simply based on achieving the look of and acceptance as the gender they want to be. The overpowering reason is the fear of not passing. Not passing exposes you to what you have feared about exposing yourself all your life—the ridicule, harassment, and the shame that accompanies embarrassment. Transgender women I know wrote about their fears:

> [I'm] hoping to go to the next party [and] scared to go alone.

> I think the fear of humiliation is something that most girls like us just learn to live with. When you describe the lengths you went to as a child to conceal your cd [crossdressing] activities, paying attention to minute details to avoid detection, it made me think that I live that way today, even as an adult.

Transgender men also told of their feelings regarding their ability to pass.

> My concern, I told her [his girlfriend] there are lots of reasons why many people don't go to such a great effort to pass. Not everyone wants to be stealth [Being stealth for a transgender person means living without others knowing that you are a transgender person.] [Passing means that you can "pass" for a person who was labeled male at birth.]

> You can "pass" and not. . . . I'm just insecure about not passing.

> Passing as male is important to me, but it's not as important to others [to] be stealth—it's quite fun actually, as it involves shocking people on a regular basis.

> I've tried being 'out' and I've tried being stealth. Life's better when I'm stealth.

I know many transgender women who desperately want to be able to function in public, but avoid such appearances. They fear appearing in public because they do not look acceptable enough as a woman. Their height too high, hands are too large, their jaws too square, or their Adams Apples too pronounced. These same girls relax, seem happy, content, and enjoy their feminine experience at transgender gatherings, where they are unconditionally accepted as a woman, regardless of how they look when dressed as a woman. Obviously, they like being a woman in social situations. The underlying reason they avoid the public is fear. The same fear all of us experience at some time in our lives—ridicule and embarrassment.

Some transgender women expressed their desire, their feminine dream, before they die as follows:

Attend a party, pass as a woman, in public for an afternoon.

Spend a few days in girl mode and be seduced by the right girl.

Be single again. Live in an apartment. Work as a man by day and live in my apartment, alone, as a woman at night.

Have a boyfriend. Go on dates with [my] boyfriend, be romantic now and then, but live as a single woman.

The only thing I would like is to pass. Go shopping with some other girls and go for lunch. It's hard to pass at 6, 2 and 235 [pounds] so [I'd] like to be 5, 8 at 135.

A bikini by the pool. . . . That would be something, and to be ogled too!!!! (In my case, not being at all passable, that would require LOTS of prep work!).

I want a big wedding with a long honeymoon on my wedding night I will be glamorous and ahh so sexy. A honeymoon in Maui where I wear a tiny bikini. I will be so thin and ahh so smooth. . . . I also want implants and I want to be castrated and get vaginoplasty [vaginal cosmetic surgery], Botox, and cheek implants.

When transgender women cease being an oddity in the public arena, they will be free and out in public even if they don't pass at all. That is what transgender people as a group must work toward. It is called acceptance. The way to get acceptance is by integrating—being in the public eye and convincing the public we are normal people. Normal for the way God made us. I believe people must get to know us individually and the biological causes of our transgenderism must become a fact, rather than a theory, for our true acceptance. Then we will eventually have an easier time in public.

I know I agonized for years because I wanted to walk in public before I died, regardless of how "authentic" I looked. I didn't do it because I was afraid of other people's reaction. I was in total terror because I thought people would point a finger at me and say, "Look at the guy in a dress" and laugh. If that happened, I thought I could never recover from the embarrassment and shame.

This fear is apparent in transgender men as well; however, the shame component is not as great, since the closet they occupied was not as deep. A woman in male attire is thought to be stylish; even being mistaken for a "butch lesbian" carries less shame with it. The greatest insult is hearing, "Look at her, isn't she cute in men's clothes!" Furthermore, transgender guys are not as visible as a guy in a dress. Women wear pants, sneaker or loafers, a shirt, and even a tie sometimes. Although transmen are typically smaller, have a smaller head, narrower shoulders, delicate features and are shorter, they go relatively unnoticed compared to transgender women.

Of course, some transgender women and men do not want their employer, friends, and relatives from the world they grew up in to find out about their secret. However, when trying to go out in public, the fear of embarrassment is the controlling factor. This is especially true of transgender women, even when they are safe from exposure to people in their past life.

This fear is mostly irrational and based on sexism. People go to all extremes to protect their identity when dressed.[1] A trans woman told me of how she planned an outing. She rented a car to be sure her car would not be seen with a woman inside. Early in the day, she got a motel room with an outside door, so she could change clothes and wouldn't have to walk through the lobby "dressed." She made sure she had plenty of coins to pay a toll at an automatic lane without having a toll worker see her. All this took place before EZPass and far from home. It could have done the CIA proud.

Some transgender women are pretty and have a feminine face, but they are not convinced they appear acceptable as a woman.

Self-confidence is totally lacking. They choose wigs that cover most of their face to hide themselves. They see through their makeup, hairdo, etc. and see the man they are accustomed to seeing in the mirror. They do not realize the probability of being recognized as their male persona is unlikely. They look different with hair and makeup and, the most camouflaging factor, they are seen in a different context.

This author describes the high level of fear she felt as follows:

> Late one night, I dressed in my feminine things, entered my garage through a common door from my house, got into my car, opened the garage door with a remote control device, backed out, and drove a few blocks to a mail box. I got out of the car, walked around it to the mail box, put a letter in the box, and couldn't get back in the car soon enough. My heart was beating so fast I thought I would faint. I thought for sure I would use up all the heartbeats allotted for my entire life. I drove home into the garage, shut the motor off, and closed the garage door with my remote device before getting out of the car.
>
> It was late at night, no one was outside their house and most people were already in their bed and fast asleep. Yet the fear was so great, so over powering, and so controlling that I vowed I would never do anything like that again and I never did.

The fear was totally irrational. However, fear is a powerfully and destructive force. The more you think about what you fear, the more irrational it becomes.

Transgender men are at a disadvantage. They are completely exposed and more easily recognized, since the masculine type of clothing, hairstyles, and lack of makeup do not provide a cover as those things do for a transgender woman. Thus, there is little if any change in a transgender man's appearance.

Those stories not only demonstrate the extent we go through to prevent our exposure, but how strong the need is to be the other sex even for a short time.

When a transgender woman overcomes that fear and finally takes the first step to ventures outside, she is generally elated and can't get enough of being in public like all the other women. Some of them expressed it this way:

About nine years ago I found the courage to step out into [the] real world. I have not looked back. I love to shop and go out.

I feel that my feminine side needs to show. I enjoy my heels at home, and am slowly venturing out.

But I have done the full public dress up route and have discovered for me that it really is not about my feeling like a woman so much as being myself, and free to express that in ways that are rather more traditionally feminine.

Personally, my appearances as a man and as a woman are completely different. I can't see a trace of the guy in a mirror. I am a different person in my appearance. I have been before relatives, friends, and shop owners who know me as a guy by name. Even though I went out of my way to say hello, every one of them thought I was some woman they didn't remember knowing. Not one ever had the slightest clue I was the guy they knew.

I knew I didn't pass in my first appearance before the public. My makeup was not very good. My outfit was okay, but it was put together hastily. I wore an unbecoming wig that covered part of my face. I went out anyhow. Nothing could have stopped me. With the protection of a professional escort plus my need and determination to walk in the street, I mustered the courage to do it. I was very happy to be out on a street in New York City. I was nervous but not as nervous as I should have been. Perhaps the elation I felt actually wiped some of the fear from my mind. I was living my lifelong dream.

When transitioning, a transgender woman hates to be addressed "Sir" and only wants to hear "Miss" or "Ma'am." A transgender man hates the word "Miss" or "Ma'am," when he wants to hear "Sir." That single word tells them if they pass or do not pass.

I remember being tired of being called "Ma'am" a lot. I wanted to be called "Miss." I solved the problem by telling people my name was "Miss." and they called me that. Sometimes manipulating your world pays off handsomely.

Acquiring the Look of the Other Sex

The first rule I have been recommending to girls I help leave the closet is to simply relax and be yourself. Ignore any stares and even any comments you overhear. This advice recently came to me in an email and echoed my feelings:

> When I was first starting out [going in public "dressed"], I met TS [a transsexual] who taught me that your attitude is more important than your looks. I didn't believe her at first, but I found it to be true. A lot of being girly comes from inside your head, and not from what you have on.

Some in the transgender community endure a large expenditure of time, a high level of discomfort, and great monetary expense to erase the "damage" puberty's testosterone caused. That is, to make themselves look like the gender they feel they are or want to be. How much time, discomfort, and expense each individual devotes to "passing" depends on what it takes to make each individual feel secure from the fear of embarrassment. Frequently, that is tempered by their financial ability to pay for it and how much they dare to change, given their circumstances (i.e., job, family, etc.).

In some individuals, only the head, legs, and hands require temporary cosmetic changes because that is what shows. The rest can be accomplished by women and men with padding and/or binding[2] and restrictive under garments. At the other extreme, no less than every hormonal treatment, every surgical procedure possible, and all the available professional training will satisfy their need. Some even pursue the acquisition of social conditioning by professionals such as those found in Miss Vera's Finishing School for Boys Who Want to be Girls[3], in New York City and Femme Fever on Long Island[4].

Many transgender men I observed imitate what they see men do. One wrote,

> Everything is broken down into the tiniest details: a certain way of walking, how to step off a curb, the length of my stride, a certain way of holding my head, and moving my arms. It's nerve racking.

Transgender women do the same thing: how they hold their handbag, how they walk, etc. I personally know a transsexual who seems obsessed with acquiring a woman's gait (whatever that is). Some professionals tell them to do that. My advice has always been to simply be you. Be yourself! They can be sure there is a woman or a man who walks and moves just like they do. Being natural and being yourself, is the most important part of passing.

The next most important thing is being relaxed. You can achieve a great look, but if you appear out of place and nervous, you will probably not achieve what you want—to pass.

This does not mean a transgender woman when wearing a skirt should sit with one knee facing east and the other facing west. It also does not mean repeatedly shoveling the food in large quantities into your mouth like a machine. It does mean being natural, polite, and generally having good manners. For transgender men passing means not pointing your pinky or being overtly dainty. It also means being natural and relaxed in the way you stand, sit, walk (heel first, then toe), and do other things like that. The best advice is to use general and appropriate behavior for the gender you are adopting and do it judiciously. Above all, be natural and as relaxed as you can be.

As one might expect, FtM and MtF transitioning are both found difficult by many transgender people. Several aspects of female and male transitioning require the exact opposite action (e.g., getting breasts and getting rid of them). Whether the individual is MtF or FtM we try so hard to pass that we tend to make it more difficult than it needs to be.

Hair has always been an important factor in grooming and distinguishing between the sexes. Transgender men should be very conservative. Keep the back and sides relatively short and the overall look not too creative. Do not get a crew cut style because it emphases a small head size and shape. Furthermore, many "butch" lesbians favor crew cuts. You are a man and want to distinguish yourself from lesbians.

If you have light fine facial hair, you need to shave the "fuzz" from your upper lip and any other place on your face. Since facial fuzz is a typical feminine feature, fuzzy leg and arm hair that is not dark needs to be shaved or preferably dyed.

The female-to-male also has breasts with which to contend. Correction is made by surgical removal (referred to as "top surgery"). Otherwise, you must endure the discomfort and sometimes harmful effects of binding. There are several different binding options available. A loose fitting vest in combination with light binding can help conceal small breasts.

One suggestion was to use control top pantyhose with the legs cut off. Also, the cotton crotch area needs to be carefully cut out to make room for the head to pass through. However, you must make sure you leave the fabric around it intact. The smaller the pantyhose size, the tighter the binding action. Some transgender guys cut the waistband because it cuts into them; however, if you do that the converted pantyhose is more prone to riding up. It's a trial and error thing to find what's best for you.

Another choice in flattening your breasts is obtaining a binder from Transitions Binder.[5] This company sells a soft and comfortable chest binder to wear. It looks like a regular tank top, but it is made in layers. The underside is 50 % cotton and 50% Lycra, so it is strong and holds you in firmly. The 100% Lycra outer layer covers it. Exact sizing is needed, so contact Transitions Binder for a sizing chart. If you are on hormones and will undergo shape changes, they offer free alterations.

If you're not too large, camouflaging the area with loose clothing or merely a loose fitting vest may be all that is needed to satisfy you. Your size, build, and desires determine what will work best for you.

Fabricating a reasonable facsimile of a penis (a phalloplasty, referred to as "bottom surgery") is surgically far more difficult than simulating a vagina. Even metoidioplasty is avoided since it requires taking a large flap of skin from the forearm to create a makeshift male looking sex organ. Therefore many transgender men prefer an artificial penis (i.e., a dildo), prosthesis, or stuffing the groin area (called "packing") before bottom surgery is considered.

It is possible for a physical female to urinate while standing. A finger placed on the labia, as described on the Internet works, but the finger gets wet. One of the best sources for instruction for the finger method is Urinelle on the Internet.[6] These are disposable cones that are frequently used by women who go camping.

Skeletal features, including height and delicate hands and facial features, are permanent. However, short men with delicate features can be found. Feminine fat distribution (e.g., wide hips, etc.) can be changed with hormone therapy. If you are impatient for the hormones to do it, liposuction can help. Even a high pitched voice can be found on some men, but the pitch of a woman's voice can be lowered considerably with male hormone therapy (i.e., testosterone).

Speech can also be a problem for FtM. Although testosterone will lower the born female voice, the feminine intonation is recognizable over the telephone. The inflection and vocabulary changes may need professional help[7] to overcome and sound more masculine (i.e., have a monotone quality).

Similarly, the male-to-female has many items to change. Obviously, surgery to construct a vagina does not seem to be difficult for surgeons, from the standpoint that this procedure has been done successfully a significantly large number of times.

Fabricating a vagina goes relatively far back in time because it has been frequently used "to correct" an intersex condition long before genital operations were used to treat gender dysphoria. The intersex baby's "correction" may sometimes have been to the wrong sex, but nevertheless, it added to the surgical experience of constructing a vagina.

The typical male beard and body hair needs to be removed since no woman wants to be a "Hairy Mary." Shaving with a makeup cover is a temporary and frequently an unsatisfactory solution. A home epilator (it looks like an electric shaver with pairs of tweezers instead of blades and cost about $100) removes hair by pulling them out. Repeated use can eventually destroy the roots. However, its use is painful until hairs are pulled often enough that the pain is reduced to a pulling sensation. Using an epilator on long hair is very painful, so shave first and epilate afterwards frequently at first. Since the hair grows at different rates of speed, it emerges from the surface of the skin at different times. Therefore, you will pull fewer hairs at each use and experience less pain. After a while, the epilating pain becomes bearable and eventually it becomes merely a pulling sensation. When pulled enough times, the root is destroyed and hair never grows there again.

Most people opt for electrolysis for permanent removal of facial hair. Electrolysis is done by an electrologist (a licensed is required, in most places). It varies from uncomfortable too painful as well as being expensive and time consuming. Most people experience treatments over 2 or 3 years for the face.

Lasers are also frequently used for hair removal. Lasers work best when there is good contrast between dark hair and a light complexion. The process is relatively painless and faster than electrolysis; however, reports indicate this method is not always as permanent as electrolysis can be.

There is also a home laser for hair removal[8]. There are other makes you can explore. They all look somewhat like a hair dryer. This may be a good answer to the hair removal problem. It is a onetime cost in the middle 3 figures. The only things cheaper are shaving and the home epilator.

With patience and hormones, the body hair may diminish to an acceptable amount since it is mostly covered with clothing, but the beard is always visible and only slightly affected by hormones. It must be physically removed.

Some transgender women cannot remove their unwanted body hair because their wife seriously objects or they feel it would "out" them at home, on the job, or at play.

Removing arm hair, which is exposed and obvious to most people, would be noticed as missing. If arm hair cannot be removed for any reason, bleaching can make it less noticeable. If sudden bleaching would also be noticed and attract unwanted questions, start doing it in the summer and blame the bleaching on the sun. If this isn't done, you will be doomed to wearing long sleeves and gloves in warm weather. Leg hair can usually be covered with beige opaque pantyhose.

Some transgender women use close shaving and cosmetics to conceal the beard. Very dark beards usually require "clown pink" cover-up under a skin colored makeup. This results in a thick layer of makeup over the face, but they see no alternative. Lighter beards disappear under skin tone concealer.

Perspiration washes makeup off and is a problem for some women especially in summer months. When this happens to a transgender woman, the beard may create an unwanted appearance. A thin coat of Gillette Series clear gel "cool wave" or other clear antiperspirant before applying any makeup will eliminate the problem.

A prominent "Adam's Apple" (i.e., trachea) can be reduced or made "invisible" through surgery, known as a tracheal shave. A tracheal shave is a comparatively simple operation and can be done with a local anesthetic. If a tracheal shave is not a possibility, wearing a turtleneck top or a kerchief tied around the neck can conceal it.

Large hands are difficult with which to deal. You can keep your nails, real or false, pointed so the fingers appear longer and slimmer. Avoid the square end fingernails, since they tend to make your fingers look fatter. Don't draw attention to large fingers by wearing a lot of rings or an unusual shade of nail enamel. The face is often flattered with bangs by softening your appearance and minimizing the visibility of the typical male brow ridge. They also help cover the edge of the wig. Don't select wig to cover your face— it doesn't hide you and is usually not flattering.

The voice is a major problem for almost all transgender people. Many transgender women pass quite well, until they start to speak. At that time, heads turn to see the man who wasn't there a minute ago. A main difference between women and men is women speak from their upper palate, almost nasal, and men speak from their throat.

Male hormones can lower the pitch of a physical female's voice; however, female hormones do not raise the pitch of physical male's voice. Only practice and coaching, from a professional, can help you learn to sound like your gender identity.

After losing the deep masculine voice "rumble," obtaining a feminine intonation, or lack of it, is the most important factor for others to hear you as a female or a male. This is especially true, since a physical man can only raise the pitch and a physical woman can only lower it enough to still sound authentic. Therefore, intonation is the most important aspect of gender speech. The singsong quality, the varying speed and the emphasis of some syllables are important features for the MtF to learn and the FtM to unlearn and avoid. Both genders are faced with a difficult task, because unlearning anything is always more difficult than learning something new.

When you speak, you are usually concentrating on, and wrapped up in, what you are going to say next, making it difficult to concentrate on the conversation and intonation at the same time. Changing your speech pattern is particularly difficult because you have been using it for decades and repeating the same pattern a large number of times every day.

Women with low-pitched speaking voices are not a rarity, but when they speak, there is no mistaking that a woman is speaking. The feminine intonation tells anyone a woman is speaking. The same is true for the masculine monotone. When you add the difference in the choice of words, there is no mistaking whether a woman or a man is talking.

As an example, I have successfully trained my voice to be in a higher pitch. Even with the help of my New York City speech therapist Christie Block[9], it takes a good deal of work between therapy sessions. With training, even a masculine rumble in your voice can be "corrected" but it takes practice.

However, in my experience, I have found the intonation is so imbedded in my speaking over so many years that it is difficult to overcome and acquire a natural feminine intonation. I know my intonation is still not truly feminine. Even when I tell strangers my feminine name at the beginning of a telephone conversation, I will frequently hear them address me as "sir" by the end of the conversation. They are not being impolite, but their mind interprets the speech pattern they hear, by the end of the conversation, they forget the feminine name and hear a man talking.

Introducing a feminine or a masculine quality to your voice requires practice and a large measure of concentration. If you think of a man speaking in a heated debate, he emphasizes some words with deep feeling and sometimes changes the amplitude of other words for additional emphasis. A woman does something similar, except she does it in a soft tone without a trace of power, anger, or animosity. A transgender man needs to learn to speak at a relatively even volume, one speed, and with little emotion or emphasis.

To sound like a woman, I learned two relatively easy tricks. They both take a good deal of practice. Transgender men need to avoid my tricks to sound like a man.

The easier trick is to sometimes raise your voice at the end of a sentence like you are asking a question. However, a mature woman, unlike a teenager, does not raise it as high or as often.

The second trick is to "spike" your voice occasionally. That is, hit a high note on a word you would normally emphasize. For example, the easier one is to sometimes raise your pitch, spike on the "sometime" and/or "pitch." If you keep trying, you can train yourself to get "up there."

Speech therapists can be helpful since they work with you to help you exercise speech patterns that can only be changed with practice. However, many speech therapists place too much emphasis on pitch. Make sure your therapist helps you with intonation as well.

If finances and/or distance from a therapist is involved, "Melanie Speaks" on the Internet[9] contains some good tips and agrees pitch is not as important as most people believe. Her lesson is also available on CD and DVD. Transgender men can benefit from Melanie Speaks by simply using an opposite approach. However, personal training and guided practice is the best method to acquiring the masculine or feminine voice you want. Unfortunately, voice therapists are not available everywhere.

The vocabulary is not difficult. Just add a few typically feminine words once in a while. For example, "cute" is okay, but "adorable" is better. If you want to be a man, you need to avoid adorable at all costs. Also, men frequently use words that are definite and committing, whereas women avoid them. Although indecisiveness is not always a feminine quality, when women speak, they often sound that way (e.g., *I am going* is masculine and *I ought to go* is feminine).

Transgender women must remember they are not trying to be a feminist. Regarding speech patterns, they are trying to be the stereotype of a woman.

I have not ignored pitch. I have concentrated on it for years and still do. I find singing along with a recording of a female vocalist when I drive anywhere (alone) is helpful. Eventually, after hundreds and hundreds of replays, I am able to reach Shania Twain's higher notes—notes I could not reach when I started.

As previously mentioned, testosterone will lower the pitch of transgender men's voice; however, the resulting voice is not always satisfactory. Therefore, a monotone and a masculine vocabulary are important additions.

Surgical attempts to raise the pitch of the voice from the male average of 125Hz (100-150Hz) to the female average of 195Hz (170Hz-220Hz) have resulted in unsatisfactory outcomes. Either the pitch was not raised enough or it was raised too much. When the pitch is raised too high, it causes a mismatch between the pitch and natural resonance, resulting in a weird sound that is definitely not a female voice. I heard a woman who had this surgery in a conversation in London. She spoke in a high pitch, but you wouldn't want to listen to her for long. It simply did not sound normal but rather like that of an alien from another planet.

One new surgical method has been developed at the Yeson Voice Center, Seoul, South Korea. They claim voice feminization can be achieved by shortening the vocal folds, which they claimed is quite simple. The vocal fold shortening increases the voice frequency and thus raises your pitch. This newly developed high technology vocal fold surgery technique is said to be effective.

The vocal folds method was introduced at "The Voice Foundation's Annual Symposium: Care of the Professional Voice" which was held in Philadelphia, from May 29 to June 3, 2007. The Center says that after the surgery, the recuperation takes 2 months in order for the scars to heal. Also, a 4 week therapy and rehabilitation program, will teach you how to make sounds properly with the reduced vocal folds and have better results of the voice feminization surgery. The 2 month recuperation period doesn't sound wonderful. I would opt for intonation practice.

Other desirable actions to help a male-to-female appear as most women include hormones and/or padding. Some male-to-female individuals are impatient and can't wait for hormones to do their job or hormones did not do enough to satisfy them. They then turn to surgically enhanced breasts, derriere, hips, and/or plumping the facial cheeks. They also turn to stomach liposuction to rid themselves of their beer barrel belly. Facial changes to lift the eyebrows, pull the hairline forward, implant hair into the scalp to cover male pattern baldness, and/or make their hair thicker, make the nose more delicate, make the lips fuller, and whatever you can possibly think of, and some you can't think of, is obtainable from surgeons that specialize in feminization work. The facial procedures are commonly referred to as "facial feminization."

Some desirable attributes to appearing as a man include hormones and binding (the breasts). Some transgender men turn to surgery to remove their breasts. They are also impatient and can't wait for hormones to make fat redistribution changes. They turn to liposuction to redistribute the fat on their hips and derrière. Some transgender men get every possible surgery and turn to other specialists that offer masculinization training.

My transitioning started before puberty. As a child in my bathtub, I manipulated my genitals to demonstrate they can be put out of the way to look like a girl. One time, the manipulating caused an orgasm. I didn't know what it was. It was a pleasurable feeling and a little frightening at the same time; however, I never mentioned it to anyone because I already knew wanting to be a girl had to be a secret.

The orgasm felt very good and I ignored the frightening aspects. I repeated the fantasy many times in future baths. After that, I was the cleanest kid around because I took baths frequently to have the orgasm a la Charles Lamb's Ode to a Roast Pig.[10]

I also I remember going to my mother's dresser drawer when I was alone at home. I removed and tried on some of her things. I remember taking great care to replace the garments exactly as I found them. I did this more than once. The skirt effect of a slip or a half-slip was the best, since I didn't get to her closet. It was a wonderful drawer with its sensuous fabrics, beautiful colors, and the most wonderful floral fragrance that I love to this day.

I went to my mother's dresser drawer at every opportunity that I thought I would not get caught. Later, I found the clothes hamper was a safer source. The hamper didn't smell as nice, but a locked bathroom door, where the clothes hamper was located, prevented unexpected discovery. Besides, I didn't need to remember the exact placement of each item I borrowed to prevent detection of them being "tampered" with. I remember I put her undergarments under my regular clothes and went into the street once. It was very daring. The use of a mother's clothes is common when we are young. Many transgender women wrote in agreement with this,

> I remember as far back as Junior High School when I first tried on mother's girdles, corset, and my sister's bathing suits. I have always been fascinated with gurlie things as I cook, clean house, do laundry, and even cry like girls do. Guess I should say that ever since my teen years I've known.

> I started at [an] age when my mom and her boyfriends would go out I would go into her closet and start dressing up and I have been in the closet ever since.

> My earliest memories: I remember expressing my feminine side even before I first ventured into my mother's closet at the age of 6 or 7. I can remember wrapping a towel around my head and one around my chest and imagining myself a girl.

> I think I am pretty typical, in that I discovered my mom's nylons when I was 8 years old and never looked back. (Thank goodness). I got caught several times, by a woman who worked in my house and of course told my mom. My mom was an angel, even though she had been told she didn't really say much about it. Probably because she thought it was child's play and that eventually it would go away. It didn't happen of course.

> I did spend as much time trying on my mother's clothes as I could. I did this with reckless abandon for quite a while until I was eventually "caught." Not in the act but in the aftermath. I decided to try on some nail polish one afternoon as I dressed to the hilt. It was easy to put on but I didn't know that you needed nail polish remover to remove it. I didn't know how to get it off so I kept scratching at it and chipping it off slowly.

> I learned to put everything back EXACTLY as I found it. If a blouse leaned to one side of a hanger, that's how I put it back. If I used perfume from the dresser, I would look for the outline of the base of the bottle on the dresser that was

not exposed to dust. I learned to notice the minutest details. I learned from my older brother's experiences to never hide secret belongings under my mattress.

I also learned at an early age to be very careful with my mom's clothes. I would watch her intently as she dressed to go out, sit in her bed and just stare at her and her girlfriends as they got ready to go out for the night. Needless to say, few minutes after she left, I would go into her drawers and closets and eagerly put something on. Nervous, not to be caught and nervous to put everything exactly the way I found it. I would also lock myself in the bathroom and practice putting on lipstick. Even at that age I knew I was different.

With me it was about 3 years old when I picked up and tried on my Moms panties. My grandmother caught me and told my Mom, so for the rest of my life living with my Mom I never saw her panties in the laundry, but she knew when I turned 12 that I had this fascination and would take panties off clotheslines for excitement. I always returned them tho [though].

Transgender women frequently use the phrase, "my feminine side" because they live a double life. However, that reference is not their feminine side it is really their feminine inside!

Purging

Years later, as many of us do, I acquired some of my own feminine things. I especially loved my own pumps—black patent leather heels. However, somewhere along the way, I became disgusted with myself. I thought, "What am I doing? This is wrong and bad! It is something I should not be doing. What am I a queer? Am I a filthy degenerate, a pervert? I must get rid of every feminine garment I have and never, ever, wear anything like that again."

It was at night when I put every woman's thing I had in a large paper bag and found an empty lot not too far from home. Once I was sure no one was watching me, I discarded each item separately until the whole bag of stuff was gone. On my walk back home, I thought, "There, I did it! Now I can be normal, like everyone else." I felt clean and pure. I especially felt I was now going to be what I always prayed for, to be like everyone else.

I was normal until the next night, when I was out at the same lot trying to find my discarded stuff in the dark. I remember trying hard to find the precious shoes that were very difficult to obtain. It was awful! Everything was either gone or it was too dark to find them. I didn't dare come back when there was daylight. I thought, "Why did I do that? Why did I even think of doing that? But this is a typical action many transgender women experience.

In the transgender community, it is called "purging." Nearly everyone has done it with the same result. Sooner or later, we always start dressing again. It is true boys don't do that, but some boys cannot, not do that.

God, how much I wanted to get rid of the girl in me. She just wouldn't go away. All I could do was bury her inside me and hope she stayed buried. I always hoped for a cure from this "unnatural" feeling. Of course, a cure never came because there is no illness. My fantasies of dressing, and plotting dress up schemes distracted from my schoolwork, since when I should have been studying, I was in some fantasy about my next dress-up. The only time I was able to keep the girl buried and able to stop secretly dressing was for a few years, right after I was married. Outside of that time, I always found a safe place to hide my special things. I was really a creative person when it came to being a sneak. I was not alone in this. One girl told me,

> I hollowed out a toy in which I could hide the pantyhose I was buying at the age of ten.

After my spouse died, I was able to dress a great deal, since I was alone most of the time. I only did this at home.

Leaving the Closet

My need to walk in the street dressed as a woman, with makeup, a skirt, nylons, and heels was something I wanted more than anything else. I thought I must do it once, just once, before I die.

Although I tried to think about how appearing as a girl could be done, I just couldn't think of a way to do it. That desire was not realized because I felt I could not survive from the pointing fingers ridiculing me and people laughing at me. By chance, I bought a transvestite newspaper in New York City one night and saw an advertisement for someone who would do a makeover and escort me in the city. I thought maybe the transvestite stories I have been reading about is not all fiction.

I pursued the ad with a telephone call and later followed up with a personal visit to the escort. That itself was a difficult and brave thing to do according to my mindset. Finally, I had an appointment to hire his services. I didn't need a makeover, since I was well practiced in the art of makeup over many years. However, it was part of the deal, so I went for it!

I didn't like the makeover he did, but who cares! I was going to walk in the street! My dream for decades was going to happen and it did! We walked in Greenwich Village and eventually ended uptown at a restaurant/bar devoted to transvestites on Saturday night. His lack of attention to me in the bar, where I was nervous as a cat at a dog show, demonstrated he was as poor an escort as he was a makeup artist. I felt the problem was not ability but he had no interest in doing a good job at either task. He seemed simply uninterested. The important fact was that my impossible wish came true!

It was the spring of 2003 and cost $300 for a bad makeover and not so great an escort. However, it was the best $300 I ever spent. I will always feel thankful to him. Who could ever buy the dream of a lifetime for a mere $300?

That experience somehow led me to an organization of crossdressers in New York City,[11] where I could change my clothes, spend an evening as a woman with friendly people, and change back to guy clothes before going home. Eventually, I went to clubs with some of the girls I met there. The people I met told me of Femme Fever on Long Island. Femme Fever is the web site of a boutique, occasional parties, and a web group, where transgender women can post questions, express their feelings, and generally communicate with one another.

At Femme Fever parties, I met some more transgender people. I soon learned of Ina's[12] in Manhattan, the same transvestite club I went to with my escort that first night, but didn't know the name or location (nerves?). Before I knew it, I was shopping in New York City, going to the theater, and eating in restaurants dressed as a woman. I even was sightseeing while "dressed" in London, Thailand, Seoul, and Hong Kong. I also went on a cruise of the Caribbean that had a group of 20 transgender women.

I thought about why it was very difficult for me to peek out of the closet. A transgender man described his problem and it expressed my dilemma perfectly:

> The reason it took me so long to come out was because I was always worried about my family thinking less of me, strangers thinking less of me, losing friends, and I was worried this facet of my life would negate every positive thing I did. I learned this week, especially, that that was never the case. My own fears got in my way of getting close to the people, who love me most, and I regret the years of silence between us, but I know we can catch up.

Before coming out to their family, many transgender women and men have negative thoughts about what may happen as a result. They wonder what they are doing to themselves and those they love. They think coming out to the family is an act of stupidity because they have a good life—a life other people would die to have a wife or husband they love and children they adore. They ask themselves if they want to risk giving all that up for a life they don't know much about. They also ask themselves am I willing to risk breaking my wife's or husband's heart for a questionable outcome. Can they risk possibly destroying their children's role model for an unknown outcome. Will the courts take away all my rights to my children?

Nurture, the socialization process, enables transgender people to control their need to reveal their inner gender. The need to control their real gender varies from individual to individual and between transgender men and transgender women. Some never tell anyone. Others feel they must tell a loved one. There is a natural and compelling need to be honest and free themselves of the deception and hiding. Those who have a measure of control over their compelling drive to be open and honest, do it with careful planning and break the news slowly and considerately. Others are desperate to climb out of the closet. The following describes how two transgender women handled telling their wife according to two different needs. The first one tried to display a bit of femininity over a considerable period of time. She said after several months of this.

> I made all the hints and gave these time to grow in her mind. The reason I did this was to cushion the shock when I came out to her. Before I finally came out I thought about if I

really needed to do this. I thought about it and decided that I needed this so badly.

Another told of her method and why it differed:

Slow and easy would have been a lot nicer, but I was getting ready to kill myself so I had to own up all at once. And no, it didn't turn out so well. That's a huge problem.

Transgender individuals have many doubts. The most troubling one is whether this is the best choice for their happiness and the happiness of those they love. They question if they are really a transgender person. Many wonder, just as I wondered, if honesty is all it is cracked up to be. In this regard, one transgender woman said,

Honesty is the best policy, except when it isn't.

Most of us have no personal experience with transitioning. We only recently learned anything about transgenderism and even lack a proper language for talking about it.

Once I told my family, I actually told everyone! I stopped hiding and sneaking. That is the best part. Honesty is absolutely all it is cracked up to be. I am now a woman all the time, which is good too.

The hormones give me a wonderful feeling of peace. I feel more comfortable, calm, and relaxed. I love my soft and smooth skin and what I feel inside. I adore my increasingly less aggressive nature. I recently had a complaint about being kept waiting in a routine manner, when an emergency brought me to the doctor. In the old days, I would have said I have a complaint in a typical aggressive masculine way. However, sans testosterone, I presented it as a suggestion (for improvement). A guy doesn't approach situations that way. A woman, like me, with estrogen up to her eyeballs, has a less confrontational approach to problem solving.

Most people would say I was always a nice person, but I simply feel like a nicer person and I like me better now. I am lucky! I "pass" easily with my natural gestures, my appearance, and even the way I sound. I find I can speak naturally and people see a woman therefore they hear a woman. Over the telephone they can't see me so they hear a man. I don't even think about being a woman anymore because I am now sure I am one. Furthermore, I am not trying to convince anyone of anything as I may have in the past. I believe I am a woman, with masculine conditioning, even before hormones changed me chemically. Have an operation? I know I don't need that. I am as much a woman as I could possibly be. Furthermore, if you don't look between my legs, I am as much of a woman today as anyone who did not grow up as one. If you don't think so, ask New York State or the U. S. Department of State. You can even ask my therapist.

Readers may wonder why I describe a life story under the heading of transitioning. I feel this demonstrates that transitioning is a lifelong journey. It is not having an isolated genital operation, starting a hormone regimen, or any other event or combination of events.

Coming Out

I was "out." Since I told my children, I was really out. An important part of transitioning is said to be "coming out." That is, telling everyone what you are. Saying you are something other than what you previously led them to believe you are.

Transgender people generally experience a feeling of relief that coming out provides. The act of coming out has a complex set of meanings. When you come out, when you experience the Final, Final Stage, you expose yourself to everyone as a transgender person and admit you have been concealing your true self from everyone, usually for decades. If a sex altering operation is planned, coming out is a prerequisite, as specified by the current revision (i.e., revision 7) of Dr. Benjamin's regimen prior to an operation. Transgender women and men—those who pass and are perceived as the gender they wish to be, are fortunate. Coming out occupies an important part of their sense of identity. That is, they can finally live the part they feel is compatible with and who they really are. After coming out, some think they will live a normal life, a mundane one, for a change. Wrong! It doesn't ever happen! You are "Trans" and will need to make many adjustments. Life as a different gender is quite different.

Some in the transgender community take an opposite view of the act of coming out. They feel coming out is a betrayal of their true gender. They prefer to feel they begin to live in the gender they "are." It is not a transition. It is who they are and always have been! Their past in another gender was a false identity that they would rather forget. It is okay to feel that way too; however, I feel it is a bit dramatic and a fruitless argument. I don't reject my experiences as a man. In fact, I cherish them. It wasn't all a downside. It permitted me to live with an amazing and creative person and have wonderful children, their spouses, and adorable grandchildren.

Coming out helps serve to break the cycle of torment and self-condemnation. You hid as if your true self was bad and shameful. It destroys the facade of lies and deception you hated, but felt forced to adopt. You rid yourself of the implication that the past deception is preferable to being open and honest. It sounds silly to me now, but there is an implication you are doing nothing more than standing up as an individual. As an individual you are expressing your basic and natural human right.

On the negative side, when you come out, backlashes or other negative reactions to your coming out are caused by transphobia and sexism. However, from my view, it is worth it.

CHAPTER 8, The Personal Cost of Being Transgender

An Unacceptable Need

Life is not easy when you are a transgender person. Transgender people have a continuous series of challenges to face. They struggle with one difficulty after another. There are difficult medical, physical, and employment issues, not to mention relationships regarding family and friends.

It takes a fairly strong person to deal with what is regarded as an unacceptable compelling need to be your feminine or masculine self when the world insists you are not. A critical conflict is the need to express your true gender (e.g., dress as your true gender) while simultaneously complying with society's demand that you appear the way people expect—always present as your birth label.

This dressing need is obviously more difficult for the MtF. Everyone knows the tomboy will grow out of it when she meets her first boyfriend. Later in life, in men's clothes, the woman is just being stylish or comfortable. The FtM may not have social difficulties until later in life. On the other hand, the male-to-female variety finds wearing feminine clothes especially difficult. Being feminine or wearing a single feminine garment is not tolerated from an early age. Such a boy is said to need someone to "make a man out of him." People avoid him because he is commonly thought of as one of those homosexuals or a sexual pervert—worse, a pedophile.

For those who are not strong enough to withstand the confusion, pressure, and ridicule, thoughts of suicide are common and often likely—at best the frustrating situation is depressing. The need to be your true self and your inability to cope with the roadblocks others put in your path are too much to bear. It is demoralizing to be told "you are crazy." "You look ridiculous and nothing like what you are trying to look like." "It's unnatural for you to want to be the other sex and God will not accept you that way!" They hear many derogatory things that people say for their own self-serving benefit. They can't live in their present state and they can't see any way to be who they truly feel they are. Stressful is a mild description of the situation.

Kate Winslet, a British actor, summed it up in her story in *Becoming Myself, Reflections On Growing Up Female*[1] as follows:

We girls were quite tomboyish, allowed to behave like boys, so we had that privilege, whereas often with boys, they are questioned if they behave like girls. People say, 'Oh God, which way are they going to go?' That's tremendously unfair for boys and men, to be expected to be brave and bold and not cry in front of others, particularly in front of women. I always thought of that as a great tragedy.

Deprivation

When you are quite young, you understand what is expected. For MtF, you like girl things, but know having them is impossible. If you want a doll, it's too bad for you. That is a girl's toy! One transgender woman wrote of her disappointment with a gift when she was young, but she suddenly realized it was a wonderful gift:

> One fateful day I received a puppet as a gift from my mother. At the time I had wanted something else. Something I thought would allow me to fit in with the boys . . . snappy pop things. My mother, concerned with my safety opted for the puppet instead. I was enraged and remember throwing a tantrum and pouting.
>
> After I thought about it I think I liked it better than the snappy pop things. After a while, Zoo Loo the Zebra was born. Zoo Loo quickly grew from that bitter seed into my greatest childhood friend and ally. He was easily my most expressive and complicated personality of all my puppets that I had started collecting after that time. For unknowing to me and possibly even my mother, she had provided me something I really needed; a license for a boy to play with dolls.

When you are quite young, you understand you may not be yourself. You may not act naturally. You may not talk about what you would like to talk about. You may not do the things you want to do. You may not hang out with the girls. You don't need to be very bright to figure out there is a way to avoid ridicule, fit in, and be what people expect you to be—just act like everyone else. You can do it! Just look at what the boys do. Act like them, talk about what they talk about, do the things they do, and stay with the boys. In fact, if you can be more of a boy than the real boys, it is even better. One transgender girl's comment about this was,

> I tried to be very macho. I was like, maybe if I do enough stuff like that, my brain will flip over and be a boy brain, like rock on, let's go to the strip bar!

When I was young, I didn't try to be more boyish, but I was definitely not a sissy. Some transgender girls can't help their girlish mannerisms and pay a dear price. However, if you can control it, you had to be stupid and ask for constant harassment if you acted like a girl. You could not even be a little like a sissy or show any signs of being feminine.

I knew my taboos! I played sports with the guys, but never pursued a game and really didn't enjoy it much. I never wanted to be in a fight and usually avoided them. However, if I was in a fight, I could never hit someone with all my strength. I watched my brother fight and noticed he put his total strength into every one of his punches. Although I tried, it simply was not my way. I couldn't do that. It simply was not my nature. I was a tall kid, so fortunately I rarely got involved in fights.

Winning a fight was important for your male persona; however, I remember winning in a game was nice, but not the least bit important. It rarely lighted any competitive spark in me. To this day I don't like to play games and have difficulty staying concentrated on them. It just isn't important enough to keep my eye on the ball, actually and figuratively. I always knew and accepted I was different.

It is a difficult life. Some of the difficulties encountered result in the following:

a) A Closeted Group: most boys and men know that boys don't do that. They are a transgender person and "closeted" because of the ridicule they fear they would experience, if it became known that they wanted to be a "sissy girl." It is too difficult to be in the open. When considering whether there is a need to be secretive, they realize that anything else would be self-destructive in relations with their family, their employment, their friends, and nearly every aspect of their life. This applies to girls also. Most girls become withdrawn and as invisible as they can because the other girls don't let you into the group. "You really want to be an icky guy?"

b) Feeling Like an Outsider: Knowing you are different makes you always feel like an outsider. When you have friends, you seem to always have them in groups. You rarely feel that you are a best friend to a particular person in the group, exclusive of the others. For a time, I did experience an exception when I had a best friend, a girl. It was when I was on the young side to have a girlfriend, but old enough get away with it. My parents thought it was cute of me. I said she was a girlfriend, but we were actually buddies. It was just the two of us. We never bothered with the outside world. It was like each of us traveled halfway to the other gender and we both were in between a boy and a girl.

c) A Need to Fall Silent or Change the Subject: In ordinary conversation, it is painful to always find a need to fall silent or change the subject because you are in constant terror that you will slip up and someone will discover your awful secret. You can rarely claim the freedom of expression that most people take for granted. The freedom you need to simply exist as yourself is never available.

d) An Isolated Feeling: Women can consult with girlfriends about almost anything, intimate or not, unless the subject is their transgenderism. Guys are not "allowed" to discuss intimate details of any kind or any sexual feeling with a male friend.

Unlike transgender people, nontransgender people can always feel they are part of a group. A transgender man spoke of the isolation as follows:

> Think of how many times a day a nontransgender person "comes out." When a woman mentions her husband, when a man and woman talk about their kids, when heterosexual couples talk about getting married. Imagine how hard it would be to never talk about your significant other, or to not hold hands because you're scared of getting verbally harassed, physically harmed, or even killed. Imagine how hard it would be if you had to hide who you are because you are afraid of losing your job.

A Socialization Difficulty

A socialization problem is typical of many transgender individuals. Some transgender women said it this way,

> My big problem was communicating. [I] became the quietest person in the room when any tg [transgender] issue came up.

> In school I found out rapidly in the company of other boys my age that I was not one of them. They were rough and played games boys play. I liked to read and the playground was a frightening place for me. The lunch recess is where the pecking order would fully bloom. I would try to hide in the shade away from the heat and the other children. I look back on my entire academic career and I am astonished at how much fear there was in each day. . . . At that age I felt more affinity with the girls.

> In first grade boys were just starting their indoctrination into athletics by their proud fathers. My quick indoctrination was from the class bully who taught me the word "Faggot" when I failed to catch an oblong shaped ball I'd never seen before. My second indoctrination was from a fastball pitch to the head on my first attempt to swing a bat. My athletics career was over from that day forward. My father still tried of course. There was wrestling, basketball, soccer. I would do my best to avoid the ball or drop it on purpose and position myself behind the coach so he could easily forget to put me into play. I became a master of invisibility.

> Personally, I had socialization problems I feel were greater than most transgender people. In adult life, I largely grew out of it, but it was not overcome completely. I just don't understand how socialization comes easily to some people. I observe two people who I am sure just met each other and seem to have a great deal to say to each other. I see them talk to each other for an hour or more. I can't imagine what they talk about.
> Even at the gym I say a few words to someone I know and it ends there. I see those same people talking for a long time. I say to myself I came to the gym to work out, not talk. I don't necessarily

want to waste time in idol conversation, but I secretly would like to be able to, at will, like others seem able to do without any effort.

Typically, transgender people always have socialization problems in some form. They acquire guilt, shame, and regret, which are powerful emotions. In addition, when you are a transgender individual, you experience nearly constant anxiety caused by several factors. For example, you are anxious when you are not able to express your inner self. You fear discovery when you even think about it, let alone when you assume the other sex. This, plus you have all the everyday problems most people experience in the course of life.

"If you feel anxious long enough, you can also develop a state of depression," says Nada Scotland, M.D.[2] Doctor Scotland's statement may explain why many transgender individuals experience depression. Trans men experience depression from this later in life, since the permissiveness they experience meets disapproval later in life. Tomboys grow out of it, but some don't.

Dating is another source of depression for transgender men and transgender women. Finding a partner is very difficult for a transgender man. A nonlesbian woman wants a 100% man and thinks intimacy with a transgender man would be a homosexual act; a gay man wants a 100% man; a lesbian wants a 100% woman. The pickings are slim for a transgender man. For the transgender woman, dating is also a source of depression for parallel reasons. Basically, each person prefers intimacy with someone who both is and wants to be physically and mentally the gender they want.

The best and only chance a transgender person has for romance might be with a bisexual person. A second choice might be a gay or lesbian in denial.

Young transgender people are a bit freer regarding the manner of dress, since an androgynous look is stylish for both sexes and usually acceptable. Although their life is as problematic as for us older folks, a good deal of society is now aware of transgender people and accepts them.

Psychological Cost

Guilt, shame, regret, anxiety, and depression are each individually capable of having a devastating effect on one's self-esteem. Each is common in the transgender community. In combination, the emotions involved can be very debilitating. I have experienced all those emotions. I somehow managed to function well in all areas of life in spite of that, at least in the eyes of others. Perhaps that is what drove me to always try to do more and do a better job than anyone else could do and anyone expected me to do. I feel lucky in that regard.

All those negative emotions call for distraction. I was able to distract myself by becoming focused on my work, family, gardening, or something else that allowed me to escape most detrimental effects. My natural ability to totally immerse myself in an activity and focused on it served me well in this regard.

Several transgender friends do not cope well with all the emotions involved. To add to this problem, the therapist population is not always well trained and equipped for treating a transgender person.

I recently was with a friend who was a virtual wreck because her therapist was pressuring her to make life changes she was not ready for. That is not a therapist's job! A therapist should make you comfortable with yourself and help you decide when to take a particular action, not tell you what to do.

My friend was being pressured to take action she felt would have ended her employment and family relationships. She needed time to meet the challenges presented by the emotional and psychological stresses stemming from the negative attitude of her spouse and the general public toward gender variant people. Finding ways to deal with an aggressive therapist on top of these problems merely added to her stress. As a result, she could not think logically or clearly and seemed close to a breakdown.

The 2 most common emotional problems transgender people face are guilt and shame. Frequently, individuals feel they are doing something wrong or inappropriate when they crossdress. I know I felt guilty when I bought women's clothing. I believe this was because I felt I had no right to be spending money on something I shouldn't own in the first place. Wearing women's clothes? That was something I was not entitled to do. That was for women! Boys don't do that! Guilt, from this situation or simply from knowing you are engaged in something considered wrong, eventually results in a feeling of guilt and shame.

Shame, psychologists tell us, is a negative feeling of self-worth. It took nearly a year of therapy for me to become conscious of the fact that shame was dictating the major part of my life—my thoughts, actions, and decisions. I always felt my secrecy regarding crossdressing was to protect my loved ones. I never realized my secrecy's purpose was mostly to conceal my shame. Shame was controlling me. I found once you are conscious of shame, it becomes easier to handle. It is never easy to deal with shame, but it does get easier. John Bradshaw[3] expressed my situation and experience perfectly:

> Shame begets shame. . . . I came to see that shame is one of the most destructive forces in all human life. In naming shame, I began to have power over it.

The transgender individual sees a hostile world filled with condemnation and contempt for any person's deviation from what the rest of the world considers as normal. Almost all gender deviants must express their true gender somehow, someway. It is an internal driving force that they find is beyond their ability to stop. Psychologists feel one's biology demands you express it. A Biological Imperative is uncontrollable for most people.

Another reason transgender people feel guilty is because they haven't told their parents, spouse, best friend, or children about their gender issues. I personally hated the dishonesty involved in deceiving those I loved. I felt I had to hide the girl from them because if they knew my secret, my transgenderism, it would demean me in their eyes and destroy any perception of me serving as a role model. The only way I could endure the necessary deception and hiding was to make a game of it—to outsmart everyone. Scheming and planning ways to go unnoticed while doing something anyone can, and everyone will, tell you that you shouldn't be doing, was the game.

On the other hand, there is often a source of regret in having hidden the girl in you for so long. I waited a lifetime before I lived, even part time, expressing my feminine feelings in front of another human being (i.e., in public). My only regret involved not getting out of the closet until about 14 years after my spouse died. Before she died, I felt there was no way out of the closet and the closet is where I belonged anyhow.

Actually, staying in the closet was a relatively easy choice, since I didn't know there was any other alternative. I thought that coming out was not an option, since no man can survive trying to appear as a woman. However, if I knew then what I know now, I could have realized my femininity, enjoyed the pleasure of it, and experience the peace of mind, the one I wanted desperately all of my life, 14 years sooner.

I often wonder how many transgender people still believe there is no life other than the one people expect of them. I was computer savvy, well-educated, and fairly intelligent, but I didn't find a transgender world existed until 2003. If I hadn't followed up on an ad in a transvestite magazine, I still might not know an accessible transgender community exists. The actual number of transgender people must be far larger than is now estimated. Some of them contact me, but are too fearful to let me help them out of the closet. I have had others tell me of their desire to "dress" but can't drive themselves to do it because of some kind of attachment to their male life that they fear losing. Still others want to be a woman but feel their physical appearance makes it impossible so some turn to being a "queen" in a gay relationship.

There are many cases of transgender women who experienced getting out of the closet just to be urged to get back in and stay there. However, once out it can rarely be done. Some transgender women said,

> In order to keep peace, I have had to go back into the closet. I have told the family therapist and family that I will not ever dress again and will work hard to suppress my feelings. I have lied to them all and dress occasionally and go out. It is terrible not to be able to trust those you love and the ones that are supposed to love you

> When I told my wife she [went] off the deep end and told me that I must go back into the closet for the sake of my family. I told her, "I could not nor would I even if I could, this is who I am . . . and this is who I was [and] should have been all my life." Well the worst happened. I am now waiting to sign the final divorce papers.

I saw similar situations to the ones above from younger transgender girls—transgender kids (see Chapter 2—The Meaning of Sex, Gender, and Transgender—Comparison of Gender and Sex). When they were caught and promised punishment if they dressed as a girl or wore a girl's garment again, they didn't refrain from "dressing." They were simply more careful to avoid detection. Long before you became an independent adult you learned the girl you thought you buried inside simply would not stay buried. She kept coming into your consciousness and there was nothing you could do about it except turn her free and let her have her way. Transgender men experience a similar problem when they do not grow out of being tomboys.

Due to the stigmatization of transgenderism, the most frequent problem faced by the transgender population is depression. Even with depression, a good deal of transgender people hesitate to get help because of the shame and the lack of sound help they usually get. They are frequently faced with the fact of being discounted, misdiagnosed, or characterized as pathological by inexperienced mental health professionals.

Another prevalent problem in seeking professional help is finances. Many transgender people are unemployed or underemployed and do not have insurance or the necessary funds, due to frequently experiencing discrimination in employment.

The cost of hormones and therapy required for transitioning is high. Only recently has Medicaid been covering transition costs but not everyone is eligible. The Affordable Care Act helps with the cost of transitioning. However, many people fall between the cracks of Medicaid, medical insurance, and self-financing. The possible need for transgender men's breast removal or transgender women's hair removal and/or some optional surgical procedures may drive up expenses beyond affordability. When this is added to the associated cost of transportation to a doctor specializing in transgender issues plus the costs of recuperating from surgery in a distant hotel, with or without insurance, proper treatment, and care are frequently unaffordable. This lack of adequate finances is another cause of depression. Furthermore, with the right-wing control of all three branches of the federal government, coverage of costs under the Affordable Care Act or Medicaid is in question.

Still another source of depression comes from ones self-image. A male-to-female transgender person looks in the mirror and sees whiskers, an Adam's apple, a tall (unfeminine) hairy body with its shoulders too broad for a female. A female-to-male transgender person sees breasts, a feminine shaped beardless face, a short person, a generally feminine person, with hips too broad for his waist and a smooth hairless body. The inadequacy seen, in contrast to what they want to see, is depressing.

Fear is one of the strongest emotions everyone feels at one time or another. The transgender population is no exception to being fearful. Transgender men are as much in danger from transphobic people as transgender women. In fact, both are fearful all the time and have even more things to fear than other women and men. They need to be cautious of the sexual predators as genetic women. However, the added danger of transphobic people makes it necessary to be extra cautious. A source of fear may also be nonviolent and simply come from being alone and feeling isolated.

Transgender people are hated for disturbing the "natural order" of things. Both transgender women and men suffer at the hands of the rampant transphobia of many people, especially religious fanatics.

The Bathroom Problem

A large amount of fear, as well as a component of humiliation, is the bathroom issue. This issue never occurs to most people. To everyone it is like gender was thought of at one time. Either one or the other is appropriate. A woman uses the Women's and a man uses the Men's. It is so simple there is nothing to even think about. However, for the transgender person, there is a decision involved—sometimes a frightening decision. Do you go to the room appropriate for the way you are appearing or do you use the one appropriate for your birth sex label? It sometimes even comes down to legality and more important safety.

Not many places have unisex bathrooms or gender neutral bathrooms. You are forced to make the decision whether to use one or the other. In either case, there are hazards because there is no good choice. In one case, you are not where the public believes you technically belong. In the other case, you are unsafe. In some states, it's even illegal for a someone labeled male at birth to use the women's restroom. It is not much of a problem in New York City and some other jurisdictions, where you may use the restroom in accordance with the appearance you present. When I was dressing part time, I always had to think twice about how I was dressed before I made that selection.

Several transgender women have told me that when they attempt to use the Men's Room while dressed en-femme, they invariably hear, "Miss you are in the wrong room." I fear if they were perceived as a man dressed as a woman, they might have experienced bodily harm. Transgender men said,

> I have spent so many hours avoiding public multi stall bathrooms that I have damaged my bladder and put pressure on my kidneys. The problem was a daily one. I'd think about where I was going, what bathrooms I'd have

access to, how much I drank during the day, whether I'd be with people who could help stand guard.

I'd been in men's rooms before, but only the kind that are singles, you know lock the door behind you type. Here was a public one with men going in and out. I felt no nervousness or wrong. I was a man. Heart and soul and now body wise looking. No one blinked an eye. This may all sound strange, but it was the first time I had EVER been comfortable in a public restroom.

All my life I have cringed and lived in fear of going in a public bathroom. I always, always felt out of place. I was afraid someone would scream and run out, or verbally accost me, or find out I wasn't supposed to be there. I didn't fit there.

I hated washing my hands, it meant standing there with maybe someone else as they primped and fixed hair and makeup. I felt as if I were trespassing. It was hard not to run out most times. . . . Sometimes I would sit in the stall for 15 minutes or more waiting till it was clear before I came out. That feeling never went away, never lessened, never let up.

The bathroom is a problem for the male-to-female also. When I first started to go shopping, I had to preplan where I would go. I lost a list of bathrooms that accommodate one person at a time that a clever girl made. Later on, since I passed well, I would sometimes stand guard for another girl and tell her when it was clear. She would then dash into a compartment and stay there until I gave her the all clear signal that everyone had left and she would dash out. Hand washing was never considered. Getting out fast was the only consideration.

Terrified of Exposure

Transgender people have many things to fear. High on the list is exposure. Exposure of being a transgender person jeopardizes relationships, jobs, family, and friends. All transgender people fear exposure; however, transgender women are the most fearful.

Perhaps their greater fear of being exposed is because of the high degree of shame involved. Even those that do not have job loss or family rejection to fear, nevertheless are terrified of exposure because it would indicate they are a sick person—the kind of person to avoid. Only a sick person would seek to go from a "superior" man to what has been thought of for millennia as an "inferior" woman.

All this makes a transgender person's life difficult. Society's lack of understanding the true nature of transgenderism adds to the need to be invisible and a highly closeted isolated group. I understand I carry a natural bias, but after careful consideration, I feel it is accurate to say transgender women are subject to more abuse than transgender men. I don't mean to minimize the problems of transgender men; however, they have less to fear than transgender women. Generally, they never escape other's perception that they are female and the public treats females more gently than males. However, that does not shield them from the harm and even death at the hands of extremist transphobic people.

Fear is usually fed by thought of the humiliation. When in public, transgender people are frequently embarrassed since they are stared at, laughed at, harassed, and heckled if they do not pass perfectly. Transgender girls wrote,

> I have been out in public places a few times—just short trips to get gas or grab something at a drive through window. Once I went to buy some nails at Walgreens. Every time it has been scary as hell and humiliating. All of these experiences have resulted in some pretty shocked reactions from people, from gaping mouths to people bursting out in laughter.

> How do you get past this? Every time I get a weird glare or a smirk I just want to shrivel up and hide in my belly button: How did you make the transition from the closet to public life?

A lot of people are transphobic. They forget that transgender people are still people. Different in the way they dress and think of themselves, but still human and deserving the right to live peacefully and happily. The general public doesn't know that transgender people are like everyone else in every way other than the way they happen to regard their gender (i.e., as different than their physical sex label).

Psychotherapy and Selecting a Therapist

Deciding to see a psychotherapist can be a difficult decision for some people, since in the past it implied you had a serious mental illness. That is no longer true. Seeing a therapist is a self-improvement step frequently used to help you better accept yourself and/or cope with a specific problem. For a transgender individual, it is safest to see a therapist before taking hormones and/or having an operation. Doctors usually prefer you see a therapist to be sure you are ready, since a doctor's prime objective and credo is to first do no harm. They want to be sure your decision to transition is based on sound reasoning.

Even if you are not transitioning with hormones and/or surgery, an important reason for seeking psychotherapy is the need to cope with your gender conflict. It is distressing for a transgender person to be caught in the middle between being the woman or man they feel they really are and the man or woman society is used to and insists they are. Therapy is good for the conflict every transgender person faces. However, when the need to "be yourself" is a strong pull in one direction and your need—actual or perceived—to stay in the closet is a strong pull in opposite direction, it's time for the help of a therapist. The stronger the conflict, the more destructive the conflict can be, if left unattended.

Generally speaking, psychotherapy can improve the quality of your life, but before selecting a therapist, you need to understand a therapist will only help you with problems you may have, think you have, or don't even realize is your underlying problem. However, she or he is not a problem solver, but will help you either solve or cope with your problem.

The second most difficult part of seeing a therapist is selecting one. There are psychiatrists, psychologists, social workers, counselors and others who engage in psychotherapy. You may come across degrees and titles, in this context, that are confusing such as M.D., Ph.D., PsyD., LCSW, CSW/R–CSW, CSW/P, CSW, ACSW, CSW, and perhaps others.

An M.D. (Psychiatrists) can prescribe psychotropic drugs and that generally is not what a transgender person requires. Psychotropic drugs are sometimes used in severe cases of depression and other mental illnesses. Most transgender people generally seek psychotherapy strictly as part of their transitioning or gender conflict.

That leaves psychologists (Ph.D., PsyD.), social workers, or counselors (basically all those other acronyms above) for help transitioning. Psychologists generally have more schooling than the others and have a doctorate degree, while social workers and counselors generally hold master's degrees. However, education is not the only determining factor in a therapist's ability to help you.

When selecting your therapist, you should first consider competency. Insist on a licensed therapist. A state licensed therapist is the only way to be sure the person has had adequate training and supervised practice. If an acronym follows the name, ask what the letters stand for in the event you need to check further. Training alone won't insure a skilled therapist, but choosing a properly trained therapist will give you a better chance of finding one.

Another factor of competency is the skill of the therapist. A good portion of what makes a competent therapist is skill, since therapy is, at least partially, an art. Unfortunately, this is difficult to determine ahead of time by examining credentials, conducting interviews, or any other means. A good choice might be a recommendation from someone whose opinion you can trust, who can recommend a therapist based on their personal experience with favorable attributes similar to what you seek. Just remember almost everyone believes his or her therapist is the best therapist.

Although I have had some successes with the recommendations of my doctor(s), other professionals, and professional organizations, I wouldn't favor their recommendations, since they are usually giving turns to those whom they know, but have no personal treatment experience with that person. Thus, they may know little about their attitudes or actual abilities. Getting recommendations from other transgender individuals may be helpful. Additional information may be available on the therapist's website or networking page (e.g., Facebook and LinkedIn).

A favorable indication of competence is the professional organization membership(s) and post licensing courses taken. This indicates the therapist is active in the field and is keeping up to date with new developments.

The most important attribute a therapist can have, after competency, is your mutual comfort level when communicating. Also, outside of unlawful and destructive activities, you need to feel your therapist accepts you "as is." You must also believe strict confidentiality will be observed. All licensed therapists abide by ethics and codes that require confidentiality with exceptions only for extreme or dangerous situations. Trust in confidentiality is important for you to be completely open and honest with the therapist.

My view of therapy is that therapists are facilitators. They help you think about your issue(s). You need that help because, as Henry Ford once correctly said, "Thinking is a difficult process. That is why so few people engage in it." Your therapist listens as if it were you listening because listening is what therapy is all about—you listening to your thoughts. You are forcing yourself to think about your issue(s), openly say what you think, and consciously listen to your thoughts. The therapist may help you pursue a thought deeper and prompt you to go further with it, but you are responsible for the thinking.

The gender of the therapist may be important for your comfort level and may affect your ability to speak openly and honestly. I tried both genders and had a preference.

It is difficult to say why I had a preference because I'll never know if it was the demeanor or gender of the therapist that made me more comfortable with one over the other.

Experience with transgender patients is another attribute to seek. You need to find a therapist who generally understands the transgender woman and man (we are sort of special), but you shouldn't sacrifice competence for experience with transgender people. However, you should look for both attributes—your perfect "fit." You need to watch out for therapists with a practice that claims a laundry list of specialties. You should prefer more of a specialist whose specialty meets what you seek..

Some state licensing or state psychological associations will share any complaints regarding your prospective selection. Although people rarely complain about their therapist, it is a good idea to check this out.

The location of the therapy may be important for practical reasons such as ease of access or transportation time and cost. You will probably need to attend sessions on a regular basis over a period of time. Acceptance of your medical insurance plan can be a very important factor in your choice. If cost is an important consideration, ask if the therapist uses group or other methods that reduce the cost.

It is a good idea to interview more than one psychotherapist, and the telephone is a good vehicle for that. A telephone interview can answer many important issues. Over the telephone, you need to first identify yourself, state you are looking for a therapist and why. Be brief and then get down to business by asking any questions you need answered. You can learn the therapist's credentials: the license, the issuer of the license, experience, and membership in professional organizations. Also, judge the professionalism during the telephone call. Does the psychotherapist seem confident and professional in her or his presentation? Confidence is good, but it is a bad omen if you perceive a know-it-all attitude or you are being talked down to.

Start being honest and open from the first moment of the first time you speak to the therapist. Say you are checking with other people as part of your decision making process. If you feel you are not a good match—and you don't need to know the reason—say it plainly and ask for a referral.

If you feel you may be a good match for each other, schedule an appointment for an initial meeting. Ask whether you will be charged and how much. Some therapists charge a full fee, while others will waive their fee entirely. There is nothing wrong with discussing this since there are all sorts of arrangements.

Some therapists do an "intake" appraisal of exactly what you need and recommend a therapist that would be a best "fit" for you. This frequently also involves a fee.

You may feel a little uncomfortable in an initial meeting, but generally you need to feel the verbal exchange is easy, open, and honest. You need to be comfortable talking about yourself and, later, the business aspects of your therapy.

The psychotherapist should have an essential understanding of the problem(s) or issue(s) with which you are concerned and must be willing to discuss his or her expertise when asked. If you are not comfortable with the therapist in the initial interview, keep looking for someone else.

The psychotherapist should also be clear about the business aspects of the relationship such as meeting times, scheduling, fees, and methods of payment. You need to be told how much the fee is and whether she or he accepts your insurance. Does she or he offer any cost options such as group therapy?

If finances are a significant concern in your decision about whether or not to enter therapy, there are places that offer reduced fees or no fee services. Some community health centers such as Callen-Lorde Community Health Center[4] in New York City provide health services for whatever you can afford. Free and low cost health centers in other cities can be found on the Internet. Most public libraries have computers and employees who can help you search the Internet. Many community health centers offer the services of psychotherapy, endocrinology for hormones, pharmacology for prescription drugs, and total medical care. Also, universities and training institutes often offer treatment at a reduced rate by supervised trainees. Furthermore, many mental health centers and LGBTQ Centers near your residence may also offer health services usually free or at reduced cost, depending on your ability to pay. Your county health department is a good place to start when looking for less costly therapy.

CHAPTER 9, Transphobia—Transgender Discrimination

Transphobia refers to prejudice against those people who identify with a gender that varies from the gender label applied to them at birth. It is frequently based on a transgender person's changing physical appearance and/or sex to resemble the sex they feel they are—their brain sex. Transphobia is expressed at all levels of society. It is seen at the personal, interpersonal, institutional, and cultural levels.

It is interesting to note that the continuous change in the names used to describe transgender people throughout history demonstrates the lack of understanding of the phenomenon.

History

According to some popular interpretations, transphobia was started with the writing of the Hebrew Bible, but that is misleading. Transgenderism existed long before any Bible was written or any thought of it being negative behaviors. We find they existed in most cultures and religions. The Vedic people (who evolved into present day Hindus) wrote of it around 1500-1100 B.C.E. They spoke of transgender people as the third sex. They wrote that the third sex was inborn and not an acquired perversion.

The third sex was recognized as a normal and natural occurrence among Romans, Native Americans, Hindus, Pacific Islanders, and most cultures. Transphobia is believed to have originated in ancient times coinciding with the denigration of women. The writing of the Hebrew Bible was a prime cause of the spread of transphobia. In recent history, transgender people were originally thought to be the same as homosexuals and homosexuality was banned in writing by the Bible. Transphobia was established in writing by the Bible. It was spread throughout the world in the fourth century by Christian invaders and in the seventh century by Islamic invaders.

In 342, Emperors Constantinius and Constans,[1] recently converted to Christianity, ruled that punitive measures be applied to "passive" homosexuals, those men who marry men as if they were women. They declared same sex marriage, which involved the roles of husband and wife, illegal. In the year 390, perpetrators of homosexual acts were subject to being burned alive.

Homosexuals were used as scapegoats for famines and pestilences. Earthquakes were also attributed to homosexuals. From 550 AD. (the same year the Abrahamic Laws outlawed the practice of sex between men) homosexuals were blamed for all disasters. At that time, acts of homosexual people (back then homosexual people included transgender people) were translated to English as abominations in the Hebrew Bible (i.e., the Hebrew word *to'ebah* describes a prohibited act, a detestable act). It says that mankind shall not lie with mankind as you would with a woman.[2] Transphobia, the wearing of the other sex's clothes, was also interpreted as a *to'ebah* in the Bible's Deuteronomy 22.5 (see below under Religion).

It was a common practice all across Europe and throughout history to subject homosexual/transgender people to mutilation, burning, other forms of torture, or murder. A recorded example of both participants being punished occurred in 1482 C.E.. A knight and his squire were both burned at the stake for sodomy in Zurich, Switzerland.[3] Both partners were usually punished; however, the passive partner (i.e., frequently the transgender one) was singled out for physical punishment before he was put to death.

Homosexual behavior between women was unheard of, mostly because women were the property and under the strict control of their father or their husband. In a harem or similar setting, however, who knows what all that giggling was about.

Religion

Transgenderism is not a religious matter. If anything, it is a biological variation. Although it has not been proven, evidence tends to support that belief. It is the belief of medical researchers and scientists. Nevertheless, it is discussed here, since many Moslems, Christian Fundamentalists, and Orthodox Jews insist it is a religious issue.

Transgender discrimination is hardly a new phenomenon. Discrimination is legitimatized by the Bible's Book of Deuteronomy that says it is a *to'ebah*. It never was an *avera*, Hebrew for a sin.

A *to'ebah* is the same prohibition as when your daughter wears jeans (i.e., pants), when a man wears a garment with wool and linen mixed, or extended to apply to a woman wearing a garment with polyester mixed with another fiber.

To'ebah appears 22 times in the Hebrew Bible and, for the most part, describes one of the most ignored passages in the Bible today. Most people wear articles of clothing commonly, or in the past, worn by the other sex. Most people don't know and don't care if fibers are mixed in their clothing. I even bought a pair of pants once that I thought was woolen, but the label read it contained several different fibers. I found the contents totaled 120%. I still have that gem of a tag somewhere.

Never the less, most religious people do not like transgender people, based on Deuteronomy 22.5, which says,

> A woman shall not wear that which pertaineth unto a man, neither shall a man put on a woman's garment; for whosoever doeth these things is an abomination unto the LORD thy God.

Some people even want to inflict punishment in the name of God because the Bible says people should not wear the clothes of the other sex. Since people believe what is written in the Bible is God's word, we must consider those words as they were written. Who are we to question the word of God? But that doesn't prevent me from wondering why He thought wearing the clothes of the other sex is detestable—an abomination.

I constantly think about and question everything; including what people say was said by God. Most people take God's word without question, but I simply can't help thinking about these words and wondering why He said what is attributed to Him. When I was young, I thought I was the only one who analyzes and questions God's word. I worried that it was like questioning God and is a bad thing to do. Since then I learned religious scholars do the same thing all the time. I am not a religious scholar, but I welcome their company.

Some people feel violating Deuteronomy 22.5's *to'ebah* (detestable act) is so bad that the death penalty should be inflicted for violating those words. I don't understand why God did not classify it as an *avera*, a sin? That is a very interesting point. What the haters feel is a capital offense (i.e., punishable by death), God didn't think was a sin. Detestable, but not a sin!

Because the Bible is often used as an excuse to harm transgender people I was prompted to take a close look at it.

The Hebrew Bible's prohibits of wearing the clothes of the other sex was adopted and spread by Christianity and Islam and through their invasions to many lands and cultures.

The abomination word was chosen to translate the Hebrew Bible's word "to'ebah". Since our haters feel violators should be punished with death, it seems odd that God called it a to'ebah, an abomination, and not an avera, a sin in Hebrew.

A study of Deuteronomy Chapter 22 reveals that it is clearly devoted entirely to human relations except for Verses 5, 6, and 7. Verse 5 prohibits wearing the clothes of the other sex and Verses 6 and 7 describe how to deal with a fallen birds nest. Verses 5, 6, and 7, the clothes and birds nest reference, seem to be an anomaly unless they also have a human relations meaning.

Because the 4 Verses before number 5 prohibits hiding from your neighbor to avoid helping him. It seems logical that Verse 5 means you should not wear the clothes of the other sex as a disguise to avoid helping your neighbor. But how is a bird's nest related to human relations like the rest of Chapter 22?

Could the fallen bird's nest represent a destroyed home and the contents homeless infants that you should take care of? Although wearing inappropriate clothes as a disguise has some merit, the bird's nest thought might be a little farfetched even though the following verse, Verse 8, mentions building a home, Yes, although misplaced, Verses 5, 6 and 7 must say what they mean. Don't wear the other sex's clothes and how to deal with a fallen birds nest, period!

Transgender people know they shouldn't wear the clothes of the other sex yet are mysteriously driven to do so. I know an Orthodox Jewish transgender woman who is tormented by the use of the word abomination because an inner force drives her to cross dress in opposition to her deep seated religious beliefs. That mysterious inner force is so powerful and so near impossible to resist, it must be God's will.

There are 2 methods of determining a person's gender. One when we determine someone else's gender and another method when we determine our own gender. When we determine someone else's gender we do what doctors do we use a person's genitals. When the genitals are covered, we use an indication of gender such as clothing, hair styles, etc..

When we determine our own gender we use a different method. As a child, when we first recognize there are both boys and girls, we know which one we are. We don't pick a gender! We know which one we are intuitively—it's automatic! It comes from somewhere inside us—our brain gender tells us. That explains the irresistible drive to dress like our inner and true sex demands. One transgender girl said,

> When my father caught me with nail polish, he said if he caught me doing that again he would send me to school dressed as a girl. I was such a dumb kid, my one chance and I blew it!

She added, that incident didn't stop her, she just became "more careful" when she "dressed."

Also convincing that we are born knowing our true sex, is so many observations of intersex children and boys born with a penile deformity. They had their genitals surgically made to look like a girls', because boys' genitalia is not successfully simulated. They were raised as girls, never told of their operation, and yet they eventually insist they are really male.

The mystery is compounded when you listen to transgender kids relate their early experiences and thoughts. You learn they started life believing they were not the sex people assumed they were at birth and wrote on their birth certificate.

Quotes from the stories of born girls and boys cited in CHAPTER 1—Comparison of Gender and Sex are a testimony to that. Also, one girl related her kindergarten experience:

> The teacher said the girls curtsy and line up here and the boys bow and line up over there. I curtsied and lined up here with the girls, of course. The teacher instructed me that I belonged with the boys, over there. I obeyed the teacher and went to the boy's side, over there. All the children laughed at me. That laughter taught me that even though I really belonged here with the girls, I better keep that a secret and stay with the boys or the children will laugh at me.

Most children intuitively know their own true gender. A born girl related, "Mom, Dad, there is a man inside me". Transgender people always talk about the man or woman inside them. Our birth doctor saw an indication of our sex not our sex. Gender is a feeling and not visible. It is like a headache. You can't see it or show it to anyone but you know it is there because you feel it.

Furthermore, there are 182,000 Intersex children born each year. Many have ambiguous genitals and some even have genitals that look like the other sex. Genitals are like clothes. They are only an indication of gender and not our gender.

To convince the reader of this let's turn to God's word, the Bible again, for the official answer. I remember something Samuel said. Oh, not to me personally. I'm not that old in spite of the rumors and especially since I started lying about my age. I didn't hear it, I read it. It is written in the Bible, of course. To quote Samuel 16:7,

> Man looketh on the outward appearance, but the LORD looketh on the heart.

The King James Bible says something very similar. John 7:24 says,

> Jesus commands you to look beneath the surface, so you can judge correctly.

The Koran says:

> The Almighty knows what's in the heart and will judge us according to our intentions.

Most children heard their parents say over and over, "be a good girl" or, "be a good boy." They hear that even before they learn to speak. Most accept the word of their authority, their parents. Others wonder why their parents mistakenly think they are the other gender.

The doctor who delivered us took one look at us and without any thought decided which gender we are. Worse yet, medical science can even see the presence or absence of our visible sex organs before we are born. Doctors are not endowed with God's ability to look inside us—to look in our heart, beneath the surface, and determine our intentions.

A simple conclusion is we are not wearing the clothes of the other sex, but we are wearing appropriate clothes. We are merely correcting the error our mother's doctor innocently made, which falsely led our parents to think and temporarily convince us we were the wrong gender. Those Fundamentalists, Orthodox, and other religious adherents have also been misled. The consensus believes transgenderism is bad. However, that consensus is wrong!

I remember in a math class in high school, all the students had the same answer to a problem, except me. I insisted on a different answer and stood my ground. The teacher worked the problem out on the board to prove the consensus was correct and found the consensus to be incorrect. The consensus is not always correct. It wasn't easy to be alone, to which most transgender people can testify, but I turned out to be correct.

Similarly, I am sure God does not go by consensus and is on the side of transgender people. He worked out the human problems long ago. He sees our struggle to stop wearing clothes inappropriate for our inner gender, our true gender. He judges us by what is in our heart and not by our outward appearance. Only He can know our intentions. I am sure He looks at transgender peoples' determination in the face of discrimination, and too often martyrdom, to conform to Deuteronomy 22.5, His written word with appreciation and approval. Because of that, I know God has given transgender people His blessing for standing fast!

Just as passages in the Hebrew Bible have been interpreted to demonstrate support or a lack of support for transgender people, a large number of passages in Christian Bible and Koran do the same. After all, we were created in God's image.

The only thing I can do to conform to Deuteronomy is stop wearing the clothes that "pertaineth unto a man."

Anticrossdressing Laws

In the mid nineteenth century, many cities in the United States started to pass laws making it a crime to dress as the other sex. They were referred to as the Anticrossdressing Laws. The flurry of laws coincided with a wave of scientific and medical advancements that seemed to be replacing religion's moral force. These laws were intended to "stem that tide."

Most of these laws came between 1848 and 1956. However, Cincinnati, Ohio passed such a law as recently as 1974. Anticrossdressing Laws were enacted in localities all across America. A New York woman, who liked to dress as a man, could wear no more than 3 items of men's clothing at one time.[4]

Almost coinciding with all those transphobic laws, in about 1869, Karl Heinrich Ulrich and Karl Kertbeny issued the first known statement by scientists to remove the Anticrossdressing Laws. They said the origin of transgenderism is biological. Incidentally, at that time, Ulrich and Kertbeny recognized and published their belief that homosexuality and transgenderism were 2 distinct and separate phenomena.

They coined the word homosexual and they separated homosexuals from gender inversion people. The term gender inversion was an early term for homosexual and later was often used to referred to what eventually became called transvestite in 1910).

When challenged in court, proponents of these Anticrossdressing laws claimed that:

1. These laws are necessary to prevent crime;
2. These laws are a safeguard against fraud;
3. Society's gender norms should be protected; and
4. These laws are a way to discourage homosexuality.

The United States courts of the 1970s struck down the Anticrossdressing Laws and rejected these arguments as unconstitutional.

Employment

It is not widely known that wherever there are no specific laws outlawing transgender discrimination, a transgender woman or a transgender man can be fired from their job merely because she or he is a transgender person. This is true even if they dress "conventionally" on the job. If they are allowed to remain on the job, they are frequently forced to quit due to harassment by fellow employees.

I personally know a transgender woman who was mercilessly taunted and tormented on the job, although she never dressed as a woman at work. She was not a "swishy" type either. Her gender expression was somehow recognized. She was either observed by someone off the job, or her failure to join the boys in their outside activities gave her away. In any case, her tormenting started and once started never stopped. She eventually had to quit her job.

This is the same kind of discrimination faced by nontransgender and nongay feminine acting men and nonlesbian masculine acting women who are not a transgender person. It is therefore imperative that gender expression be included along with gender identity in antidiscrimination laws.

This need is demonstrated by the famous case of the United States District Court decision, Price Waterhouse v Hopkins.[5] The verdict was in favor of a woman, a senior and successful employee, who had been denied a partnership because she was too masculine in looks, language, and management style. She was told to wear makeup and jewelry, and to take a course at a charm school. She was a genetic woman, not a lesbian nor a transgender person. On the basis of discrimination, she won the case based on Title VII's, sex discrimination clause.

A 2009 study of discrimination, "Injustice at Every Turn," was made to investigate employment discrimination against transgender people.[6] The report, titled "National Transgender Discrimination Survey," involved a total of 6,456 transgender and gender nonconforming individuals in the U.S. and its possessions. The results indicated the very poor economic and psychological conditions transgender people experience. A follow-up study in 2015, the United States Trans Survey (USTS) involved 27,715 respondents. This study yielded essentially the same picture as the previous study but included many more aspects of a transgender person life and experiences.[6]

Both studies found: discrimination is pervasive among all ages, at all locations, among all races, and is most severe for people of color. Transgender people have a poverty level of 29%, double the U.S. average and 3 times the unemployment of other U.S. citizens. The treatment of transgender people in most aspects of life is inhuman and a disgrace to our country.

Transgender people experience 8 times the psychological distress in the month prior to completing the survey and 40% attempted suicide in their lifetime compared with the U.S. population (5%) (Note: a more recent study showed 1.6% of the general population and 41.0% of the transgender population attempted suicide in their life-time.)

Mistreatment of students in school was particularly distressing. The majority of transgender students experienced some form of harmful discrimination: 54% were verbally harassed, 24% physically attacked, and 13% sexually assaulted because they were a transgender person. The mistreatment was so severe that 17% felt forced to leave school. The abuse that transgender youths experience at home and in school is the most damaging to society.

Harassment, mistreatment, or discrimination at work, in seeking health care, and trying to obtain shelter in homeless shelters are inhuman and disgraceful! Many transgender people said they had only been able to support themselves by working in the underground economy (e.g. becoming sex workers or selling drugs).

The American Civil Liberty Union reports it is legal to fire someone for being lesbian, gay, or bisexual in many places and the legality of firing transgender people is even more widespread.[7]

Sometimes transgender people lose their jobs when they begin to transition. One transgender woman sued the Library of Congress. She was qualified for the job researching terrorism by virtue of her similar military terrorism experience. She was told she was overwhelmingly qualified for the job and she was hired. However, when she later told the hiring manager of her plans to transition before she started the new job, the decision to hire her was reversed. In the case of Diane Schroer v. James H. Billington, Librarian of Congress, the District Court's conclusion was:[8]

> In refusing to hire Diane Schroer because her appearance and background did not comport with the decision makers' sex stereotypes about how men and women should act and appear, and in response to Schroer's decision to transition, legally, culturally, and physically, from male-to-female, the Library of Congress violated Title VII's prohibition on sex discrimination.

Some progress has been made. In December 2009, Governor David A. Paterson of New York issued a proclamation forbidding employment discrimination against gender identity and expression. This applied to New York State employees only. New York was only the seventh state to protect public employees from discrimination based on gender identity or expression.

In January, 2016, Governor Andrew Cuomo used his executive authority to protect transgender people from harmful discrimination; however, this can be reversed by any subsequent governor. Therefore, we now we need the New York State Legislature to pass the Gender Expression Nondiscrimination Act (GENDA). It covers employment and other protections from harmful discrimination. GENDA has been introduced repeatedly and passed by the New York State Assembly, but the State Senate has never put it to a vote. We need a GENDA law in New York and similar laws in many other states.

On September 14, 2014 the Equal Employment Opportunity Commission (EEOC) filed lawsuits against two companies accused of discriminating against transgender employees. This was the first time the federal government has brought suit under the Civil Rights Act of 1964 to protect transgender workers. One complaint was filed in Florida and the other in Michigan. They are the most ambitious steps in a series of aggressive moves taken by the EEOC in the past several years to advance LGBTQ rights under existing laws. These lawsuits aim to give the full force to Title VII's prohibition against sex discrimination and is an attempt to ensure it helps eliminate unlawful discriminatory barriers to LGBTQ applicants and employees. EEOC General Counsel David Lopez said of his ruling, "It seeks to ensure employers aren't considering irrelevant factors, like gender-based stereotypes or gender identity, in making employment decisions."

Partially based on the Diane Schroer v. James H. Billington, Librarian of Congress and similar cases, on December 18, 2014, the United States Justice Department's Attorney General Eric Holder stated, "I have determined that the best reading of Title VII's prohibition of sex discrimination is that it encompasses discrimination based on gender identity, including transgender status.

Although Title VII has been favorable toward transgender people, a Federal law specifically providing transgender people and all LGBTQ people with protection from harmful discrimination has been filed. It is in Congress under the name of the National Equality Act of 2015 It is needed, since Title VII is not always applicable. If a law specifically prohibiting transgender employment and other forms of discrimination, it would ultimately result in fewer occurrences of this form of discrimination and possible litigation.

The Department of Defense announced in July, 2016 that it plans to end the ban on transgender people serving openly in the military. In a statement they said, "We recognize there are transgender soldiers, sailors, airmen and Marines—real, patriotic Americans—who I know are being hurt by an outdated, confusing, inconsistent approach that's contrary to our value of service and individual merit." In addition, a spokesman said, "The Defense Department's current regulations regarding transgender service members are outdated and are causing uncertainty that distracts commanders from our core missions." In July, 2016, the harmful discrimination against transgender people in the military was ended.

It was inspiring to see this progress and it gives added energy for us to continue working for positive change.

President Obama went one step further. He made history on July 21, 2014 when he signed an Executive Order that not only barred harmful discrimination against LGBTQ people who work for the federal government but included all those who work for federal contractors. The President said we should all be judged based on the work we do and not on who we are.

On January 30, 2017, newly elected President Donald Trump seemed to be negating all President Obama's Executive Orders but stated he will leave Obama's order outlawing harmful discrimination against LGBTQ people intact.

The Secretary of Defense, in July, 2017, stated he needed six months to decide on the effect of transgender people in the military. The results were expected to be the same as the 18 countries that now have transgender people openly serving in their army (Australia, Austria, Belgium, Bolivia, Canada, Czech Republic, Denmark, Estonia, Finland, France, Germany, Israel, Netherlands, New Zealand, Norway, Spain, Sweden, and the United Kingdom).

In August 2017, Trump violated his word and first outlawed the admittance of transgender people to the armed forces and then notified the Secretary of Defense that he can discharge transgender people already in the armed forces at his will.

Trump ignored his January promise to leave the LGBTQ rules in effect, ignored the previous Secretary of Defense's statement, and the study in progress by his current Secretary of Defense. He was not interested in if the study's results would be for, against, or indifferent regarding transgender people. He was a bigot or bent to bigots in his staff.

To sum all this up, we must fight ever harder for a universal human rights law.

Human Rights

Transgender people are also subject to discrimination in credit, housing, restaurants, retail stores, hotels, health care, and other public accommodations. In many places they do not have simple human rights or equal protection under the law. Such protection is taken for granted by others.

Denial of medical treatment is particularly inhumane and experienced by transgender individuals. Two cases demonstrate transphobia is sometimes encountered when medical treatment is needed.

One such case involved the refusal by 20 physicians to treat a transgender man, Robert Eads,[10] for ovarian cancer. He subsequently died of cancer.

Another case involved a transgender woman. Tyra Hunter[11] was a passenger in a car involved in an automobile accident. When rescue workers discovered she was a transgender woman, they backed away and stopped administering treatment. After being taken to a Washington, D.C. hospital, she was refused treatment. She later died in the hospital.

A transgender woman on Long Island, New York, wrote,

> I've seen paramedics deny T-girls [transgender girls] medical care. I got to experience that one first hand after I was beaten and the medics refused to treat me after I was found out. The cop . . . picked me up threw me in the back of the squad car. He then drove me to an Emergency Room at a local hospital.

This is not a problem from the past. The Indiana Star Press reports a male-to-female transsexual named Erin Vaught says she was called names and left waiting when she went to the Emergency Room at the Ball Memorial Hospital on July 18, 2010.[12] Ms. Vaught was coughing up blood. She says a doctor eventually told her the hospital didn't know how to treat transgender people. The Indiana Transgender Rights Advocacy Alliance and Indiana Equality complained to the hospital, where the complaint has resulted in a Sensitivity Program for hospital personnel.

The denial of medical insurance coverage by some companies is particularly transphobic and inhumane. Even psychological services are sometimes denied. In June 2008, the American Medical Association released a pertinent statement supporting the transgender insurance coverage issue, as follows: [9]

> Resolved, That our American Medical Association support public and private health insurance coverage for treatment of gender identity disorder as recommended by a physician.

Six years later, in 2014, we saw a major advancement in removing the bigotry of denying health benefits to transgender people. New York State moved to require insurance coverage for transgender health care in private insurance and Medicaid. Also, a decades-old rule preventing Medicare from financing treatment of transgender people, including gender reassignment surgery, was overturned within the Department of Health and Human Services. Two weeks later, the U.S. Office of Personnel Management announced that government contracted health insurers could start covering the cost of gender reassignment surgeries for federal employees, retirees, and their survivors.

In what many have deemed an historic measure, the IRS on November 11, 2011 announced that it would allow transgender taxpayers to deduct the cost of gender reassignment surgery from their taxes as a medical expense.

The IRS officials announced its intent, via a "notice of acquiescence," to abide by a 2010 decision that held that some medical expenses from such surgeries could be deducted from income tax filings. The "acquiescence" also effectively ends an almost decade-long battle that Rhiannon O'Donnabhain, who was born male, waged against the IRS to deduct $5,000 in expenses she incurred to bring her anatomy in line with her gender identity.

The IRS had previously claimed O'Donnabhain's procedure was entirely cosmetic and, as such, not subject to a deduction. O'Donnabhain said she brought the lawsuit in an attempt to force the IRS to treat "sex-change" surgeries the same as appendectomies, heart surgeries and other deductible medical procedures.

The Australian Commonwealth guidelines on the recognition of sex and gender, passed the Sex Discrimination Amendment Act on June 25, 2013 without a vote. It defined the 'X' as a gender marker which would encompass "indeterminate/intersex/unspecified" categories. The policy extends the use an 'X' gender marker to any adult who chooses that option and can obtain a certifying letter from a doctor or psychologist. This applies to all dealings with the Australian Commonwealth government and its agencies. The option is being introduced over a three year period. The guidelines also clarify that the Australian Federal government will now collect data on gender, rather than sex. The "gender identity" attribute protects transgender people with non-binary identities.

On April 15 2014, the Supreme Court in India directed the federal and state governments to include transgendered people in all welfare programs for the poor, including education, health care, and jobs to help them overcome social and economic challenges. The Court also noted that it was the right of every human being to choose their gender without regard to gender surgery. All documents in India will now have a third category marked transgender.

The Affordable Care Act (ACA) of October 2015 prohibits health insurance companies from denying coverage because of pre-existing conditions, which was the major basis for denying transgender people insurance coverage. Section 1557 of the law also blocks companies from discriminating against transgender people in general, since this law will also apply its non-discrimination provision to transgender individuals. Coverage for the costs of transgender surgeries and hormones is also covered by the ACA. However, the ACA has only been adopted by some states and the District of Columbia. This law needs to be extended to all states. Conservatives need to understand that health care is a human right and not a political issue.

Vitally important, we need the Congress of the United States to pass the National Equality Act that protects gender identity and expression and thereby granting us basic human rights. This has had a measure of relief in the form of a presidential memorandum directing hospitals receiving Medicare and Medicaid funds to give LGBTQ patients the compassion and security they deserve in their time of need, including the ability to designate someone other than an immediate family member to make medical decisions and have visitation rights.

Furthermore, the Hopkins case demonstrated individuals outside the transgender community also need the federal law. Masculine behaving women and feminine behaving men need this protection. These nonconforming gender expression people, who are neither a gay nor a transgender persons, are also subjected to discrimination and harassment based on their gender expression.

There is help for gender nonconforming people from miscellaneous legal organizations throughout the United States (see APPENDIX II, Transgender Legal Assistance Organizations). However, these organizations need laws with which to work and such laws are only available in some parts of the United States. Up to now some other parts of the United States have only had Presidential and Gubernatorial Orders to help in this area. We need all-inclusive laws to insure all transgender people have basic human rights.

On May 23, 2014 the Departmental Review Board (DRB) an arm of the United States Health and Human Services Department (HHS) ruled that the blanket rule excluding elderly transgender people (and disabled people) from receiving Medicare benefits was unjustified. The 3-decade old rule cannot be automatically applied in the future.

This groundbreaking decision recognizes the procedures transgender people seek as a medical necessity and an effective treatment for individuals who do not identify with the sex indicated by their genitals. The ruling had wide-spread implications. Aside from offering coverage for sex reassignment surgery, hormone therapy, and psychological services, this government ruling lead to insurance companies including Medicaid to follow suit. The Affordable Care Act (ACA) did that and has prevented many legal battles that would have been necessary to establish this principle as past experience would indicate.

Unfortunately, only some states and the District of Columbia offer ACA benefits and therefore provide health care for low income transgender people.

Safety

Women's safety is another important issue. Women, in general, need to be safety conscious because they are in general physically weaker than most men and easy prey for a thief or a sexual predator. An example of the precautions taken by most women is they "automatically" lock the doors after entering their car.

Transgender women need to be doubly careful. They are weakened to the strength of a woman by hormones and therefore also easy targets for thieves and sexual offenders. In addition, they are also prey to transphobic people who hate "any man who wears women's clothes and/or wants to be a woman." Another danger is a man might be attracted to a woman who he learns is a transgender woman and he becomes violent because in his mind the individual made him a homosexual.

Transgender men are in a similar situation. They grew up without much testosterone and are therefore generally smaller and more easily overpowered than those who had the endurance, strengthening, and height advantages of testosterone during puberty.

Wilchins, in a 1998 video "Transgendered Revolution," said,[13]

> Transgender people are never killed from 300 yards away with a high powered rifle; they're always killed up front and personal. . . . People want to see us die. . . . There is a level

of almost unhinged deranged violence about gender hate crimes.

In 2010, a Federal Hate Crimes Bill was passed by Congress and was signed into law by the President. This legislation increases the penalty for hate crimes against gender variant people in the same manner as for racial and religious hate crimes. The discouraging effects of this law regarding crimes against transgender people is important. However, equally important is it gives a measure of federal legislative and presidential recognition in United States that gender variance is a recognized and legitimate state of being. I believe this is the first step toward acquiring transgender human rights at the federal level and will help in acquiring recognition in other jurisdictions sooner.

In other areas, the Department of Housing and Urban Development (HUD) announced a series of proposals on August 19, 2010 intended to ensure core housing programs are open to everyone, regardless of sexual orientation or gender identity. Furthermore, HUD also announced the first national study of discrimination against members of the LGBTQ community in the rental and sale of housing.

Human rights laws that include transgender women and men have been passed in some jurisdictions. New York City, the State of New Jersey, the State of Iowa, and over 100 other states and jurisdictions, which includes 60% of the U. S. population (over 180 million people), have laws extending human rights to gender variant people.[14] In spite of the fact that there has never been a reported problem of a transgender person committing a criminal or antisocial act because such a law (see Appendix VI) is passed, human rights inclusion is still resisted in many other places.

I don't think many people understand that transgender people experience widespread discrimination and abuse in many areas of life. I am confident that eventually the U.S. Constitution will be extended to protect the human rights of all people in all areas and not just the actions of the governmental agencies.

The framers of our Constitution, by specifying protection to religion and other classes of citizens, effectively excluded those not specifically mentioned. If they had said what Thomas Jefferson believed,[15] every human being on this continent would have their human rights protected.

We are starting to see more governmental involvement in all aspects of LGBTQ people's lives. In October, 2009, the Health and

Human Services Department created a National Resource Center for LGBTQ elders,[16] proper treatment of transgender healthcare from Medicaid and Medicare participants, and inclusion of LGBTQ people in the Hates Crime Law.

Source of Discrimination

Transphobia finds some of its more modern roots in the fact that until 2013, the American Psychiatric Association (APA) classified transgenderism as a psychological disorder (i.e., pathological—a mental disorder). Some of those in the field said it was necessary to classify transsexualism as a "disorder," so medical insurance will cover the treatment (i.e., hormonal and surgical sex reassignment). Broken bones are not listed as mental disorders, yet they are covered by insurance. Other surgically correctable biological variations, which transgenderism is closest to, are in the biologic disorder or variation category. They are not defined as a psychiatric disorder and are covered by insurance.

A report from an Amsterdam meeting, "Moving from Intentions to Action," urged the reclassification of transgenderism to "gender dysphoria" in the APA's Diagnostic and Statistical Manual and the World Health Organization's International Classification of Diseases. This change was made by the APA in 2013. It provides a diagnostic category that would accommodate the needs of those gender identity variant people who require insurance coverage for medical care of their transgenderism, but without the stigma attached to a mental disorder.

The past implication that transgenderism is a mental illness lingers and flies in the face of the fact that there is no treatment that converts transgender people's gender identity to become identical with their physical sex. Brain gender cannot be changed. No amount of psychotherapy has ever been successful in altering anyone's gender identity. The only treatment available is with hormones and/or surgery to bring a transgender person's physical sex into better alignment with their gender identity.

Except for the social stigma, most transgender people are not suffering, they do not have feelings of distress, nor are they experiencing difficulty in functioning. Most require no treatment; therefore, most have no need for a diagnosis at all. If transgenderism is a mental illness, then millions of people worldwide are mental cases due to this reason alone.

The APA committee that dealt with gender identity was accused of being stacked with pseudo scientists, such as Doctors Kenneth Zucker and Ray Blanchard, who are in favor of promoting antiquated reparative and aversion "therapy," which has been declared unethical by their peers at the World Professional Association for Transgender Health (WPATH).[17] I call this reparative therapy, sometimes called aversion therapy, modern words for torture. They are designed to drive one's gender identity into those deep, dark, and solitary closets. Since October 1, 2012, California law prohibits the practice of reparative therapy. This prohibition is slowly spreading throughout the United States.

The old approach of the APA was described as "junk science" by most people in the field and only led to greater and greater persecution of transgender people. Some people in the field reinforce antitransgender bigotry. In 1950, Ray Blanchard said there are two distinct subtypes of MtF transsexuals. Members of one subtype, homosexual transsexuals, are best understood as a type of homosexual male. The other subtype autogynephilic transsexuals are motivated by eroticism. Contrary to that, many transgender women are living as gay men (see Chapter 4 - The Homosexual Connection).

J. Michael Bailey[18], a psychology professor at Northwestern University, believed the idea that transgender people are women trapped in a man's body has little fact in science. Of course, science has theories, but few facts regarding most aspects of transgenderism. At any rate, I wonder what special clairvoyant ability Professor Bailey has that enables him to read people's mind and feelings?

If one subtype of transgender people is homosexual and another subtype driven by an erotic desire to be a woman, why am I both not attracted to men and willing to surrender my erotic virility to hormones to live more like a woman? This is not valid, since bigotry rarely is, if ever, rational. Unfortunately, these old beliefs seem to live on.

It is uncanny how so many transgender people have experienced the same, or very similar, experiences with being or wanting to be a female from a very early age. It is equally uncanny how we fought the need to express our femininity before we knew others like us existed. My observations of transgender men indicate the same thing.

In 1869, Dr. Ulrich said homosexuality has a biological cause (and that included gender inversion people, at the time). Magnus Hirschfeld said the same thing in naming the transvestite around 1910. Harry Benjamin said it again in 1966 at the conclusion of his

17 year study of transgender individuals. In between those times, other researchers repeated the same thing.

In June 2010, the WPATH, formerly the Harry Benjamin International Gender Dysphoria Association, Inc. released a statement urging the depsychopathologisation of gender variance worldwide. WPATH is the foremost international authority and mental health authority regarding transgenderism in the world. They issued the following press release on May 26, 2010. The statement is as follows:

> The WPATH Board of Directors strongly urges the depsychopathologisation of gender variance worldwide. The expression of gender characteristics, including identities that are not stereotypically associated with one's assigned sex at birth is a common and culturally diverse human phenomenon, which should not be judged as inherently pathological or negative. The psychopathologisation of gender characteristics and identities reinforces or can prompt stigma, making prejudice and discrimination more likely, rendering transgender and transsexual people more vulnerable to social and legal marginalization and exclusion, and increasing risks to mental and physical wellbeing. WPATH urges governmental and medical professional organizations to review their policies and practices to eliminate stigma toward gender variant people.

WPATH further suggested the term gender identity disorder places a stigma on transgender individuals and it applauded its coming replacement with gender incongruence, although it favored gender dysphoria. Gender dysphoria was the official description that was finally adopted.

This was long overdue and especially timely for the 2013 DSM revision and reissue in May 2013. The discrimination spread by Dr. Zucker has caused lasting damage. When the State of Colorado tried to include transgender people in their civil rights legislation, full page ads appeared depicting transgender women as sexual predators in restrooms. This is how transgender women are portrayed. A similar protest occurred in Maryland.

That is bigotry, not based on knowledge or common sense. Perhaps women would prefer to have transgender men use the ladies room. Their chromosomes say XX (female), but their bearded face, balding head, and masculine appearance and attire is unlikely to be a comfort for women rather than a transgender woman who looks, acts, and even thinks like them. I do not believe they would like bathrooms excluded in any law. If given a choice, I believe women would prefer women, in fact, rather than women by birth label that look like men in their restroom.

The bathroom issue is slowly dying. In April, 2015, the Equal Employment Opportunity Commission (EEOC) found that the Army discriminated against a transgender civilian employee when it required her to use a single-user restroom at work and reprimanded her for using the women's restroom when the single-user restroom was unavailable. The EEOC concluded that Tamara Lusardi, a Software Quality Assurance Specialist in the U.S. Army Aviation and Missile Research, Development, and Engineering Center in Huntsville, Alabama, "was subjected to disparate treatment on the basis of sex" in violation of Title VII of the Civil Rights Act of 1964.

The EEOC also found that Lusardi's supervisors subjected her to a hostile work environment by continually referring to her with male pronouns as a way to "humiliate and ridicule" her. The commission called the behavior "offensive and demeaning." In July, 2016, the military allowed transgender people to serve openly.

As previously indicated, 60% of the U.S. population (180 million people) live in areas with gender rights laws and nothing bad has happened. I have not been able to find any transgender sexual or other crimes. There has never been crimes as a result of transgender nondiscrimination laws (see APPENDIX VI, Survey—No Assaults Due To Transgender Nondiscrimination Laws). When transgender people go to a toilet, they are interested in one thing only. That is, doing their business and getting out. They are women and also sit down behind a compartment door. There are no reported cases of women or children being abused in restrooms by a transgender woman or sexual predators. Sexual predators avoid lighted places where an "intruder" may appear at any moment. They prefer a dark alley or other assurance of privacy.

Furthermore, sexual predators are expressing power and wearing women's clothes would defeat their purpose. However, this is an obstacle faced by transgender people each day in some communities. The situation of a transgender woman in the ladies' room is more like, who is more frightened by a chance meeting, the woman or the mouse?

The consequences of the unfair mental disorder stigma are perpetuated by the old APA classification. A transgender man, speaking of his situation at his place of employment said,

> There was the fear that I would start meeting the other men in the men's bathroom and, would they freak out since they knew my history. I just keep telling myself that I was using the men's [room] everywhere else in my life and that I was handling it okay, and that we're there just to use the bathroom. You go in, do your business, leave.

In addition to the restroom ads in Maryland in 2007, a Maryland extremist group, Citizens for Responsible Government, dedicated a web page to denouncing transgender civil rights based on the old APA's DSM. It stated,

> Gender Identity Disorder is classified as a mental disorder by the American Psychiatric Association. Legal protection against discrimination based on mental illness is not provided for any other disorder, and there is no rational explanation why it should be offered for this one. Those who wish to assume a 'gender identity' contrary to their biological sex are in need of mental health treatment to overcome such disturbed thinking, not legislation to affirm it.

This was also the case in New Hampshire. In 2008, a similar argument was used to deny civil rights. On the other hand, Dr. Kelley Winters,[19] a writer on issues of transgender medical policy, is most noted for her statement to the medical society,

> It is time for the medical professions to affirm that difference is not disease, nonconformity is not pathology, and uniqueness is not illness. . . . It is time for diagnostic criteria that serve a clear therapeutic purpose, are appropriately inclusive, and define disorder on the basis of distress or impairment and not upon social nonconformity.
> It is time for medical policies which, above all, do no harm to those they are intended to help.

Many countries are far ahead of the United States. In 2002, the British Lord Chancellor's office published a "Government Policy

Concerning Transgender People." It categorically states transgenderism is not a mental illness. Furthermore, in May 2009, the French Government declared "transgender identity" is not a psychiatric condition in France. Sweden has also declared transgender individuals are not pathological.

In 2004, the UK introduced a Gender Recognition Certificate (GRC). If you have medical treatment for gender variance and choose to live in the gender role that differs from your birth label, you can obtain a GRC and a new birth certificate in your "adopted" gender without a genital operation. The one limitation is you cannot remain married. However, once you have a GRC, you are free to marry or enter into a civil union. There is nothing like that anywhere in this country.

In July 2014, New York City passed a law creating a Municipal Identification Card so that residents who face obstacles to obtaining government-issued identification (ID) can more easily acquire it. The law will help transgender people, who often have difficulties securing an accurate ID with gender markers that match who they are. This new law makes New York City the first governmental entity in the nation to allow transgender people to self-designate their sex on ID cards, without the need to provide medical or other documentation to confirm their sex. Such documentation is often extremely difficult for poor or otherwise marginalized people to obtain.

On June 5, 2014, New York State change the rules for revising the sex marker on birth certificates. New York State no longer requires a surgical operation for the birth certificate gender change. New York City, which has separate rules, followed the State's example on December 8, 2014 . Like the state, the New York City Council passed a law that no longer requires a surgical operation to obtain an amended birth certificate that reflects the way they live their lives.

Some transgender people reduce the effects of discrimination by shedding all traces of the fact they ever were a transgender person. It is possible to change all references to one's sex and name in many states and the federal government, if you have sex reassignment treatment and a court ordered name change. Without an operation, gender treatment, or a court ordered name change, it is still possible to change some identification regarding your sex marker and your name, but as indicated above the procedure varies by jurisdiction, if it is allowed at all.

Every state has its own rules. The two states with a liberal regulation are California and New York. In California, you are not required to have genital surgery to have your name and sex designation changed on your driver's license. Merely submit a form requesting it and provide a doctor's letter stating you are being treated for gender identity dysphoria. The New York Division of Motor Vehicles (DMV) will change your sex designation with a similar doctor's or therapist's letter; however, it is difficult to change your name on a New York driver's license without a court-ordered name change. Even if the name on your birth certificate is different than your driver's license, you need either a court order or documents totaling six points on their list of acceptable documents. The difficulty with the DMV is that most documents on their list need your Social Security number and name to match. This problem is faced in other states. Social Security will not change your name without a court order. Gender can be changed with a doctor certifying a genital operation has taken place; however, there are some exceptions and they sometimes relent on requiring an operation for a gender change. The operation requirement will probably be replaced in the future with completion of treatment (i.e., top surgery or hormone therapy).

This has been a less vital issue, since October 6, 2011. At that time the Social Security Administration stopped including a person's gender when communicating with employers.

In June, 2010, the U.S. State Department issued new rules regarding the sex notation on passports. You no longer need to have a genital operation to change the sex marker (i.e., notation) on your passport. You need a medical doctor's letter stating you have been treated for gender identity disorder (I believe they have not changed "disorder" to "dysphoria"). If the treatment has concluded, you get a regular ten year passport (note: hormone treatment as maintenance of your appearance still qualifies you for a regular ten year passport). However, if your treatment is still in progress, a two year passport with the sex marker change will be issued.

It is still nearly impossible to get your name changed on a passport without a court-ordered change. The policy states if you can show you have been using the name exclusively for five years or more, you don't need a court order. However, there is a complication. Many of the documents required to prove your name is used exclusively, such as banks, driver's license, credit cards, utilities, and others, require a social security number (with matching name) or other nearly insurmountable name change requirements since the 9/11 terrorist attack. The Social Security Administration will only change the name on your record (i.e., card) with a court-ordered name change.

I feel it is now a Catch 22, which was not intended when the regulations were established. My position with the Passport Agency is I use my assumed (i.e., common law) name exclusively. It is other people who do not! They insist on using my birth certificate name.

Until the Affordable Care Act (ACA), transgender people suffered the lingering disadvantages of the DSM-IV mental illness classification, but even today rarely experienced any of the purported benefits that were used as an excuse to justify the maintenance of the mental disorder classification. Many insurance companies, including Medicaid, did not cover hormone therapy even when it was determined necessary by a doctor. Sex reassignment surgery was classified as cosmetic, elective, or used some other excuse. They refused surgical coverage even though it is considered medically necessary in many cases.

In September, 2012, the Transgender Legal Defense and Education Fund (TLDEF) won a case against the MVP Health Care (an insurance company) for genital surgery coverage. The threat of a law suit, together with substantial medical opinion, and the TLDEF backup, convinced the insurance company to cover the surgical expenses.

In spite of the TLDEF victory, only the Affordable Care Act forces many insurance companies to cover transgender medical treatment(s). Today, those covered by the ACA can get insurance coverage for transgender medical treatment. Other good news is the Internal Revenue Service allows all hormone, surgical, and associated expenses as income tax deductions.

Probably the most wide spread impact of the previous mental illness classification by the APA is the belief that the transgender phenomenon is synonymous with a mental condition and is even associated with sex maniacs. This means we need to take precautions for which one should not have to be subjected. It is best for a transgender man or woman to stay far away from children. We are believed to be pedophiles so we are unlikely to be employed as a teacher of young children regardless of how much we love children.

To save myself from unfounded accusation, persecution, prejudice, and intolerance, I can never dare to be friendly towards children in my neighborhood, as I always was in the past. I love children and would never harm or hurt a child. Yet I know I can no longer be friendly with any of them because I would be suspected of being a sex maniac and a pedophile. Again, social interaction is denied by prejudice.

Jennifer Diane Reitz, referred to in Chapter 1, has a similar perception of the situation. She stated that she could never work in a day care center. She can't hope to become a grade school teacher or any job that might help overcome her sorrow of being a childless transgender woman.

The APA's long standing blind spot regarding the transgender phenomenon remains a serious problem because their mental illness classification endures even after it was changed.

Doctors in Europe had been using hormones and surgery to align a transgender person's physical sex with their brain sex for more than 50 years before doctors in this country did. The Europeans learned a long time ago that changing ones brain sex to be aligned with one's physical sex is not possible. Doctors in this country resisted altering the physical sex to match the brain sex, which always was and still is, the only the effective treatment for gender dysphoria.

After the 1949 legal opinion by California's Attorney General Pat Brown against genital modification, doctors were frightened away from performing such operations. Pat Brown's legal opinion said the destruction of healthy human tissue in genital modification operations would expose a doctor to criminal prosecution.[20]

Brown's legal opinion frightened doctors. Therefore, the few genital operations that were performed were done in secrecy between the 1949 opinion and 1966. In 1966, Dr. Harry Benjamin published his book, *The Transsexual Phenomenon*. It contained his 17 years of research that called for the same treatment for transsexuals as Magnus Hirschfeld promoted in pre-Hitler Germany. Benjamin's work quickly changed the entire medical and legal concept of transgender patient treatment. Thus, that phase of medical antitransgender discrimination ended.

Some people oppose transgender rights for religious reasons. Furthermore, critics of transgender antidiscrimination legislation in public accommodations insist it would mandate unisex restrooms. This is difficult to find creditable, since no one examines genitals before anyone is admitted to a restroom

Transgender women, at whom this discrimination is aimed, have been using women's restrooms for a long time without any incidents. Opposition is not really about bathrooms. Simple bigotry is most likely the only reason why some people oppose transgender rights and use bathrooms as an emotional argument. Transgender women are not aggressive; they are as nurturing as other women.

Although transgender rights have been won in spite of the bathroom issue, bathroom discrimination remains an important and significant obstacle to transgender rights. Since opponents to transgender civil rights no longer have the mental disorder issue, their only remaining excuse for their bigotry is the bathroom issue

Unfortunately, transgender advocates and organizations that advocate for transgender human rights avoid mentioning the bathroom issue. I was advised by a national civil rights organization, "Don't mention bathrooms!" They believe they can avoid the issue; however, it cannot be avoided because opponents of civil rights use it! The bathroom issue must be faced head on. Regardless of whether the opponents believe it or use it as an excuse, opponents make it an emotional issue and use it effectively against transgender human rights. Therefore, we must face it.

The issue is in our favor if we use it to help our cause. First, roughly 180 million people now live with transgender civil rights laws and nothing bad ever happens (see APPENDIX VI, No Assaults Due To Transgender Nondiscrimination Laws). Second, we need a "Chromosome Day" that I have advocated for since 2010. On that day a demonstration needs to have transgender people use the bathroom indicated by their sex label at birth. The public needs to know what it is like to have transgender men with their beards, balding heads, and men's attire in the ladies room. That is the only effective way to fight the emotion our opponents use.

Transgender men look like other men in men's rooms and transgender women look like other women in women's rooms.

Transphobia also comes from unexpected sources, such as some Intersex organizations, feminists, and from within the transgender community itself.

Some Intersex organizations refuse to accept transsexuals as an Intersex phenomenon and bar them from joining the organization.

Some feminists feel transsexuals cannot call themselves women simply because they have not grown up and experienced the oppression and social conditioning women experience. Feminists also say being a female is a complicated mixture of physiology, cultural conditioning, and lived experience. What they don't realize is we understand what they are saying; however, we transgender women generally have a Biological Imperative to live like a woman and get as close as is possible to being a woman. We want to be as close to being a woman as someone who spent the early part of their life as a male can get.

Today, the notion that gender is purely a social construction is outmoded. The old feminist theories are changing along with the rest of our culture. We are learning gender identity is inherently rooted in the working of the brain. Many things previously thought to be in the realm of upbringing, choice, or subjective experiences has been disproven. Furthermore, in her bestselling book, *The Female Brain*, Louann Brizendine claimed all those feminine characteristics are actually "hardwired into the brains of women (see Chapter 1, Endnote 6)." She believed we do not acquire feminine characteristics (e.g., empathy and sensitivity). We are born with them. I believe she would agree that the same principle applies to transgender women, since we are also born with these characteristics. Dr. Milton Diamond, an expert on human sexuality at the University of Hawaii, said,

> We don't come to this world neutral; that we come to this world with some degree of maleness and femaleness which will transcend whatever the society wants to put into [us] (see Chapter 1, Endnote14).

Transgender discrimination comes from within the transgender community also. Some postoperation transsexuals do not accept the transgender banner. They feel the only "true transsexual" is one who has already had a genital operation. They say anyone else is somehow inferior and merely playing with gender or just a guy in a dress. This is opposed to Dr. Benjamin's definition. After studying transsexuals for 17 years, he concluded that transsexuals may be grouped into three categories: Type IV Transsexual (Nonsurgical), Type V Transsexual (moderate intensity), and Type VI Transsexual (High intensity). Only one True Transsexual type was a genital operation candidate—Type VI. Be that as it may, a postoperation transsexual is legally a woman who can drop the transsexual label, and go stealth. However, many postoperation transsexuals do not do this. They stay in the transgender community for companionship and social interaction after their operation. Many do not venture outside this community, frequently because they do not fit in elsewhere and have no alternative for social interaction.

On the other hand, some postoperation transgender individuals refuse to accept the designation transsexual as Christine

Jorgenson did. They insist on describing themselves as transgender individuals. They feel transsexual implies something sexual and they prefer to identify with transgender—"crossing" genders.

The United Nations Charter's Universal Declaration of Human Rights (1948) has been used, outside the United States to promote equality. Article 27 of the Covenant on Civil and Political Rights states,

> All persons are equal before the law and are entitled without any discrimination to the equal protection of the law. In this respect, the law shall prohibit any discrimination and guarantee to all persons equal and effective protection against discrimination on any grounds such as race, colour, sex, language, religion, political or other opinion, national or social origin, property, birth or any other status.

Of course, at the time Article 27 was adopted, sex and gender were considered the same thing—either male or female. However, the "other status" has been used successfully to include transgender people. In 2004, transgender people were starting to get named in UN reports. That was a new and welcome development.

In recent years, many organizations promoting transgender human rights have been formed in many parts of the world. The most recent was when transgender women from ten Asia Pacific Countries and areas came together in Bangkok, Thailand on December 23, 2009.[21]

They protested against discrimination and marginalization by forming the world's first Asia Pacific Transgender Network (APTN). After three days of intense meetings, it was decided the APTN, which was composed entirely of transgender women across the region, would promote transgender women's health, legal, and social rights.

Similar to the basis for most phobias, transphobia is primarily based on fear promoted by the ignorance of people against those who are different. The best way to overcome this fear is to make transgender people more visible in the public eye. This is easier said than done, since transgender individuals harbor so much shame it "forces" them into the closet of secrecy. However, transgender visibility is increasing slowly but surely. Most educated people overcome their prejudice if they read a brief description of the transgender experience. I feel transgender visibility by celebrities in the news tell a positive story that advances acceptance.

Recently, transgenderism is becoming better understood. This is being achieved with public education. Notable among these efforts was a New York Times editorial printed on May 24, 2015. The editorial outlined the injustices that are still inflicted on transgender people. The editorial pointed out how unjust the denial of restroom access, health care, employment, and other life necessities are for transgender people.

CHAPTER 10, Life's Complications

Marriage Complications

Transsexual marriages are less tenuous since the "marriage equality" ruling by the Supreme Court. However, precautions may still be needed. Regardless of the same sex "marriage equality" ruling, if the marriage is shown to be fraudulent or achieved through deception, the marriage can be voided, if challenged. This would be the case if it can be shown one partner did not know the marriage was to a transsexual.

When there is a monetary gain such as an inheritance, any relative, even a very distant and previously unknown relative, can sue to void a marriage. A court could declare the marriage void and the surviving spouse would lose all marital rights to property, children, other assets, and every other inheritance right.

All couples that involve a transsexual should consult a lawyer[1] to do what is necessary to preserve the martial rights of each party. The minimum you will need to protect each party is a declaration that the transgender status is known to the spouse (to prevent claims of fraud or deception). In some cases, a lawyer should decide if other documents may be needed such as: adoption of any children; co-ownership of all property; a strong will; a durable powers of attorney (to insure the mate can make health and property decisions, when necessary); a personal relationship agreement including each spouse's rights and responsibilities regarding finances, property, support, children, and/or any other issues in their specific situation; and any documents involving medical decision making, money, property, children, or other documents to prevent gain to anyone from challenging the legality of the marriage and to be sure the vital attributes of the marriage are maintained. If third parties have nothing to gain, they will not challenge the marriage in a court.

Since laws vary from one jurisdiction to another, each time you move to a different jurisdiction, you should consult an attorney again. In any case, it is important to know and deal with marriage laws, same sex marriage laws, and transgender laws to be on the safe side.

The need for extra-legal precautions were previously more imperative due to some past court rulings (before the "marriage equality" ruling).

In 1999, Christie Lee Littleton, a transsexual woman, in a medical malpractice suit, alleged her husband's death in 1996 was preventable and the result of an incorrect diagnosis. The Fourth Court of Appeals (Texas) denied Lee Littleton any legal standing as a marriage partner.[2] Although her female gender was recognized by the State of Texas, the court invalidated her seven-year marriage to Jonathon Littleton on the basis it was a same-sex marriage; therefore, illegal and void. An appeal was upheld and the Supreme Court would not hear the case.

Because Christine had no legal standing (as a wife) to bring the suit, the malpractice case was not even considered.

In still another case, a son sought to inherit his father's total estate. A Leavenworth, Kansas County Probate Judge, Gunnar A. Sundby[3] said, "J'Noel Gardiner was born a male and remains a male for purposes of marriage under Kansas law. The marriage between Marshall G. Gardiner and J'Noel Gardiner is void." This ruling was based again on the fact that a person's chromosomes determine what one's sex is; therefore, the marriage was an illegal same sex marriage. The Kansas Supreme Court upheld the lower court's ruling. The spouse had no spousal survivor rights.

The situation was not always dismal before the "marriage equality" ruling. Some courts have cited both the Zhou study and the Kruijver study findings regarding the Brain Sex Theory of Transgenderism. Also, an article by Dr. William Reiner[4] of John Hopkins, "To Be Male or Female, That Is the Question" was quoted by a judge as saying a person must determine their own sexual identity and the organ that appears to be critical to psychosexual development and adaptation is not the external sexual genitalia, but the brain.

In 1997, a trial court in Orange County, California affirmed the validity of a transsexual man's marriage.[5] His wife sought to invalidate the marriage in order to deprive her husband of his parental rights regarding the couple's child. The child was born via artificial insemination. The court held California law recognizes the postoperative sex of a transsexual person for all legal purposes. The transgender man did not lose the right to maintain a relationship with his child.

In 1976, a New Jersey superior court upheld a transsexual marriage. The Hardberger case involved a man who paid for his mate's genital operation and lived with her as man and wife for two years. When they separated, she sued for support. The lower court sided with the transsexual: "If the psychological choice of a person is medically sound, not a mere whim, and irreversible sex reassignment surgery has been performed, society has no right to prohibit the transsexual from leading a normal life." The New Jersey appellate court agreed.

This kind of question only arose when someone had a monetary or other gain in having the marriage ruled void. Usually, it was a relative who wanted the rights to an inheritance. In the Gardiner case, a son wanted to inherit the entire estate. In the Litttleton case, an insurance company sought to avoid paying malpractice compensation. In the Hardberger case, the ex-husband tried to avoid alimony payments.

The "marriage equality" ruling by the Supreme Court took away the right of states to void or nullify the marriage of committed couples. In our world, interracial marriage was also outlawed only a short while ago. Furthermore, the same sex marriage issue was important for all transgender people because sex change is not recognized in some states. However, a transsexual's marriage can still be declared void if deception regarding a partner's transsexual status was unknown to the partner.

The federal Defense of Marriage Act (DOMA), specifying marriage is between one woman and one man, was ruled unconstitutional regarding Section 3 on July 8, 2010 by U.S. District Court Judge Joseph L. Tauro. He ruled Section 3 of DOMA—which denies federal benefits to same sex married people—is unconstitutional.[6]

The objections were brought by seven same sex married couples and three widowers from Massachusetts, where same sex marriage was legal at the time. Under the ruling, the plaintiffs were declared entitled to the same federal spousal benefits and protections as every other married couple. This case narrowly targeted some aspects of DOMA.

On March 26, 2013, the United States Supreme Court heard two same sex marriage cases. One case challenged DOMA and the other challenged California's Proposition 8, which prohibited same sex marriages.

Both rulings came down on June 26, 2013. Justice Anthony Kennedy wrote the 5 to 4 majority decision. He said that the act wrote inequality into federal law and violated the Fifth Amendment's protection of equal liberty. He said, "DOMA's principal effect is to identify a subset of state-sanctioned marriages and make them unequal." Edith Windsor, the 84-year-old woman who brought the case against DOMA said that the ruling "ensured that the federal government could no longer discriminate against the marriages of gays and lesbians." She did not know the ruling also affected transgender people.

In the second case, the court's decision said that it could not rule on a challenge to Proposition 8, a ban on gay marriage in California passed by voters there in 2008 because supporters of the ban lacked the legal standing to appeal a lower court's decision against it.

At that time, the court did not rule on the constitutionality of gay marriage, but the effect of the decision will be to allow same-sex marriages to resume in California. California Proposition 8's 5 to 4 majority decision was written by Chief Justice John Roberts.

There was another pertinent bill at the time, the Respect for Marriage Act (RMA HR3567). It would nullify state amendments baring same sex marriage, and treat all people equally regarding marriage rights. The same sex marriage ruling nullified the need for this law.

An interesting note (out of the past) was that a same-sex transgender marriage was always possible if one partner in a marriage transitioned, had the records legally changed to indicate the transitioned to sex, and the original couple remained married. For example, a married woman who transitions to a man and remains married to his original husband results in a man married to a man. They were in a same-sex marriage, but remained legally married.

A transsexual marriage can be heterosexual. For example, a postoperative transsexual has his legal sex changed from female-to-male and marries a woman. It is a heterosexual marriage if the jurisdiction they are in recognizes gender reassignment and the transsexual person has his sex changed on legal documents. However, this issue is of little importance since the Supreme Court ruled a same sex marriage is a legal marriage.

Interfacing with the Police

A good rule for transgender people and all people is avoid doing anything that puts you in an adversary position with the police. It has been proven that one cannot win an argument with a police officer. This does not mean when dealing with the police you will face discrimination and poor treatment. It merely means you *may* face discrimination and poor treatment. In nearly all cases you will be treated respectfully, but you never know when you are dealing with a transphobic cop. It is like a lottery you don't want to win because those transphobic cops are out there.

If your car is stopped by a police officer, you need to keep your hands on the wheel or the dashboard in full view while the officer is present. If possible, before he comes to the side of the car, have your insurance card, your driver's license, and ownership paper ready. After the officer arrives, don't go to the glove box or a purse without permission. She or he may think her or his life could be at risk with the wrong person getting a weapon from it. Keep your hands in sight, be polite, and answer any questions honestly, but don't say any more than an answer requires. The officer will treat you accordingly.

Furthermore, violating some laws, such as driving under the influence of drugs or alcohol, will result in you being jailed. That may result in physical harm to you and even your death, if you are in a cell with those of your birth-assigned sex. Short of that, you can suffer inhuman conditions. Not all prison systems offer protection for transgender inmates from other inmates.

Transgender women, usually cross dressers, have the most to fear. Some had encounters with the police and reported the following experiences were generally good:

> My nightmare: I was stopped by a state policeman for speeding when I was in soccer mom attire. But I just showed my regular license and registration. He did do a "double take" (which I appreciated) but that was all. After he had written up my ticket, I had to ask whether how I was dressed would be on the report. He just said, 'Why? You were speeding.' He was just totally professional.

> I've been stopped about 15 times, always the same result. They look at my license, check me out to make sure I have no priors, and say don't do it again.

> I show my male license and ID and have never had a problem. Cops have seen it all.

> If you get stopped just show your Lic[license], reg[registration] and ins[insurance] card. If you show a phony ID you can be arrested for Criminal Impersonation. Most police if not all have stopped TG's. And of course

don't drive drunk, because if you do get arrested it won't be a fun experience.

Sometimes a police officer is playful in their disrespect, as the following girl explained:

I have gotten stopped a couple of times. [He] made me get out [and] walk inline in my heels. Otherwise [he gave] just the smile.

The best way to handle a police "stop" is to be courteous, answer all questions honestly, and do not offer too much information. Some transgender women wrote to tell how they react or would react to a police stop while driving.

I got a letter from my therapist about my GID and keep that in my purse. And yeah even more of a reason not to get drunk and drive. I'd hate to have to deal with that while dressed.

In my opinion just look the officer in the face and tell him the truth. If you're in the process of changing to your desired sex then he/she will probably understand.

I was stopped at 2 A.M. and had a letter from my endocrinologist, but I never showed it. He asked where I was coming from, where I was going, if I had anything to drink and if I feel okay to drive. I answered all his questions honestly. Even that I had 2 drinks before dinner and one at 11 P.M. He then released me after making sure his partner saw my male license and the girl driving. I didn't get a ticket for driving at 70 in a 55mph zone.

I got a letter from my therapist stating that I'm undergoing therapy and this is how I present myself. [I] never had a problem.

But so long as your driver's license says MALE answer to/offer that name to Police. It is not illegal to be out dressed but we do not have the same protections everywhere.

Depending how far along you are in transition you can carry a letter from your therapist explaining your current status.

In dealing with the police, never show false identification. A few transgender women wrote about it and aside from it being a felony said,

> I do happen to know a lot about the ID issue. Unless you are an illegal immigrant, using a fake ID, driver (license), passport, or any other government issue ID is a federal crime since 9/11. Knowing many police in various departments I would agree that they have seen it all and there are a fair # that dress themselves.

This can get sticky. You DO NOT want to get caught with a PHONY ID!

One girl wrote about poor treatment, but didn't say how she was beaten,

> So for those who think it's only when you break a law you're living in fantasy land. I . . . learned early on you're not going to win an argument with a cop on the street and have never tried. I've seen too many T-girls and Gay men lose this argument. I've seen paramedics deny T-girls medical care, I got to experience that one first hand after I was beaten and the medics refused to treat me after I was found out. The cop there picked me up threw me in the back of the squad car. He then drove me to an Emergency Room at a local hospital.
>
> Now that laws are changing we stand a better chance of survival. Some said I gave too much info the only problem is today they have computers in their cars and if you're caught lying its worse. Everyone can arm chair quarter back . . . but I have one thing over a few friends. I'm still alive. Some friends were not so lucky.

One girl reported being the victim of a highly transphobic cop who seems to have a problem with transgender women,

> I was in my car on the road to Quincy Illinois. As I drove down to Quincy I was driving at a pretty good clip, about 75

or 80 M.P.H. most of the way, not a lot of traffic. As I passed an Illinois State Trooper going the opposite direction I saw him hit his lights and turn around to come after me. I didn't play games so I pulled right over, put the car in park turned the engine off and got out my driver's license, registration and insurance card.

He walks up to the car and says I clocked you doing 79 m.p.h. in a 65 or 70 m.p.h. zone. He asked for my driver's license and I just handed him everything. He came back in a few minutes gave me my registration and insurance card back and walked back to his car. A little while later he comes back with a ticket asking me to sign it, when he says you know your driver's license says male on it. I said yes that will be corrected Monday. [He] looks at me and says what do you mean? I proceed to tell him that I'm a transsexual and my surgery to fix a birth defect would be on Monday.

Then comes the questions. Do you have drugs in your car? I tell him no. Are you carrying contraband? I say no again. Can I check your trunk? Sure I have nothing to hide.

Then comes the accusations. Did you steal these tools? No, I'm an electrician, they're mine. You're an electrician? Yes sir. Did you steal this Laptop? No its mine

Sit on the ground in front of my car and don't move. He now starts to go over every inch of my car. I'm crying as I watch him pull everything out of the car including the car seats, spare tire and anything he could. The whole time telling me he didn't believe me, that I ether stole everything or I was moving drugs. He checked in the gas tank, under the hood he crawled under the car tried to pull my doors apart after he looked down in the windows.

An hour later I was allowed to start putting things back in my car. After I signed my ticket and got back in my car, I started to put everything back. Then after all that he would drive behind me for the next 5 to 10 miles. I thought for sure he was going to kill me. I will never forget badge # 5727 of the Illinois State police, AKA as the Gestapo or S.S.

I could not stop crying. I didn't sleep well that night. The next day I got up and took a shower got dressed then went to meet a friend for breakfast, the whole time scared still that the trooper from hell would pop out from somewhere and start all over again. As my friend . . . tried to have conversations with me and show me the town and the local Architecture, I just keep telling her I want to get back on road and get out of Illinois. A few hours later I was on the road again and I didn't stop till I hit Ohio. In Columbus I stayed at a Best Western and got a good nights' sleep.

The lesson from the voices of experience above is don't drive if you think you might possibly be legally drunk. If you are stopped by a police officer, be respectful, answer all questions honestly, briefly answer any questions, and do not offer more information than is necessary. Simply answer all questions without going into details or elaborating.

It is rare, but if the cop wants to search your car, tell him a car and trunk search is fine, but if any disassembly of the car is necessary, it would be okay if it takes place at a police station. Years ago jewelry salesmen carried valuable inventory on their sales calls. When asked for a car search they protected valuable samples by agreeing to a car search at a police station. The cop probably will drop any thoughts of disassembling your car. If he continues, other officers may try to talk the cop out of it because in their mind they may have to be a witness if a complaint is lodged. This is effective even if you are not in a position to actually complain.

I know of another case where a trans woman who did not break any law but was submitted to very degrading and inhuman treatment at the hands of several policemen. She was made to stand in the rain for almost 30 minutes while they searched for guns and they refused to get her umbrella from her car or allow her to sit in her or their car. They made her remove her wig so they could find any guns she might be hiding under it; they searched her person most disrespectfully, and committed her to a psychological examination at a medical center. The police searched her house for weapons and left her in the night at a medical center far from home without returning the keys they took from her. It took her hours to get the police to tell her that her keys were in her garage at her home. She had no way to get home in the driving rain late at night. Her cell phone was dead by then and she had no money for a cab. When she finally got home, the keys were nowhere to be found.

There are insane and hateful people with authority out there. We must be careful. Never turn your keys over without a search warrant, since that implies voluntary agreement to a search. There is little you can do except sue afterwards.

Transgender Incarceration

Transgender individuals face serious and special problems when detained or incarcerated by the police. They face three major areas of concern: disrespectful treatment, unsafe or unhealthy housing, and failure to receive appropriate medical treatment.

Disrespectful forms of address are depressing and demeaning. It demoralizes an individual when someone addresses them incorrectly and with a malicious intent, such as a deliberate emphasis and taunting voice. Everyone, in prison or out, should always be addressed in accordance with their gender identity and not their genitalia. If you are not sure, simply ask, "What name do you prefer I use? What pronouns should we use to address and describe you?" If an individual desires another form of address, she or he will tell you.

Too often, law enforcement personnel think it is sport to torment, harass, and demean transgender people. This is a serious issue and everyone should know that ignoring another's' basic dignity is helping to destroy a human life. Even transgender people detained for trial are abused this way. They may be found guilty at a later date, but they are not guilty of any crime until they are convicted. However, guilty or not, they and everybody deserves to be treated courteously and respectfully.

Housing transgender persons using their birth sex label exposes them to serious dangers, including the risk of physical and/or sexual abuse, and even death. Transgender women are particularly at risk in a male lock-up. This is a very serious problem in some places.

Even New York City, with its model human rights law, has eliminated special housing for transgender (and gay) inmates, presumably as an economy move. This poses a serious danger to them and can force a transgender inmate to choose between an isolated lockup for 23 hours per day or possible abuse in the general prison population.

Isolated lock-ups are being employed in the face of a state court ruling in 1982. In the case of the Schipski v. Flood,[7] the Appellate Division of State Supreme Court (Second Department) ruled that Nassau County, New York's policy of holding protective custody jail inmates in isolation 22 hours a day was unconstitutional.

Denying transgender people hormone therapy exposes them to serious medical and psychological problems. Until September, 2011, the U.S. Bureau of Prisons said,[8] "Inmates who have undergone treatment for gender identity disorder will be maintained only at the level of hormones which existed when they were incarcerated in the Bureau." In other words, if an inmate cannot show there has been a doctor's formal diagnosis of gender identity disorder/dysphoria (GID) and previously began a legally prescribed hormone therapy regimen, they will not be treated with hormones, nor will they be given other appropriate medical attention.

Incarcerated transgender people were frequently denied continuation of hormone therapy exposing them to serious medical problems associated with withdrawal. Those who obtained hormones in the black market, usually because they could not afford the legal route and those wanting or needing to start transition were denied treatment.

Medical provisions outlined in Federal Bureau of Prisons policy always allowed for the diagnosis of mental disorders while incarcerated. The policy also provides medical attention and treatment for people living with diabetes and HIV/AIDS as well as those who have sustained injuries in prison. Until 2011 when the guidelines were changed, the Federal Bureau of Prisons singled out transgender inmates as excluded from proper medical treatment for gender identity dysphoria.

In September, 2011 the policy was finally changed to conform to the World Professional Association for Transgender Health (WPATH) guidelines. It is hoped that the personnel administering the new policy will execute it properly and humanely.

San Francisco has a transgender inmate policy that is far more appropriate and more extensive than even the new federal prison system's policy. Rather than the brief memo the Federal Bureau of Prisons policy has, San Francisco's policy concerning transgender people is 24 pages long. It covers the subject completely and properly. The policy includes everything from screening employee candidates for transphobia, and other biases, to psychological evaluations of inmates that can lead to the start of hormone therapy.

Too often, transgender prisoners are denied prison jobs and access to recreation equipment. Jurisdictions with prisons that are too small to properly accommodate transgender inmates should arrange their transfer to facilities that can properly handle the special needs of transgender women and transgender men.

In Boston, Massachusetts Federal Judge Adam Wolf ordered the state of Massachusetts to pay for sex-change surgery for a murderer, Michelle Kosilek.[9] The ruling was based on the WPATH Standards of Care and the testimony of medical professionals in the field that a gender operation is the only cure for gender dysphoria in cases such as the one under consideration. Hopefully, this ruling will change federal prison policies and in other jurisdictions regarding proper medical care for transgender individuals. Proper medical care includes psychotherapy, hormones, surgery, and any other needs that may be found in the future.

Almost all states in the United States and counties nationwide lack any formal policy on housing transgender inmates. Therefore, most are housed according to their genitals, not their gender identity. Even those who have breast augmentation through hormones or an operation are housed according to their genitals. This is a disgrace! We are supposed to be an enlightened, humane, and compassionate country. Placing a transgender woman in a cell with men would place her life at risk and invite sexual abuse. This is as cruel and inhuman a punishment as you can get and it needs to be corrected without delay.

In April, 2015 the United States Department of Justice filed a brief supporting a transgender prisoner's right to hormone treatment. The suit was brought against the Georgia Department of Corrections. This was reported to be the first time the United States Justice Department had taken action in support of a prisoner's effort to compel hormone treatment for gender dysphoria, the diagnostic term used to refer to discomfort or distress caused by a difference between a person's gender identity and their sex label given at birth.

Recent court rulings are starting to force appropriate change(s) in many other places. The BBC reported (January 15, 2010) a first positive breakthrough in transgender prisoner treatment is Italy's action in opening the world's first prison exclusively for transgender inmates in a town near Florence.[10] The nearly empty former women's penitentiary has been specially equipped as a detention center for transgender inmates. The prison includes its own library, recreation center, and agricultural land.

Every little detail of human treatment and human dignity must be fought in nearly every location. Activists must also work toward having their local police include transgender sensitivity training to avoid any misunderstanding regarding transgender peoples' needs.

Sports—K Through Olympics

The sexes are separated in many sports because women and men have many physical and physiological differences that need to be leveled out to help make competition fair for all participants. However, it is widely recognized that the separation of the sexes in prepuberty children is absolutely unnecessary, since sex differences do not present themselves until hormones start having an effect on their physiology. Even after puberty creates a physical difference, the need and wisdom for the separation of the sexes in noncompetitive sports is questionable.

In competitive situations, there is a fear that men, masquerading as women, could dominate women's sports due to their high levels of testosterone. Testosterone significantly elevates certain physical attributes in the performance of sports. For example, testosterone gives men better endurance due to a larger and greater number of oxygen-carrying blood cells and a greater strength due to more muscle mass. There are still other advantages: Men derive greater strength than women due to the use of leverage in physical activities that a longer skeleton provides. A longer skeletal frame also provides a longer stride for faster running and other sports.

In the 1930s, Mildred "Babe" Didrikson,[11] a great women's all-around athletic champion, won several medals in a variety of events, especially in track and field. Many reporters remarked about her masculine appearance. Others suspected she was really a man and was committing gender fraud. Things didn't quiet down until she married and later participated only in golf. She was simply too masculine for the stereotype of a woman. This serves as an example of discrimination based on gender expression.

Sex transition is an extremely complex process. It involves all sorts of medical, various therapeutic, and specialized legal considerations. It is a long and involved process and cannot be reversed successfully. Therefore, it is highly unlikely someone would choose to undertake this irreversible operation to gain admittance to women's sport competition. Furthermore, if a sex change operation is involved, masculine level hormone production ceases, which in a short time would eliminate testosterone's advantages.

Many people connected with women's sports still fear gender fraud will take over women's sports. The most positive way of determining birth sex was the Barr-Body Gender Verification Test, which determines one's chromosomes. This test adopted by the International Olympic Committee was later abandoned. The test checks an athlete's chromosomes to determine if he or she was labeled male or female at birth. There is still no way to alter your chromosomes, which makes it a sure test to determine one's sex label at birth. However, the test was not used after the year 2000 because a problem came to light with the Renée Richards[12] case.

The most famous case, still within many people's memory, involved Dr. Richard Raskind, a tennis champion, who transitioned from male-to-female and sought exemption from the Barr-Body test. She wanted to compete in the 1977 Women's U. S. Open Tennis Championship. There was no possibility she could pass the Barr-Body test.

Richards won the case in the New York State Supreme Court and competed in the U. S. Open as a woman in 1977. Judge Ascione ruled the Barr-Body test is an accepted sex determinant, however,

> Richards' circumstances warranted consideration of other factors. . . . When the plaintiff, for his own mental sanity, finds it necessary to undergo a sex reassignment, the unfounded fears and misconceptions of defendant [International Olympic Committee] must give way to overwhelming medical evidence this person is female.

Judge Ascione's ruling said sex is determined by other factors in addition to chromosomes. It was an important legal decision for transgender rights. Sport participation should be available to everyone, including transgender and Intersex people. The questions regarding in which gender group should transgender or Intersex athletes compete should be determined by the effective sex of the individual.

The inclusion of transgender athletes in the women's or men's sport group they belong, should not be confused with men masquerading as women to compete in women's sports. One such case was the East German athlete, Dora Ratjen,[13] a high jumper in the 1936 Olympics. She was found to be an Intersex person and barred from further competition. Years later, he was living as a man and admitted he was forced to compete as a woman by the Hitler Youth Movement.

There has always been a movement to exclude transgender women from competing in women's sports. This was based on their generally larger skeletal size and their advantage from the effects of testosterone. If transgender competitors are prohibited from playing as women because of a presumed genetic advantage, should we exclude nontransgender women born with genetic advantages (e.g., greater height)? Should they be similarly prohibited from playing as women? Should women with Marfan's syndrome,[14] which varies but can cause growth as high as seven feet, be excluded from competing in women's basketball and volleyball? Should women having congenital adrenal hyperplasia,[15] which gives them high strength and better stamina be excluded from women's sports?

There have been cases of a transgender woman being tested for women's competition with their anaerobic threshold and lung capacity that scored well. However, they fell well within the normal range of female performance in these characteristics.

There were several cases involving Intersex individuals in the 1930s.[16] Some athletes were not even aware of an ambiguous gender identity until their gender was challenged.

An interesting case that was widely publicized 20 years ago involved Helen Stevens[17], who won the gold medal in the 100 meter sprint at the 1936 Berlin Olympics. She beat Stella Walsh,[18] a Polish American, and was challenged by a Polish reporter. Stevens was proven to be a female; however, 60 years later, it turned out Walsh was the transsexual. In 1932, Walsh broke the women's 12 second barrier, won 2 Gold and several other medals. Some felt she won these honors unfairly.

This issue of where a transgender athlete "fits" is relevant for all age groups, including school gym programs and competitive sports involving school, national, and international competition. Although transgender and Intersex athletes should be included in sport competition, there is a need to be fair to both transgender and nontransgender athletes. Therefore, it is legitimate to ask if a transgender man should compete as a woman or as a man. Should a transgender woman compete in women's events or men's events?

An example of possible unfairness includes the taking of testosterone, which is frequently part of a transgender man's transition. Testosterone is known to increase muscle mass and raise the count of oxygen-carrying hemoglobin from the lungs and to all the cells. Thus, transgender men can have an advantage over women in strength and in endurance, and even over men, if "extra" testosterone is taken. The larger skeletal size of transgender women, their taller stature, and larger feet and hands than those of most females can be an advantage in women's sports.

Who can compete in a gender-specific sport came to a head during the Cold War between the U.S. and Russia. Similar to Nazi Germany, Russia was accused of entering men in women's events to win more medals than the U.S. and other countries, demonstrating the superiority of the Communist political and economic system.

After sex testing was introduced in 1966, some Eastern European track and field athletes disappeared from women's sports, without any explanation. Specifically, shot putter and discus thrower champions were never heard from again. This included Tamara Press from the Soviet Union, who was the shot put record holder from 1959 to 1965. Also, her sister Irena, a hurdler and pentathlon athlete suddenly disappeared from the scene. They both had masculine appearances, so when they no longer tried to compete, they were both accused of fraud and the use of steroids.

When sex testing was first introduced, degrading and embarrassing means, including genital checks, were used to make the sex determination. Those inappropriate methods have since been abandoned.

The issue of transgender athletes' participation in competitive sports is complicated by the participation of Intersex athletes. Intersex athletes had a mix of female and male appearing genitalia. Frequently, their genitals were made to appear femalelike and they were raised as females because the conversion to femalelike genitals was surgically possible, whereas the conversion to malelike genitals was not. In competitive sports, these athletes competed as women because that was what they, and everyone else, thought they were. However, not all were female. As discussed in a previous chapter, some were, in fact, male. Many Intersex athletes did not find out they were born Intersexual until their sex was challenged in the sports setting.

One such case involved an Intersex athlete, Erika Schinegger of Austria. Erika competed in Olympic events first as a woman and then as a man. She was on the Austrian National Ski Team and won the women's downhill ski title in 1966. She was later given the Barr-Body test when it was introduced for Olympic competition, and found to be chromosomally male. She was no longer permitted to compete as a woman. Later she had several genital operations, changed her name to Eric, married a woman, and fathered children. He later competed in cycling and skiing as a male.

In an effort to be inclusive and remain fair to the other athletes, in 2003, the Executive Committee of the International Olympic Committee (IOC) approved and published a policy that they called the Stockholm Consensus. The IOC was the first organization to address the issue of where transgender athletes belong regarding sex segregated sports. It follows the recommendations of a committee of IOC medical doctors. The approval of transsexual athletes to participate in Olympic Sports depended on specific criteria.

Those who transition before puberty should compete with those born in that transitioned sex. Thus, MtF should compete in female events and FtM should compete in male events. Masculine women and feminine men, who are not a transgender person, should compete with others having the same birth sex label. Transitioning after puberty involves other factors. These factors are less degrading than those of the Cold War era, but still demeaning.

According to the IOC policy made effective in 2004, transsexuals who undergo sex reassignment are eligible to compete with the "transitioned to" sex group; however, they must have specific medical and surgical procedures such as genital operations involving genitalia changes and gonadectomy. Also required, is legal recognition of their reassigned sex on a driver's license or similar documentation. In addition, hormonal therapy appropriate for the sex must be administered in a verifiable manner and for a sufficient length of time.

If that is not enough, the IOC policy specifies a confidential case by case evaluation. In the event that the gender of a competing athlete is questioned, the medical delegate (or equivalent) of the relevant sporting body has the authority to take all appropriate measures for the determination of the gender of the competitor (e.g., physical examination).

These requirements seem overly harsh and demeaning. However, in spite of the harshness, there was still some skepticism of this IOC policy, since many coaches and athletes feel transgender women would still have a competitive advantage over other women. They base their assumption on the height, skeletal size, strength, and other physical and physiological characteristics of transgender people that are not changed surgically. This argument is countered by the existence of a range of size, strength, and other attributes that has always existed among women.

Female-to-male transsexuals may compete as men provided their testosterone level is within the normal range of birth men.

Unfortunately, these harsh IOC standards have been adopted by other jurisdictions.

The IOC policy also addressed the bathroom, locker room, and shower facilities issues and suggested ways to deal with them. Their suggestions recognize that many schools still segregate transsexuals from others in "gender neutral" facilities. However, they basically say when "gender neutral" bathrooms are not available, it is generally accepted that students should be allowed access to the bathroom corresponding to the gender with which they identify. In other words, treat transgender people like everyone else only if all else fails!

Mostly, the IOC describes policies in use to address real or imagined complications when dealing with transgender individuals (i.e., hotel sleeping arrangements, dress codes, etc.). They usually seem to condone the isolation of the transgender athletes.

Be that as it may, the IOC was the first to issue a policy at that level. The International Association of Athletics Federations (IAAF) followed with the same policy. Soon after that, the Canadian government provided $71,000 to Sport Canada to get transgender people into sport competition. Canada is the first government to grant money for the express purpose of giving transgender athletes access to sports.

In 2008, Washington State, via the Washington Interscholastic Activities Association (WIAA) issued a policy that seems fair to transgender athletes' dignity and keeps a level playing field for others.[19] The policy applies to all school levels and provides a procedure for determining eligibility with deadlines for filing requests and appeals. It also provides deadlines for responding and acting on the request or appeal.

WIAA specifies a board of at least 3 professionals consisting of physicians, psychiatrists, psychologists, and licensed mental health professionals familiar with the WPATH's Standards of Care. Also included in the process are a school administrator (from a noninvolved school), a WIAA staff member, and a WIAA assigned facilitator. A facilitator assists the school and student in preparation and completion of the WIAA Gender Identity eligibility appeal process. The process involves a statement of persistent gender conflict that can come from the student, parent, or health professional; a current transcript; school registration information; plus any other pertinent documents.

This policy is consistent with the dignified treatment of transgender athletes. It provides an appeal procedure and recognizes the WIAA policy will likely need to be reviewed and revised to reflect increased medical understanding and evolving societal norms. It is hoped other state athletic organizations, the IOC, and the IAAF will adopt a similar policy.

The Women's Sports Foundation[20] endorses the WIAA policy and recommends it to school boards and others. The Ladies European Tour organizers amended their rules in 2004 to allow transgender athletes to compete also.[21]

In 2011, the National Collegiate Athletic Association (NCAA) adopted a policy regarding the participation of transgender athletes that is the most enlightened so far[22]. It is fair to male and female athletes, fair to transgender students, maintains and respects privacy, and promotes inclusion of all students.

Gender expression is also an issue. Caster Semenya,[23] a South African woman, won the 800 meter gold medal in the woman's race in Berlin (2009). She appeared too masculine for her competitors to accept defeat. She had a low voice and was somewhat masculine appearing. Her validity to compete in a women's race was challenged. As a result, she spent almost a year having officials investigate her sex. It was estimated during the time of the investigation she lost $250,000 in prizes and appearance fees.

The exact testing Ms. Semenya had to endure has not been made public. I would guess hormone levels and chromosomes were an important factor, but she was eventually "certified" to be female. Gender discrimination does not necessarily involve transgender people; however, the transgender community fights for the rights of women and men with an atypical gender expression. Basically, it is the same issue—the fight for everyone's equal protection under the law.

It would be understandable if testosterone levels, which increase endurance and muscle mass, were high as a result of using hormones as a supplement; however, if a woman has a naturally high level of testosterone due simply to individual differences, it would be unfair and inaccurate to declare her ineligible to compete in women's sports. This is just one example of the need for those with an atypical gender expression to have specific human right guarantees.

Although MtF transgender athletes might conceivably enjoy some competitive advantage, Dr. Jean Wilson, editor of Harrison's Principles of Internal Medicine, said,[24]

It is also true that people are not equal in athletic prowess in regard to height, weight, coordination, or any other parameters, and it follows that this is just another way in which athletes would not be equal.

Furthermore, Wilson later said,

It is important that all society, including sports organizations, recognize that gender development is not always clear cut. The only appropriate way to assign these people to one or the other sex is to allow them to choose for themselves.

Many people may subscribe to the above ideas; however, not many will when it comes to sports.

The fair approach to deal with transgender women and men in competitive sports seems to be a perennial problem. As knowledge increases, it becomes increasingly obvious that traditional notions of gender are inadequate and discriminatory.

Transgender Immigration

Transgenderism is no longer a legal reason to be excluded from entry into the United States.

Most situations involving transgender issues can be handled with little or no professional legal help. However, that is not true when United States immigration laws are involved. It is frequently confusing, often changed, and has exceptions to their rules. There are even some exceptions to the exceptions. Therefore, most of the time, if you are faced with immigration issues, particularly when asylum or marriage is involved, it is best to seek professional help from a lawyer. Of course, if immigration authorities detain you or someone you are sponsoring, you definitely need a lawyer.

Furthermore, as a transgender person, it is also important for you to know your rights regarding housing, treatment, and other life-sustaining elements when incarcerated, in the event you or the person you are sponsoring is detained.

Make sure your lawyer is experienced in immigration law. Immigration law is complex and sometimes irrational. Therefore, it is important for your lawyer to be a member of the American Immigration Lawyers Association (AILA).[25] The AILA is a national association of attorneys who practice and teach immigration law. A further advantage of using an AILA member is in some districts and in some cases, when all regular immigration channels have failed to produce the result you seek, a member can have the Liaison Committee of AILA submit a special form to the district office. It is often quite helpful in resolving an individual case.

It is not common for an AILA member to have worked with a transgender client. If she or he uses the wrong name or pronoun, it is probably not a sign of disrespect or rudeness. You should simply and politely inform your attorney and staff of the correct name, pronouns, etc. to use both when speaking to you and referring to you when speaking to others.

Choosing an Attorney[26]

There are great lawyers who charge more and there are others who operate more efficiently and can charge less. It is always a good idea to comparison shop. I feel the most important attribute a lawyer can have, after competency, is the ability to provide a comfortable environment when communicating with her or him. Furthermore, an important attribute is how accessible will she or he be to discuss your case after you are "signed up."

An indication of this can be detected in an agreement that is written in plain English and appears to be even handed. You might try to have the agreement specify the frequency of personal case discussions with the attorney and prompt notification of a change in the status of the case, such as submitted forms, received communications, replies, etc. It is important that you are kept informed.

When selecting your attorney, the local bar association is the place to check if the attorney is licensed and in good standing. Ask about past client complaints. Immigration rules change frequently it is best to find a lawyer who limits his or her practice to immigration law. Furthermore, since there are a variety of subspecialties within immigration law, it is best to find a lawyer familiar with your particular type of case (e.g., employment, family, asylum, deportation, etc.) You need to watch out for lawyers where immigration is one practice area on a laundry list of claimed specialties. You should seek a specialist specifically in your problem area.

A modest ratio of paralegals to the attorney is a good indication of how close to your case the lawyer is likely to be. More than two paralegals per lawyer in one firm may indicate an overload of work and your lawyer won't have the time to talk to you about the case. The use of email and other technology sometimes indicates the ability to deliver legal services efficiently with better quality and less expense.

The law firm's marketing and promotional materials frequently indicates quality and polish in the way the firm presents itself to its clients, and this is possibly an indication of how the firm will present itself to the U. S. Citizenship and Immigration Services (USCIS).

If cost is a problem, many lawyers also offer an unbundled service. That is, instead of handling a case from beginning to end, a lawyer will prepare only parts of the case or simply provide the client with a lawyer's expertise. This could help you submit green card application or other routine type transactions yourself, with the help and consultation of a lawyer, who will review your application. A lawyer who is willing to work this way will provide just the amount of expertise you need and can afford. Although the American Bar Association approves of this approach, some lawyers may not.

Many people simply are unable to pay for an immigration lawyer. However, you may still be able to have an immigration lawyer help you. Some lawyers work with legal organizations and take on a limited number of reduced or no fee cases. You will be screened by one of these community organizations to determine if your case is the type of case that is appropriate for a referral and will screen you to be sure you are in fact unable to pay.

Don't use this book as legal direction. It is intended to provide some basic information on the most common immigration issues involving transgender individuals and a small overview of the rules in general. There is usually no short cut to consulting an immigration lawyer.

Basic Immigration Rules

No one is admitted to this country if she or he is likely to become a public charge or has a criminal background. Their Legal Permanent Residence (LPR) application will be denied and there is no appeal. Immigrants with HIV were excluded before 2010, but no longer can be refused entry on that basis.

The first rule when dealing with the Immigration Service is to always tell the truth and never withhold any facts. If any lie is uncovered, the application will be denied regardless of its merits. Failure to disclose information truthfully and completely could be interpreted as an attempt to commit fraud and will lead to the application being denied.

Even if a name change occurred a long time ago, the transgender person's birth name must be shown as a previous name in making an immigration application. It is a mistake to be anything but truthful and complete on immigration forms and during interviews. Also, having accurate identity documents is especially important for noncitizens. It is best to obtain a legal name and gender change before applying for immigration and/or naturalization to insure proper identity is maintained or established.

Before 1990, either sexual orientation or gender identity was grounds for denying entry into the United States. That section of immigration law was removed in 1990 and those phenomena now do not have any legal bearing on an application for an LPR status or for citizenship.

An application for a tourist visa can be denied if custom officials believe the applicant ultimately intends to remain in the United States. Transgender spouses are regularly suspected of "immigrant intent". It is best to seek entry into the country with the proper type of visa. One can demonstrate there is no intention to remain here permanently if there are strong family ties, real estate ownership, a good job, or other circumstances indicating a return to the country of origin is favorable in some way.

The easiest way for a transgender person, or anyone, to obtain permanent residence status is as a refugee from discrimination in their home country. It must be shown there would be personal danger if she or he returned to the home country. However, once refugee status is claimed, the refugee cannot return to the homeland for any reason. When holding refugee status, any return to the country of origin would violate the terms of the visa, and it can be cancelled. The bright side is that a refugee can obtain a green card (i.e., a work permit), citizenship, and other advantages more quickly than nonrefugees.

A transgender immigrant can obtain a green card and other documents in their transitioned sex if they have a genital operation. Many immigration agents do not always apply the rules as intended. If you believe that is happening, you may ask for another agent before starting the appeal process.

Before appealing the application of a rule, you should check it for changes, since rule changes are constantly being made. This is particularly true of transgender issues. Activists are constantly working to help the transgender population live better and we are actually making progress at an ever increasing rate.

Generally, a foreign national—who is being sponsored for an immigration visa by a spouse, who is a citizen, or by an adult son or daughter—can proceed with their applications for immigrant status from within the U. S. They can even have their unlawful presence "forgiven" as long as the original entry to the United States was lawful and a valid visa was used. If, however, the foreign national entered without inspection by crossing the border illegally, then that foreign national cannot proceed with a green card application from within the United States, even if he or she marries a United States citizen. There is an exception to this exception. Foreign nationals who fall under the former 1996 amnesty, the former §245(i) of the Immigration and Nationality Act, can pay a penalty and have their illegal entry forgiven as well.

As previously stated, immigration laws are involved and complicated. When it comes to immigration laws as applied to transgender issues, the immigration laws are even more involved.

It often seems easier for an immigrant to return to the country of origin to get proper gender and name records established. However, there is an important rule you need to know. If the visa used by an immigrant already in this country has expired, a harsh rule of nonreturn for 3-years and 10-years is applied. If a visa has expired more than 180 days ago, the immigrant will not be readmitted to this country for 3 years. If the expiration occurred over one year ago, the immigrant will not be readmitted for a period of 10 years

Many types of visas (e.g., such as tourist, business, skilled worker, and nonimmigrant) do not allow any changes or alterations to the status of the visa holder while still in this country. The immigrant must return to the country of origin and obtain a different type of visa. Again, there are exceptions for immediate relatives and those seeking asylum. They may alter their visa status while in the United States.

Your legal status as an immigrant is important when dealing with immigration laws. If you "walked across a boarder" without authorization, you are an illegal immigrant. Also, if the length of stay stamped on your visa has passed, you are illegal, even if your visa is still valid.

Student Visas

A student visa is a good route to permanent residence in the United States. The easiest way to get permanent residence status is to have a close relative sponsor you. The next best choice is one of the two student visa types[27] (the Vocational "M-1" or the Academic "F-1"). The student visa route to permanent residence is complex, but a good choice.

To obtain a student visa, you must enroll in an "academic" educational program, a language training program, or a vocational program and your school must be approved by USCIS. Choose a field of study that is needed in this country so you will not be displacing an American worker in that field or location.

In addition, you must be enrolled as a full-time student, proficient in English or enrolled in courses leading to English proficiency, and self-supporting during the entire proposed course of study. Furthermore, you need to demonstrate that you do not intend to remain here after your course of study by maintaining a permanent residence in your home country.

After you obtain a visa and enter the country as a student, the next objective is to be sponsored for residency by an employer. This involves several steps enumerated below:

1. A student visa does not allow you to work, but after you are here, if you can demonstrate a hardship, you can obtain a work authorization. Alternately, there are different rules regarding employment for F=1 visas during school and both types of visas at the end of the course of study.
2. Get employment in your field of study or an allied field taking advantage of the Optional Practical Training Program.
3. You need to find an employer in a job related to your course of study so after completing school, you can stay here for one year of work.
4. Just prior to the end of the year, have the employer act as a sponsor for a long term work visa.
5. With the long term work visa, you can eventually apply for LPR status through the same employer.

Only someone with an LPR can apply for citizenship. Until U.S. citizenship is obtained, the holder of LPR status is still a citizen of the country of origin and must travel with their original passport.

It is important to remember at the time a foreign national applies for student status and completes the Optional Practical

Training Program, she or he cannot have the intent to remain in the United States, permanently.

Finally, often it is the sponsor that files the LPR application.

It is possible to become a student with a visitor's visa. Consult the immigration service for the current special rules you need to follow.

Marriage Issues

One of the primary principles of the United States immigration law is family unity. As a result, one of the easiest ways for an immigrant to get LPR status is with a marriage based immediate relative visa. This is sometimes referred to as a spousal visa. Most of the rules for spousal visa also apply to the fiancé visas. However, with a fiancé visa, you must marry within 90 days of immigration.

With a marriage visa, some violations of the original visa may be forgiven. One advantage of a spousal visa is it allows the immigrant to apply for a green card while still in the United States.

The Department of Homeland Security rules blocked many transgender issues that involve documentation, including immigration issues. Compliance with the old rules that governed documentation was made quite difficult since 9/11.

Since June 2010, surgery is no longer the determinant of gender when changing passport data and is being applied to other documents regularly.

Prior to the Supreme Court's ruling affirming same sex marriage, when addressing transgender people's issues, the Immigration Service was faced with two factors in determining if a spousal visa will be granted. First, what gender should be used when issuing documents? The second was what criteria to use for the purpose of recognizing a marriage for applying immigration rules.

Things changed immediately after the 9/11 tragedy. Complications also mounted before the "marriage equality" ruling. Three possible solutions regarding transgender immigrants were considered by the Immigration Service:

> Option One was to use the born name and gender in all cases and for all purposes. This option, it was felt, would lead to the approval of same-sex marriages and the applicant would not look like the identification picture.

Option Two was to use the changed sex for identity documents and the birth sex label for marriage. Internally, this was thought to be inconsistent, but the identity documents would at least look like the applicant. However, same-sex marriage would be recognized when a transgender man marries a woman.

Option Three involved the use of the transitioned to gender for both identity and marriage. This approach was the most internally consistent, defensible, and logical, given that marriage-based cases are generally governed by state law. It also stated that this option would avoid the potential recognition of same sex marriage. However, this approach would be "politically controversial."

Option Two was recommended to then Secretary of the Department of Homeland Security Tom Ridge who subsequently approved the recommendation.

Shortly after that, a memo issued by a district supervisor named Yates[28] became known as the Yates memo. The Yates memo led to the belief there is only one universal transition all transgender individuals undergo and that is genital surgery. Of course, this is not a fact. Some people may undergo one or many surgeries as part of their transition; however, many may not.

The Yates memo was widely interpreted to mean a transgender immigrant must undergo genital surgery to be considered other than their birth sex label. As a result, immigration officials would be prone to adopt this particularly unfair interpretation for many transgender men. Most choose to undergo chest surgery, but not genital surgery. Most transgender men do not seek genital surgery because construction of male genitals has not been perfected and operations are considered unsuccessful. This highly restrictive application may have been developed to avoid the possibility of recognizing any seemingly same-sex marriages.

In spite of the foregoing, if a previous marriage is involved, there was a landmark case called the Lovo-Lara case. A North Carolinian born a man transitioned to a woman and tried to obtain a permanent visa for her husband, a man from Honduras. His name was Jose Lovo-Lara. Lovo-Lara had a temporary visa to work here. His wife petitioned the immigration authorities to have him receive a permanent status before his temporary visa expired. The petition was denied as a same sex marriage. The ACLU appealed the case to the Board of Immigration Appeals. The ACLU argued that since the wife has a valid North Carolina birth certificate and that certificate recognizes her as female, their marriage was a valid heterosexual marriage under the laws of North Carolina. The ACLU claimed the U.S. government should accept that fact and apply it to granting permanent status to a partner of a heterosexual marriage. The Board of Immigration Appeals agreed with the ACLU. Thus, a spousal visa was granted.

The Lovo-Lara case became a basic principle of U.S. immigration law in such matters. The whole thing boiled down to immigration recognizing any marriage that is recognized as valid in the jurisdiction where the marriage took place. However, one other test must be met. The circumstances of the marriage must not be opposed to public policy.[29] Therefore, if a state allows same sex marriage, and a federal law does not, the marriage would be contrary to public policy and not recognized for a spousal legal resident status.

Although the Defense of Marriage Act (DOMA) had been repealed altering public policy, you had to remain alert since future laws could affect public policy. Public policy was always likely to be in a state of flux. Thus, the Immigration Service depended on the laws of where the marriage took place and where you reside to determine the legality of the marriage. Also, immigration policy may consider state laws that do not recognize sex changes. This unstable condition was a strong reason to engage a lawyer.

After considering all these factors, a transgender couple had to play it safe and marry in a jurisdiction that will recognize their marriage and their sexual transition. If the wedding took place in a location without same sex marriage that did not recognize your marriage as heterosexual and you want to get a permanent visa for your noncitizen spouse using marriage as the basis, you had to get remarried in a more accepting location.

To complicate matters further, in many cases the new location may not marry people already married. As a result, some couples have been known to get a divorce and remarry in a jurisdiction that will recognize their marriage. If your marriage is recognized as heterosexual, you need not be concerned with the passage of a pending law.

However, one other factor had to be considered. If the place where you reside did not recognize a gender change and same sex marriage, that place would not recognize the marriage as heterosexual and legal. Therefore, you had to relocate so your marriage is not against the public policy of the place where you reside.

There were a great number of combinations of circumstances that could take place. The variables that were susceptible included, but were not limited to: does the transgender party or parties birth certificate(s) indicate their new sex, has a legal name change taken place, was the marriage considered not a same sex marriage where it took place, and does the couple now reside in a place that recognizes their marriage. If any immigration issue required the services of an immigration lawyer, the marriage issue was definitely at the head of the list.

A foreign national who is being sponsored for an immigration visa by a different sex spouse, who is a U. S. Citizen, or by a U. S. Citizen who is an adult son or daughter of a foreign national can proceed with their applications from within the United States and have their unlawful presence "forgiven" as long as they originally entered the United States lawfully with a visa. If, however, the foreign national entered without inspection, by for example, crossing the border illegally, that foreign national cannot proceed with a green card application from within the United States even if he or she marries a U. S. Citizen.

There is an exception to this exception that applies here, as well. Foreign nationals, who have been in this country long enough may fall under the former §245(i) of the Immigration and Nationality Act. They can pay a penalty and have their illegal entry forgiven.

The Board of Immigration Appeals does not strictly require an amended birth certificate to recognize gender correction. The Board does require some kind of official recognition by the government of the foreign national that the individual has changed a gender marker. For example, a Philippine national transitioned and married in the Philippines. Birth certificates cannot be changed in the Philippines; however, the Philippines issued her passport as a female. That was enough to demonstrate the sex change was sanctioned in that country and the marriage was heterosexual.

Since marriage equality, many former complications have been eliminated or simplified but you must be vigilant of changes.

Asylum

Anyone already in this country may apply for asylum in the United States if she or he fears persecution upon returning to the country of origin. If you experienced transgender persecution by the government, or by others that the government didn't restrain, you may be eligible for asylum. Furthermore, if you weren't previously persecuted but expect persecution if you returned due to a change in your country or your status, you may also be eligible.

A foreign national can apply for asylum regardless of whether she or he is here lawfully. However, you must apply within one year from the date you last entered this country. If it is later than one year, you are ineligible for asylum unless an "Extraordinary Circumstances" exception can be obtained. Sometimes a mental health professional can help in this. If all else fails, the applicant may be eligible for relief under the Convention Against Torture.[30]

Cubans can apply for LPR status one year after they are admitted into the United States. A specialized LPR may be available to citizens of Haiti, Nicaragua, El Salvador, Guatemala, Honduras, and some Eastern European countries if they have been in the United States since the 1990s. They can be eligible for citizenship under the §245(i) exception.

Those with asylum status acquire unique benefits. One year after obtaining the asylum status, they can apply for a LPR status. After only 4 years, someone who was granted asylum can become a naturalized citizen. They also receive an unrestricted Social Security card, which permits them to work without an employment authorization document.

Those here holding asylum status are an exception to the general rule that an individual who has been out of lawful status cannot apply for legal status from within the U. S. The Immigration and Nationality Act made the overstaying of a visa or even crossing the Mexican border illegally a forgiven act by someone seeking asylum. There are some unlawful acts, such as using a false passport to gain entry, that are not completely forgiven, but a special waiver may be possible when applying for LPR status.

Since those granted asylum status relinquish their rights, benefits, or protections from their country of origin, their international travel will require papers called a Refugee Travel Document. If you feel you will want to visit your family at some future time, you should not seek asylum status, since such a visit would void your visa.

Applying for asylum is an area where experienced legal assistance is very important because with each step in the asylum application process, the chance of success decreases. Therefore, your first application must be the most convincing. The more persecuted social classes you can claim, the better your chance of your asylum status being granted.

After the application is filed with the U. S. Citizenship and Immigration Services (USCIS), it gets scheduled for an interview with one of the few asylum officers in the whole country. Asylum interviews are generally scheduled in 6 weeks; however, if you live far from an asylum office, you may need to wait until an asylum officer visits your area.

The interview lasts an hour or two and basically covers what is already in the application. It also touches on what you feel will happen if you return to your country and some facts about your transgender history. Your attorney is there to simply ask questions he or she feels the officer didn't ask but should know and to sum up your verbal application. He is also there to stop the interview if it is felt the officer is transphobic or in other ways inappropriate.

Part of the approval process involves the process of clearing the fingerprints of any criminal or terrorist background.

The decision on your asylum approval can vary from approval to further review and even deportation hearings.

If your application for asylum is approved, the rest is simple. If it is not approved, you really will need an attorney familiar with immigration law. Your case might be given an opportunity to do one or more of the following: submit additional data, appeal your case before an immigration judge, and appeal to the Board of Immigration Appeals. After that, it may be possible an appeal can be brought to the U.S. Court of Appeals.

Progress

All immigration cases previously referred to transgender women as "gay man with female sexual identity." The Ninth Circuit Court in a transgender asylum case in 2007, Morales v. Gonzalez, for the first time referred to the involved transgender person as a "male-to-female transsexual." Furthermore, the male-to-female in the case was referred to as "she."

The case was also important because Morales petitioned for protection based on her transsexual identity and the court granted her asylum.

<u>Storing and Hiding Clothes</u>

Concealing the fact that you own clothes society says you have no right to wear presents even more complications in keeping your transgenderism a secret. Being deceptive is definitely not good for one's mental health. In spite of that, nearly every transgender person hides her or his inner feelings regarding gender for at least a part of their life. Even those who know deception is not good for one's health do it because they feel they have no choice.

Almost everyone is deceptive for some reason at one time or other and it is not a real problem because the effect lasts for a short time. However, it is a long term occurrence for a transgender person. For some who never come out of the closet, it is a lifetime occurrence. In all cases of transgender secrecy, the transgender wardrobe must be carefully hidden from everyone.

Transgender people have a strong inner drive to express their true gender somehow and some way. The most obvious way is to cover the masculine or feminine body with clothing of the other sex. Since clothing has a sex and that is what is seen, the gender of the clothes you are seen wearing is how you are perceived. In many cases, it is the only way transgender persons have of expressing their gender identity. If you are not completely out of the closet and do not live alone, you need to keep your feminine/masculine things well hidden.

Those who live with their parents, a roommate, or their spouse need a place to store their "secret" articles. This is yet another circumstance that demands ingenuity. Where do I hide my precious clothes? It's more than that. Where do I hide my precious clothes so there is absolutely no chance of anyone finding them?

For some, the problem is compounded because they can't afford to pay much for storage. Those who can afford to pay for storage must pay by cash to avoid discovery. A monthly bill mailed to their residence, a monthly charge on a credit card bill, or a check made out to a storage provider every month may raise questions.

This is just one more example of what causes transgender people to always be alert and guard what they do. They must also be cautious with what they say to preserve their secret. One transgender woman emphasized the use of untraceable funds when paying a storage bill:

I think storage places are best and some take cash!

Many feel they must discard or give away makeup, a dress, or very guy clothes, shoes, etc. after only a single use because they don't have a satisfactory place to store them until the next time.

Aside from storage companies, some transgender people pay others to store a suitcase. Occasionally, a group is formed to share a rented apartment or a room with access day and night. If you can afford to rent your own apartment or a room, especially with an outside door, your secret life is secure and living a double life is simplified.

More frequently, there is no place away from home that can be used for storage. This is when ingenuity is needed. For the most part, transgender women have a more difficult task than transgender men because they have so many items to hide: makeup, a wig, a handbag, breast forms, bras, skirts, heels, etc. Such items are definitely feminine and you need to be sure no one knows about them. In contrast, a transgender man has fewer items to hide because most guy items of clothing have become unisex and do not need to be hidden. A breast binder is the main item for a trans man to hide. A prosthesis is more difficult to hide, but may be desired. Also, a wig may be needed to cover long hair if you can't wear a man's type short hairstyle. A hat may sometimes be used to conceal long hair and doesn't need to be hidden.

In both the transgender man and woman, the major challenge is to have a hiding place. There are several kinds of places that are used. Common places are where only "he" goes or only "she" goes, such as a tool closet or personal feminine articles are kept. If the hiding place can be locked, it is even more secure. Some transgender women wrote of their method of hiding their feminine things:

> I store some of my clothes in totes and a locker trunk I built that has my breast forms makeup wigs and over stock of thigh highs, pantyhose. As for children I used to keep my panties in my dresser until I found them in my daughter laundry basket. She used to take my thongs.

> I used to store my things in an attic space that was accessible only through a closet, which I knew my wife would never ever try to go to. I did that for years and it worked perfectly until I got tired of hiding my things and now they hang in

my closet and a shared closet with my wife. I like that better.

My wife is a true Long Island girl. . . . Anything that is out of reach, she will not venture to look at. At the moment, we have 2 homes and that affords more "Jeannie" time. I just get paranoid when she is at the other home. As another girl pointed out, you have a tendency to spread out. I search for wig hair constantly.

A lot of us gurls [girls] are married with kids and have to be discreet. When I go out I hear a lot of different ways us gurls store our clothes and the places they dress. Some have unique routines like storage places and motels. It is always interesting how others are doing it.

I used to store mine in those under bed boxes, above the suspended ceiling of my office. I also used outside storage facilities. The only problem with that is if the wife happens to pick up the mail and finds the bill.

My current spot is an area under the staircase which had no access. I suddenly realized that there was a void there that I could access from a storage room. With a little ingenuity I cut thru the drywall close to the floor, dressed off the opening and stack things in front. It has become my own little closet where I can hang up my dresses. I put in some portable storage drawers, a shoe rack, and I am all set.

I used my attic. It is one of those you entered through an opening in a closet ceiling. I built closet shelves and compartments I strategically reinforced to support my weight. I used these as stepping places to reach into the attic and place and retrieve a box of mostly makeup, pantyhose and shoes. My spouse was delighted with the custom closet I built for her. She also had skirts with elastic waists she loaned me, without knowing it. I still use that space for out of season things, but now I use a ladder in place of my stepping places.

A Dressing Room

When a transgender person must dress away from home, finding a place to dress is frequently a major problem. Some transgender people never dress outside their home. If they are in the closet, they must dress in secrecy. Before dressing, they always need to be sure the curtains are drawn, so the neighbors don't see them. When the doorbell rings, they cannot answer it and must pretend they are not at home.

If they go out dressed, they can't let the neighbors or a doorman see them dressed when they leave or return home. Therefore, they need a place to dress away from home. A great variety of methods are used. If they rent a room or an apartment to store their clothes, they can dress there and the double life is simpler.

Some do a little preliminary work before leaving home and finish dressing in their car. Other methods include: renting a motel room, using the restroom at a Dunkin' Donuts or similar place. Going to a professional for a makeover and dressing there, or calling a friend and dressing at her/his place.

Undressing in the car before going home is less difficult than dressing in a car. I know of several cross dressers who remove their clothes in their garage or basement, when coming home late at night.

I used to dress at home and do my lipstick, earrings, and wig after I drove away from my neighborhood with dark glasses to conceal the eye makeup. On the way home, the wig and earrings came off as I turned into my neighborhood. When leaving home wearing a feminine looking blouse, I wore a guy shirt over it near home if it is still light out. A bright skirt was covered with a dark cloth.

Purchasing an article of outerwear for the cool weather was frequently frustrating. Wearing a feminine looking color or even a feminine style is out of the question regardless of how much you want it, since there is no practical way to conceal it as you leave and return home. The fear of discovery results in a high level of paranoia and frustration.

When you are in the closet, every move you make has an extra consideration and frequently has a limitation. Sometimes you are forced to make a frustrating decision to not buy the item you love and really want. I loved some coats that could not be concealed and I knew I couldn't wear when leaving home. I bought a few of them anyhow just to look at and know they are mine.

CHAPTER 11, Relationship Complications of Coming Out

(This chapter describes some successful methods used by transgender people when interacting with loved ones.)

Of course, transgender people are not the only ones affected by their transgenderism. Their family and friends are also affected. Usually, when a transgender person "comes out," he or she solves some personal problems but unintentionally creates problems for their family and friends. A transgender woman friend emailed an interesting analogy pertinent to this issue:

> There's an old story about a man who cheated on his wife and was wracked with guilt and remorse. He couldn't bear it and so "confessed" to his wife. He then felt much better because he had transferred the burden to his wife. Let her deal with it!

You personally overcome your shame, guilt, and fear of rejection when you come out. At the same time, you admit you have been deceiving the people you are telling. You should expect them to be shocked at your revelation. Suddenly they have many issues to deal with. If you love, or even care about your family and close friends, you will keep the philandering husband story (above) in mind.

Family and friends are faced with a situation they frequently know nothing about. They lack the ability to understand what transgenderism really is, what it means to your relationship, and how to deal with the news. Your loved ones lack any knowledge of how permanent your inner gender sense is and what it means to your relationship. They usually wish your transgenderism would go away. In spite of that, once they understand it doesn't go away, they feel helpless. Therefore, the transgender person needs to find ways to deal with the difficult situation created by revealing their secret. It is a highly emotional thing to do for all parties involved. The degree of difficulty depends on the family.

I feel it is the transgender person's (TG's) duty and responsibility to do everything they can to help family and close friends cope with the news. Some TGs have told me they (themselves) have no problem and they feel it is the family member's problem. They prove the story of the man who confessed his philandering—let them deal with it!

It is true the family now has a problem, but the transgender person is responsible for handing them that problem and should find ways to help members of their family, and sometimes a close long-term friend, cope. As one transgender woman put it,

> One must keep in mind that our wives or kids didn't ask for any of this and they need a dad and mom so even tho [though] it is hard sometimes to do and keep in mind our feelings are not the only ones effected by our decision to be the women we wish to be and their responses to us being fem has a lot to do with how we present it to them.

Accepting responsibility for giving others a problem is sometimes disputed. On the other hand, I feel the transgender person does have a responsibility because she or he is presenting a multifaceted series of problems to innocent people. The family has been deceived for many years and suddenly feels the person is someone different from the image they always had. Your persona was a lie. They wonder why you did this to them. You are a different person than you were and now tell them you were lying to them before. How can you feel it's solely their problem?

Your feeling that you did not have a choice is not true nor is it relevant. How can you not try to help them, since you probably can? Disavowing any responsibility is not responsible. That feeling in itself is as irresponsible as the man who told his wife of his philandering and now says, "Let her deal with it."

Coming Out—General Guidelines

Should you out yourself? Some transgender individuals not only want to come out, they feel a real need to come out. The "need" involves an emotion most transgender people are incapable of defining, even though they feel it quite strongly. In any case, you need time to carefully weigh the consequences your revelation will bring—both the favorable and the unfavorable.

Coming out is a hazardous journey. If you are comfortable not coming out, at least for now that is a good road to travel. It doesn't matter how often or how seldom you dress. You must think of your own mental health when making that decision.

On the other hand, if you need to come out, proceed cautiously! Once you out yourself, you cannot un-out yourself. However, coming out may be worth it, since the favorable results are liberating. The need to hide yourself, live a double life, and constantly lie is destructive to your self-worth.

Transgender people that experience the most successful coming out also have good relations with others before coming out. Too often we tend to become angry because society makes us conceal our true feeling and forces us into a closet. You need to start overcoming any anger and establish good relations with your relatives and friends. Moral, "nice," and generally good people experience the best results when coming out.

If you plan to come out, plan it carefully and well in advance of actually coming out. You want to think of laying the groundwork in advance and determine what you will say, how you will say it, and when you will say it.

Lay The Ground Work. One successful method is to give small hints, but don't go too far at the start. Keep giving hints, trying your best to not go so far that you find you revealed your secret before you are ready to do so and you think they are ready to receive it. Hints a transgender woman would give include a demonstration of your nurturing nature, your interest in fashion, and other things typically associated with your feminine brain gender. The male brain gender would deemphasize nurturing, but show an interest in sports, cars, and anything typically of a masculine interest.

Plan What You Will Say And How You Will Say It. This is a tough one and only you know with whom you are dealing. One thing I do know is the words must be your own or you will sound like you are adding another deception to the one you carried around all these years. Give reassurance that you are the same person repeatedly. The same person he or she always knew and your personality hasn't changed. Repeat that this doesn't change your love and devotion. The only change is your presentation—how you look. I used a brief written outline of what my secret life was like. I described the difficulty of living a double life, the torment of trying to get rid of wanting to be the other sex, and a description of the detrimental effects of it all. Include the shame you felt and the fear the person would reject you—disown you.

<u>Pick Your Time To Say It.</u> Don't do anything in the heat of an argument or when anyone is angry. The best time to say those words is probably after you did something that demonstrates your love and devotion to the person you plan to tell. When you actually tell your secret, be dressed as your "audience" is accustomed to seeing you. It is a major shock to hear your secret. Seeing you dressed as a woman or man for the first time would be too much to deal with all at once. Do your telling in person, if at all possible.

You need to consider the probable reaction from the person to whom you are telling your secret. The most common belief is you are gay or lesbian. Let them know being a transgender person is completely separate from sexual preference. If you must make a statement regarding whether or not you are homosexual, do it honestly and use the sex you were always known as for a reference point.

So far their only exposure has probably been sensationalized television programs and comedians, so you will need to explain transgender is a medical phenomenon that occurs before birth. It is not a fetish, a sexual thing, a whim, a life style, or a mental illness. Many other useful facts are described in previous chapters.

Parents

Parents probably have the most trouble with learning of their child's transgenderism. Most often parents blame themselves for their child's transgender behavior. They feel they must have done something wrong in the rearing; therefore, it is their fault. As one transgender woman said,

When I came out to my parents eight years ago my father accepted it almost immediately. His attitude was "family supports family." My mom took it much harder and accepted the blame for my transgenderism. She and I dealt with it in uncomfortable silence for seven years but over the past year we began talking openly about it. She has since seen photos of me [and] has sent me holiday cards and she even picked up the dress for my first outing when I had to work and couldn't make the "door buster sale" to get it at 50% off.

It is always best to bring any issues into the open and try to discuss them. This is the case when dealing with any human relations issue.

Sometimes parents become angry that they did something wrong in rearing you and project that anger on you. When you experience this, don't deal with the anger and work on the root cause of the anger. Get the point across that medical scientists say transgenderism was not the result of anything they did or did not do. It is a chance happening in your mother's womb.

Other parents suspect their daughter or son's transgenderism but say nothing hoping their child will grow out of it. Some parents may be ashamed of their child and fear their child will be stigmatized and the parent will be stigmatized along with them. They second guess their own ability to raise children so the children turn out the way they are expected to turn out. Furthermore, some parents think they made a mistake in raising their child and try to correct their supposed error by trying to force the child into more stereotypical dressing and behavior. This attempt sometimes works in the short term; however, it usually fails in the long run.

Armed with the above knowledge, you may want to relate what research tells us to your parents. We got this way because, in the womb, something unusual happened to make our femininity or masculinity different. Explain the process of a baby's development in the womb is so involved and complex that variations are bound to occur. Furthermore, some kind of variation occurs in most births. In the case of a transgender person perhaps we didn't make or absorb all the estrogen or testosterone we should have at the exact time it was required during fetal development. Parents need to be made aware of the brain-sex theory of transgenderism. However, this will never happen unless transgender people themselves are made aware of the theory. There are scores of distinguished people in the field who believe it and feel it will eventually be proven.

Generally, parents demonstrate unconditional love for their child; however, this is not always the case. In unfortunate cases, parents have disowned their transgender child and refuse to provide a home. This stigmatization results in an alarming number of young transgender kids being thrown away or disowned by their parents, even before they reach adulthood.

Usually, parents accept their child as is, even if they blame themselves for the result. Almost every parent wants the best for their child, and they know a transgender life is not the best. It is not an easy life to deal with because parents intuitively know any variation from the "norm" causes a difficult life for their child. Parents do not want their child to face a difficult life.

Often these children believe they must live in the streets and turn to prostitution to survive. You need to know about organizations throughout the country are specifically organized to deal with LGBTQ homeless youth (See APPENDIX III - Homeless Youth Services in Some Major Cities. Appendix III includes how to locate help in other locations). These services help youngsters like you realize a life off the streets, eat regular meals, continue attendance at school, and fit into society. This is particularly important work, since kids can easily be subject to exploitation in the streets and familial abuse during adolescence, which is a critical developmental stage in your life. Unfortunately there are not enough places that care for homeless youngsters, and where they do exist, they are usually poorly funded. However, they always can offer valuable help.

If you are planning to live either sometimes or full time in a different gender, you should have an outline of a general life plan to present to your parents before you tell them. It may ease their concern. Also, if you are currently seeing or did see a gender counselor, tell them. Parents will find it comforting to know you are getting professional help. You need to give them some relief to their concern regarding your future welfare.

In one case I know, which is not unusual, the parents did not stop their love for their child. They simply didn't know how to handle the situation. A major problem for the parents was what and how to tell family, friends, and neighbors. This is an easier one for all but the youngest transgender child because the hard part was telling parents and that is now in the past. The child should solve this problem by telling all others and relieve her or his parents of a burden they simply do not know how to deal with.

One transgender woman wrote of her mother's acceptance,

> After I told my mom about me . . . she wished that I told her then she would have helped me. What that meant I never asked. I just know she is ok with it. I will never know

but if she would have help[ed] me become female, then I wish I would have said something.

Some parents typically feel isolated and don't know who to talk to about their relations with their transgender child. A feeling of helplessness and isolation ensues because they do not know where to go to learn more about their child's "condition." The common result is depression. It is the transgender person's duty and responsibility to find a discussion group dealing with similar situations for her or his parents.

Surprisingly, there are groups everywhere. However, if you don't know of a group, one can usually be found on the Internet. Another possibility is to call an LGBTQ Center and ask if they have or know of such a group, some groups are labeled SOFFA (Significant Other, Family, Friends, and Allies). PFLAG (Parents, Families and Friends of Lesbians and Gays), is the largest organization of its kind with over 400 chapters nationwide. Sometimes LGBTQ Center can only tell you how you can find one. Furthermore, parents usually need help to get started with a group. The child should accompany the parents to their first meeting. Parents are usually eager to follow up and invariably attend future meetings without assistance.

Spouses

It is best for a transgender person to avoid marriage unless she or he discusses her or his transgenderism and what it means. Many think marrying someone they love and living a "normal" life will cure them of their feelings or help them manage those feelings better. That is frequently wrong. My thoughts ran along those lines, but the girl inside me would not leave or stay buried regardless of how much I wanted to escape my transgenderism. Sooner or later that woman inside will rise to your consciousness again. There is no escaping your inner gender. Regardless of how much you try to be like everyone else and regardless of how great your love and devotion is toward your spouse, you often cannot refrain from expressing your inner gender (i.e., femininity or masculinity). The result of coming out probably will make your life and the life of your spouse somewhere between difficult and unbearable. A premature end to your marriage will likely occur as it did for this transgender woman, who said,

I have seen the pain that I have caused my wife, and I'm deeply sorry about it. We are now separated, and I don't blame her one bit. I am just truly sorry that I did not tell her the truth right from the start, which would have stopped years of pain and anguish for both of us. I will always love her, and be there for her.

There is a chance of success in a nontransgender life, if you are extremely good at self-control at the cost of your own total happiness. That can only follow if you have a relatively weak genetic transgender intensity implanted and/or a strong moderating sociological factor to help you control the need to appear as the woman or man. However, you have no way of evaluating this beforehand because the need to be your true gender seems to grow stronger with age.

If you do decide to marry, you will have a serious problem unless you tell your spouse before you get married. She or he may understand and love you anyhow; however, more wives than husbands seem to accept transgenderism in their spouse. Men have been conditioned to reject homosexuality and seem to have more difficulty with a wife presenting as a man or being masculine. Even with acceptance or tolerance, as your transgender needs inevitably grow, your spouse's acceptance and tolerance may not grow in parallel to yours. It is a rare spouse who fully accepts the transgender person's needs. Below are comments from some typical transgender women:

I told my wife and she Freaked out.

I am waiting for the divorce papers now.

My wife accepted me till I told her I was a transsexual and wanted to transition. I'm divorced now. [I] lost my house, my children, my job, and everything I built.

After decades of living, working, and building his or her persona to get along in this world, the investment a transgender person has made to fit in is often so great that the risk of walking away from the life, perks, career, family, etc. one has built up seems like an insurmountable obstacle. It seems impossible to give all that up to live according to your inner feelings, especially since you were able to do so up to now. Some transgender people can—but many cannot—contain their true self indefinitely. You either proceed in an unhappy state in the closet or bring unhappiness to others by coming out. The fact that you originally knew the only alternative was to hope for a cure, while being what society dictates you should be, is a difficult concept with which only you will be sympathetic. In a sense, you trapped yourself and now you need to decide what you will do.

When you believe marriage will either provide a cure or you have no other course, a mate is found whom you liked and later loved. You become attached and love the person more and more. This will bring the long awaited cure, you hope. You have children you adore and build a successful career. The persona you built has been successful and you may even feel cured, for a while.

At some point, you realize there is no such thing—there is no cure. It becomes more and more difficult to control your gender identity. You feel the compelling need to be yourself keeps increasing. You need to be who you are, totally, or in some cases, at least part of the time.

Although there are an infinite number of ways to deal with your conflict, there are three basic routes: (1) staying in the closet, (2) occasionally coming out of the closet, or (3) leaving the closet on a full-time basis. I believe most transgender people stay in the closet. The second most often route taken is they open the door occasionally, and the least frequent route is leaving the closet entirely. This will probably change as younger people come into the picture.

Some keep their true gender a secret from their spouse and therefore need to keep it secret from everyone else. They carry their secret to the grave. They are extremely afraid of exposure because they feel that would end their marriage. They don't want their marriage to end because they love their wife/husband and don't want to hurt or live without their spouse. One transgender woman expressed it this way:

> I am married for over 17 years with 3 kids and have been dressing since I was 13. I dress secretly and my wife doesn't know. I feel at this point of my marriage I would have more to lose by taking a chance in hoping that she accepts me. It is a chance I am not willing to take, too much to lose. Looking back, I should have told her when we first met this way I would have had a lot less to lose. If she accepted then I would not be hiding this secret and would be living a

pleasant life. [It] is painful for me to not tell her, but at this point, I will take my secret to my grave.

Some transgender people don't want the marriage to end because they love their spouse, love their life, don't want to risk losing the right to live with their children, don't want to be fired from their job, and generally don't want to be ostracized by their circle of friends. Shame also plays an important part in many transgender persons' lives and dictates how they react. We must be aware of our shame so we can deal with it.

To avoid coming out to their spouse, transgender people either dress when they are alone or on occasions when they can provide an excuse to get out of the house. You need to take precautions to be sure you are not detected on the occasions you are able to get away from the family. As mentioned previously, some use their car, a Dunkin' Donuts restroom, or something similar to serve as a dressing room to change clothes to the other sex and back again later. Some even rent spaces where they can store their clothes and change into and out of them. I know more than one person who has been doing this in the order of more than 20 years. On one pretext or another, she has a reason to "disappear" and her wife knows nothing of what she really does.

Except for the need to bind ones breasts, transgender men have less of an issue with dressing, since slip-on shoes, socks, pants, and a top such as a sweater is unisex and acceptable. Both women and men find they become good at thinking of lies to be used when the opportunity arises to dress.

Some confess to their spouse and the marriage frequently ends in a divorce, since few straight men want to be married to a man and few straight women want to be married to a woman. Even those who seem to accept their spouse's venture into a different gender don't accept it fully. It is rare, but I know some cases where the wife actually helps her husband with clothes and even go out in public with her. If your spouse accepts your transgenderism, she or he will frequently impose some restrictions and limitations to feel reassured that he or she still has the woman or man she loves. One transgender woman expressed a rare but beautiful relationship as follows:

> I came out to my wife from the start. We had a good relationship and I wanted to be honest. . . . She was glad for the truth but not too sure how it would change things. . . .

At first it was a big change for her, but not enough to end our relationship. As we grew as a married couple, she sees the joy in my eyes when I am dressed, she sees my need to dress, and she has finally recognized that I share this with her because I love and trust her with my life.

As a transgender man, it is easier to acquiring men's clothes simply because women frequently do the shopping for a man, their husband, or child. However, transgender men have a more difficult time coming out. You need to understand that your husband may see your masculinity as making him a homosexual and homophobia is usually deeply rooted.

Some spouses don't want their transgender spouse to take hormones or eliminate or acquire body hair. Some spouses need to have their partner cut their hair short. Most spouses impose some restrictions that result in their keeping their spouse "intact" in whatever aspects is felt to be important and reassuring that the spouse is still the gender they thought they married. In some cases, restrictions are invented to make sure you are willing to sacrifice something to stay together. You can never predict the reaction your coming out will bring. Some transgender women expressed it this way,

Hello my name is [withheld] and my wife is very supportive. She has me on hormones for breast development.

My dream is to have a gg [genetic girl] as a lover. Oddly, my wife cannot accept this. . . . She says that if I feel I am a woman, then she could accept me being intimate with a man, but not another female. I think she says this not to be kind, but because she feels it will discourage me from dressing.

For some transgender women, the wife's restrictions are okay and they have little trouble living that way. If you can provide something symbolic that you can both be happy with, consider it a workable compromise. Most often the wife will totally reject the fact that her husband wants to be a woman, wants to be like a woman, or even wants to look like a woman part of the time. They married a man and want him as a man or they don't want him at all. They want nothing less than a 100% of the man they thought they married. This attitude is more common among men with a transgender wife.

Although she may not say it, one type of wife feels her husband's desire for womanhood is a reflection on her own failed femininity and is embarrassed to have anyone find out. Under those circumstances, the secret became a secret they now both share.

Some wives say, "Get out, now!" At the other extreme, some feel an unconditional love for their partner. Still others feel they cannot survive financially, socially, or otherwise being alone. Some are ashamed to have people think she failed as a wife, so they become permissive. The most frequent occurrence of a permissive reaction I know of is that the wife reluctantly says once in a while is okay, but I don't ever want to see it. You can dress like a woman sometimes, but do it somewhere else because I never want to see you that way.

Other wives get hysterical, feel betrayed, cannot abide the deception, or have a hundred other reactions, mostly undesirable ones. The transgender woman feels guilty in many cases. She is sorry she ever told her wife, but the cat is out of the bag and nothing can change that. You can always postpone saying it, but once you say it, you cannot un-say it. She should have told her wife before they were married, but that demon "shame" stood in the way. Some expect or hope their marriage will cure them of the need to be a woman. The outcome of coming out is often not a happy one.

Not often, but sometimes the wife understands and we receive positive feedback from and about them. For example:

> Today, I am mature and proud to say I am still a cd/tv [crossdresser/transvestite] and loving it each day more. Married to a gg [genetic girl] who tolerates it but does not participate. At least she gives me the freedom to dress when she's not around.

> I help my hub be more fem all the time. . . . I do love and adore her and want her to have the full fem experiences she can have so she is allowed to date or have a relationship since I don't join in sexually. I have no interest in being with a woman but I do help her shop and buy things for her as well and encourage her to date or even have a relationship.

My [transgender] partner and I have been together for about a year and a half but are not married. We have our ups and downs but his cross dressing is a nonissue for us. He is strongly heterosexual but loves to dress. I can't say that I completely understand but I do completely support him. It doesn't change who he is or our relationship.

Telling one's spouse about being a transgender person is a difficult task. One transgender woman told of her way of telling her wife,

They say you can boil a frog alive without it jumping out of the pot simply by slowly turning up the heat. That's basically how I did it. I would drop hints and gauge the reaction and back off. Every once in a while I would do something a little effeminate. I would go shopping with her and actually give her good ideas for dressing—something that hetero men simply do NOT do.

One thing I can do well with my wife is make her laugh so I used it to help disarm her when I felt I advanced too far. Basically, I would keep it all theoretical and playful and never really confirm or deny and I tried to never overplay my hand.

Finally after a couple months of this I felt the time was right. I'd planted all the seeds and made all the hints. I did this to cushion the shock when I came out to her. Before I finally came out I took stock again and thought about if I really needed to do this. [She decided she must be honest.].

When I finally came out, I just told her that I was bigendered and bisexual and explained what that meant. I told her that I loved her and I wanted her to hear it from me rather than find my fake tits or something. I also explained that this is who I am. I can't just turn it off. I can hide it for a while but its still there and I'm far more happy as a girl than as a guy. Lucky for me she accepted this and has been very supportive ever since.

That wife expressed her fears at this revelation. Her biggest fear was her husband was going to leave her for a man or sleep around and she was concerned about catching some disease. This was not anything this transgender woman expected to be involved in.

That approach is a good one, since it turned out well. The shock treatment never is a welcome one.

Another somewhat successful confession was something similar to what I heard a from two other transgender women,

> I came home late one Saturday night . . . after midnight. My wife was waiting up for me, which is/was rare. "Where have you been?" she asked. Obviously, she thought I was having an affair. And, very fortunately, I had a printed piece (a) "Girls Night Out," which I showed her. "I'm a cross dresser, dear." "Oh," she replied, "that's all?" Since then we've worked out our "don't ask, don't tell" modus operandi. She never wants to meet the femme me or any friends in drag.

If a mutually agreeable arrangement can be reached, it is a successful coming out. Not wanting to see their husband appear as a woman or a wife as a man is common and understandable.

I feel the important things in telling a spouse is to avoid any lies, take it step by step, give assurance of your love all along the way and say it has nothing to do with her or him, since you were born this way.

Aside from that, there must be good words to tell a spouse you are not what she or he thought you were and you have always been the other sex or partly the other sex inside. The actual words must be your own.

I would make the following points:

- You were born a little different than other women/men.

- You were this way before you ever met her/him, so it has nothing to do with her/him.

- You didn't tell her/him before marriage because you loved her/him, feared rejection, and thought you would change.

- You were this way before you met. It is not a change in you and it has nothing to do with your love for her/him.

- You must repeat and continually reassure your spouse that your love is still strong, if it is true. Also if true, tell her/him your love keeps growing and you are more in love than when you were first married. Your spouse needs to understand what you have to say is about you, not her/him or your feelings for her/him.

- You were born with parts of a nature similar to hers/his and that may have a lot to do with why she/he married you.

If you don't get a response in some way up to this point, it would surprise me. Hopefully, things are calm so the conversation can continue.

It is important to keep giving assurance of your love. At some point, you will be asked what it is you are trying to say. If it is true, you can first say you are not gay or it has nothing to do with gay or straight because many uninformed people think transgender and gay are synonymous. You need to say you were born with some of the same nature as your spouse and, in the same breath, before anything can be said (if something is said, ignore it) you need to ask for help. You didn't want to be this way. You didn't ask for it and fought it all your life. However, it is getting harder and harder to keep that part of you hidden inside and you feel you need her/his help. You feel you shouldn't continue to keep it a secret. Keep repeating your love and that you are asking for help.

Hopefully, your spouse will eventually ask you what kind of help you want. Now, you can say what you want. It would be best to start with something like (but rephrase it in your own words):

This may sound crazy and there are a lot of others in the same boat as me. I have this strong need to dress and behave in a feminine/masculine manner, sometimes.

From here there is no telling where the couple will take it. As we have seen, in some cases the reaction approaches, "Is that all?" In other cases, your spouse may react like you had the plague.
Even if your goal is transitioning all the way, this is not the time to say it. This is something most people need to get used to a little at a time. I do not feel this is a deception. It is a display of kindness, since the fact you want to be the other sex, even some of the time, is enough of a shock for now.

Remember what was said about boiling a frog. It is like throwing your spouse in a pot of boiling water. It may be hard to understand the immensity of the shock such an admission has. It is huge! It's beyond imagination and is devastating for some spouses. If you are lucky, after revealing your transgenderism to your spouse, your marriage may evolve where your transgender needs and your spouse's husband or wife needs are both accommodated. Something each of you can live with or tolerate.

More than one lesbian told me they got married because they wanted a child, but most transgender men look at child bearing as another violation of their true gender. It all depends on his transgender intensity. Some husbands accept a wife's masculinity, thinking it is her way of showing some independence and just an expression of women's lib. If this is the case and it is enough for you to live with, go with it.

Some spouses accept, and perhaps really understand their transgender spouse's predicament. It is infrequent, but there are spouses who tolerate their partner's need to be a woman/man part of the time. In rare cases, some even remain with their partner through the transition and beyond. Does true love help to foster understanding, forgive the deception, and want happiness for their spouse, the one they love, even at their own expense? It has been known some people will make sacrifices for a loved one. It can happen as two transgender women relate below:

> My wife created my feminine persona and we two women go out to restaurants, shopping and travel together.

> And my partner, a ciswoman [nontransgender woman], loves me for being, well, me.

There is no one smart enough to predict the outcome of telling your spouse your secret. When push comes to shove, the people involved are the most important factor in total acceptance, total rejection, or something in between. However, the gentle approach is worth the effort considering human relations and the feelings you have, or may have had, for a spouse.

Sometimes whole families become closer with this news. I was on a cruise with a transgender group in 2003. Ten people of the 30 in our group were relatives of a transgender woman and were celebrating her sexual reassignment surgery (SRS). Each family reacts differently. If there is true love in the family, most members will find some way to accommodate the transgender person's newly revealed status.

Regarding the spouse, tender loving care is needed because this disruption to their life is hardest on them. The spouse of the transgender woman or transgender man is affected 24/7 by this news.

Children

If you are a transgender person and you marry, you should think carefully about having children. If you think there is any possibility you might cure the need to transition to a different gender role, having children will not cure you. Chances are if your marriage ends in a divorce, you may not even get joint custody if the judge thinks transgenderism is a sexual perversion or a mental illness. You will end up losing your children and your partner. As one transgender woman put it after being rejected by her wife,

> Sometimes I wish I had come out before kids and before marriage, but until the Internet and getting in touch with the many others that love to be more fem[ale] and lady like. I always thought I was the weird and strange and crazy one.

Generally, the younger the child the more accepting she or he seem to be of transgender people. This may be the result of growing up in a more permissive world with more exposure to romance preference and gender variations, which previous generations did not have. Perhaps young people have been exposed to homophobia for a shorter length of time or not at all. In spite of that, when it comes to a parent transitioning, children often have a difficult time.

Mostly, people prefer the status quo and young children prefer the status quo even more. As a rule they don't want change. The news that Mommy or Daddy does not look the same is disturbing. The children's idea of a parental role model is shattered. Nevertheless, individual differences are always present. Many children who don't like the idea are usually more pliable and accept the change fairly quickly.

Explaining transgenderism is a difficult because most transgender individuals don't understand it themselves. If you don't understand what it is, how it happened to you, and why it happened to you, how can you possibly explain it adequately to your child (or to anyone)?

A parent is usually a source of stability and security. You need to convince your children you are still the same person, still have the love and devotion toward them, and will always take care of them. You will always be there for them. Although this is a major change, your mission is to convince your children it is not a big thing. Nothing will change regarding your relationship and love. The only difference is the way you will look.

A father and mother represents more than stability and security. A transitioning parent makes a child fearful the same thing will happen to them when they reach the parent's age. The parent needs to convince their daughter(s) and/or son(s) the parent was born a transgender person. If the child doesn't feel he or she is the other sex or want to be the other sex by now, he or she never will. The need to be as much like the other sex as possible originates before birth, is well known to the individual at an early age, and the child would know of a need to be the other gender long before now. Transgenderism is not contagious and has not been found to be hereditary. It is best thought of as a variation during congenital development.

A transitioning parent also represents a role model of femininity or masculinity. The role model of a spouse in the child's future is also involved. The transitioning parent needs to face these issues and try to maintain previous relationships. The gender role model can be maintained with manageable effort. The spousal role model should also be maintained even if it must be demonstrated by you, without your partner's cooperation. You must demonstrate your concern and caring for your spouse (or ex-spouse).

I interviewed a young man whose father was a preoperation transsexual. I asked him how he felt about his father wanting to be a woman. He said,

I don't like it, but I accept it.

You need to be thankful if your children are old enough to understand you will still be the same person you always were. My children are grown, well educated, self-supporting, so security is not an issue. However, that does not mean it was easy to tell them their father's life was a long, closely guarded, and shameful secret. It was undoubtedly the most difficult task I ever initiated. It was difficult and highly emotional. I contemplated it for weeks and planned it carefully to inflict the minimum damage to them and my image as possible. Once my children were told, telling my grandchildren, who were 16 through 22 years old at the time, was relatively easy. Careful planning is strongly advised when telling anyone close to you. This is especially true when children are involved. The most difficult part is the problem the child will have as a result of your revelation.

Others may need to help their children understand the only difference is their transgender parent will be even closer to them by being honest and open with them, and no longer deceiving them and hiding things from them. Furthermore, many transgender parents have the additional difficulty of fitting the approach to the age of their child. However, it is not always difficult. In many cases, children can be surprisingly accepting.

Telling a very young child of a relative's transitioning may be a difficult chore. It requires an explanation in simple terms–terms they are capable of understanding. For example, the child should be told some people are born looking like a girl, but they really feel like a boy inside (or visa-versa). When they are young, it is easy to pretend being a girl, but when they get older it is hard for them to stay a girl. They are not happy inside so she (or he) is going to start looking like a boy (or girl), but will be the same person you always knew.

In many cases, the children are not told. In other cases, the child is not old enough to understand the transgender concept. In one case, when a little boy 4 years old heard the news that his father wanted to be a woman, he clasp his hands over his ears and ran from the scene.

Every child and family is different. If children have the ability to understand what transgenderism is, there is rarely any way of predicting the children's reaction in advance of telling them. Their reaction is not always apparent at first and may take a while for their reaction to rise to the surface and become known.

The major reason a grown child will reject you is often simply because you are hurting their mother or their father, your spouse. They think you are cruel, selfish, unfair, and unfaithful to the vows you swore to uphold. In an email, one transgender woman wrote,

> My oldest son (27) will no longer speak to me nor does he ever want to see me again.

They may not express any of this openly, but if you want to maintain a relationship with your children, you must face the possibility of them hating you for hurting your spouse—their mother or father. If hurting your spouse represents their view regarding the reason for your transitioning, you appear to be doing ill to an innocent woman/man (and the children) for some selfish reason. The only way to overcome this kind of resistance is to face it openly and directly. You need to discuss your transition reason and convince your children of why you are transitioning.

The best you can do is try to explain your transitioning is not to hurt their mother/father or anyone else. You thought you could control this and you have controlled it for many years. You suffered for a lifetime controlling this, you held yourself in check, and you cannot control it or bear it any longer. Your needs are becoming more difficult to contain and it is like it controls you. Again, ask for help and how you can be yourself and make it easier for everyone else, including the nontransitioning spouse. If you can engage your children in a rational conversation about your need to transition, you have a chance to maintain a semblance of a relationship with your children.

When grandchildren are involved, it is proper to leave the decision regarding exposure of the secret to the parents. They need to decide if and when their children should be told. The one problem is that if they choose to not tell them, you either will not be able to see them again or you will need to revert to your former presentation in order to see them, which may be okay or painful for you.

Researchers say young children are most accepting, but somehow they are the last ones to know. In most cases that I heard, the grandchildren are not told and certainly not told initially. Although it is not a hard and fast rule, when your child is reluctant to tell their child, your grandchild, and there is not some special circumstance or pressing issue involved, there often is some other issue involved in your child's acceptance that you need to explore and help reconcile.

Siblings

Some circumstances may require that you change your appearance slowly to get those you love used to your new look. This is the approach some transgender people use successfully with siblings. They are accustomed to seeing you as a man/woman, so start with a slight androgynous look and gradually appear a bit more masculine/feminine until eventually you appear as a man/woman.

Avoid wearing an ultramasculine/ultrafeminine outfit for a considerable time.

Younger siblings of all sexes, but particularly those of the same sex, frequently have special difficulty dealing with you because you served as a major role model. They copied you and your behavior more than may be obvious to you. They want to keep their role model intact.

Both younger and older siblings fear they are destined to follow in your footsteps and that is a major factor in accepting your status as final. Also, your new presentation may shatter your image in their mind.

For some reason, male siblings and male relatives seem to have the most difficulty accepting the new "girl in town." It is not easy for women to accept such news, but they seem to have an easier time. I have observed this repeatedly from the experiences of friends and my general reading.

An approach that has proven to be successful for a transgender woman is to dress as the man they always knew and briefly state that you are a transgender person. A transgender man's approach should parallel this. Ask if they know what transgender is and, regardless of the answer, tell them what transgender means in basic terms like you feel you are a woman (or man) inside and need to live and dress that way. Solicit and answer any questions at that time. Be sure to tell them you would like them to bring future questions to your attention.

It is good to explain the difficulties you had when you kept this a secret. It will be a part of your life they never knew. I believe it helps you gain some level of understanding of your needs to achieve happiness. At the very least, an effort to make it easier for them to understand your need to transition is a worthwhile effort.

Remember, you need to help people understand you, especially those you love because nature may love variety, but unfortunately people almost universally hate it!

Others—Relatives and Close Friends

Relatives are in two major groups. In some circumstances, they are very close to you and part of your immediate family. They should be handled as you would a parent, a child, or a sibling, depending on their age. The second group is not that close, and they should be treated similar to the way you would handle a friend. A close friend is frequently also part of your family and should be treated as family in accordance with their age.

Telling a very young relative of your transitioning may be a difficult chore. It requires an explanation in simple terms—terms the child is capable of understanding. Explaining is frequently best done by the child's parent. For example,

> When referring to a transgender man, the parent should tell the child, some people are born looking like a girl, but they really feel like a boy inside (or visa-versa). When they are young, it is easy to pretend being a girl, but when they get older it is hard for them to stay a girl. They are not happy inside so she is going to start looking like a boy (or girl), but will be the same person you always knew.
>
> She will still love you and love playing with you. The only difference will be she will take some special medicine that will make her look like a boy and she may even grow some whiskers. She will even have a boy's name from now on and we should call her that. Also, when we talk about her we will say him and he instead of what we used to say. We all love her and want her to be happy. If anyone makes a mistake and uses the wrong name or says her instead of him, we will simply correct them. It is no big deal.

Of course, a similar approach should be taken when a transgender woman is involved.

There are so many possible situations you can encounter regarding the transgender issue that common sense should guide you in each individual circumstance. If it is you who is transitioning, don't declare your intentions to become a woman or a man and walk away. Attempt to get some level of understanding first. It will prove worthwhile. Even if you fail, you will be happier knowing at least you tried your best to gain understanding.

You need to emphasize you are the same person, except you are more honest and truthful with yourself and others about your true feelings.

Employers

Coming out on the job can be perilous. Therefore, special care is required. It is different than telling a loved one, but similar because you cannot predict the outcome. Caution is needed in employment situations, if you wish to maintain a reasonable standard of living.

Generally, civil service jobs are safe, but not all government jobs are. The case of the transitioning transgender woman, Diane Schroer v. James H. Billington, Librarian of Congress, discussed in CHAPTER 9—Transphobia—Transgender Discrimination, demonstrates this.

Many large corporations accommodate transgender individuals. However, again, this is not always the case. The masculine nontransgender nonlesbian woman's case, Price Waterhouse v. Hopkins, also discussed in Chapter 9, went all the way to the Supreme Court.

In some cases, you are so good at your job the employer will hesitate to fire you for now. However, your future is uncertain in that job if a replacement for you is found.

If you are applying for employment at a company, you should research their employee policy manual. Their transgender policy, or lack of one, could help you decide whether to seek a job there. Probably the safest employers to come out with are those who accommodate and even pay for genital surgery. Some are listed in the Endnotes.[1] Student medical insurance plans at 36 schools now provide coverage for gender operations, including Brown, Harvard, Cornell and Stamford.

All the reactions we get are not unfavorable. One transgender person related what a company officer said after she told him,

> My director was very matter of fact. He's like, okay, what do we need to do so this can work? He wasn't interested in going into my personal [life], which was nice.

Even if you keep your job, the harassment from coworkers may make the job not worth having. Also, a transphobic supervisor can always find or fabricate something to use against you.

Okay, you may reach a point that coming out on the job is important enough to you to risk your employment. The safest way to insure a continuing livelihood is to find another job as a standby as you transition. If you want to keep your present job after transitioning, then you stay where you are. If the transition doesn't proceed smoothly, resign and go to the new job. In any case, many people find it more comfortable to transition and go to a new job in the transitioned presentation.

Even if your company policy manual is favorable toward transgender people, you need to go about implementing your transition in an intelligent manner. The process of coming out on the job must be done with careful deliberation. No process guarantees success. You must be the one to decide how to come out. One process that has been used for a successful transition is:

First: Know the company policy, if there is one.

Second: You need to find an executive that is most likely to be sympathetic. She or he may have exhibited liberalism on another issue.

Third: Next you need to prepare what you will say. After that, get an appointment "regarding a personal matter." with your target executive. You can't do this at a chance meeting in the hallway. The object of this meeting is to solicit advice about how to proceed with transitioning on the job. You must be prepared for your target executive to say, "Don't do it!" If you feel you can't heed that advice, you need to make it plain it is something you thought through carefully, you anticipated rejection, but your happiness dictates you express your true self all the time and that means on the job, also. You are aware of the risks and need advice on how to proceed with the greatest chance of success.

Fourth: If your job is unionized, know your union's policy and follow the same process described in the Third step, above. In addition to the Second step with whom you believe is the most sympathetic union officer.

Fifth: Once the transition is firmed up, an important point is to get suggestions from Human Resources and your supervisor regarding the accomplishment of your transition with the least disruption to the business of the company.

Sixth: It is best to write a letter to company employees explaining your identity and how the transition will be done. State how it will not affect them or their work. Explain your commitment to the company and how you will continue your job as always and you request their cooperation by simply continuing the job they have always done.

Seventh: Submit the letter to your supervisor and Human Resources and ask for a meeting to review the letter before it is distributed. The distribution of the letter will minimize the discussion and distraction you will cause. The letter should be timed months in advance of the actual transition and follow soon after declaring your intent to transition.

Eighth: Good luck.

CHAPTER 12, You Told Me, Now What?

(This chapter is a guide for people who were told of a loved one's transgenderism.)

You must remember the fact that the person who "came out" to you is the same person you always knew. In fact, if you liked that person, you probably liked her or him because of who and what they are. The manner of dress may be different and the person may even look different; however, the same person is before you. Nothing has changed beyond appearance.

Probably, the qualities you liked about the transgender person had nothing to do with gender and not in the least connected with gender. There were things like character, attitude, personality, and values you liked. These qualities are not likely to change as a person undergoes transition to a different gender role because no brain changes were made. Unknowingly, she or he was always on the transition journey. No one could see it, but they were. The coming out is merely a verbal declaration of what has been going on all her or his life.

The things you liked about the transgender person were probably linked to the fact they are a transgender person. The only noticeable change, besides the visual appearance, is an increased level of happiness that invariably happens after a person "comes out."

Being a transgender person is a difficult life. It is not any more a self-choice than left-handedness or green eyes. It happened to them and regardless of how hard they tried, they could not change it. I don't think there is anyone who tried harder than I to discard transgenderism or at least be able to keep it buried. From personal experience, no one knows better than I, that no one and nothing can alter Gods will.

You men can ask yourself, can you stop being a man? And you women, can you stop being a woman? Of course not! It is your Biological Imperative. A transgender person's need to express their inner gender is also a Biological Imperative.

Most transgender individuals generally tend to be above average in intelligence and creativity. However, their life is not always, or even usually, a happy one. Your acceptance will help make a difficult life a little easier. Rejection, or even limited acceptance, will reinforce the negative aspects of the transgender person's life

If you think carefully, chances are the transgender person you are concerned with has exhibited some characteristics usually found in the transitioned to gender. These small "hints" are not done consciously. For example, an MtF may have always been more nurturing, patient, willing to listen, understanding, and less opinionated. An FtM may have always been interested in sports and cars. Feminine characteristics are part of a transgender woman's character, just as masculine interests are a part of a transgender man's interests. You need to keep the reasons you liked that person upper most in your mind if you want a relationship to survive.

If you accept the person and wish to maintain a good relationship, there are some ways you can demonstrate it. Use the adopted name. That is, the transitioning person usually selects a name appropriate for the transitioned to gender. Using it will seem strange at first, but trust me, you will get used to it, think nothing of it, and it will become second nature to you. Use the preferred pronouns. That will become automatic also. It does take time to overcome long term habits (i.e., addressing the person in the pretransitioned way), but these small steps are important, since they demonstrate you understand, respect, and take the coming out seriously (i.e., not as a whim).

If anger ever comes into play, never ever say "Madam" in anger to an FtM or "Sir" to an MtF. Using a discarded pronoun takes time to replace and it is natural to slip once in a while. However, a discarded pronoun used in anger will permanently convince the transgender person you never really accept her or him.

The transgender individual should tell family and close friends personally. However, your offer to help spread the word to any individual or group may be gratefully accepted. You should never take this task on yourself (i.e., outing someone) without prior approval. If you do, you may seriously hurt the transgender person and your relationship. One transgender woman wrote,

> I have found out that my daughter and her mother [ex-wife] have broken my trust, and heart, by going to my social worker and others, who I have never told,. I have gotten a few emails telling me they know, not being mean yet, but it should be up to me to tell others, on my terms. It is my life.

The above sentiment is not uncommon. The transgender person needs to be comfortable with particular people knowing their gender role change, before telling them.

Parents of a Transgender Person

Many parents, especially mothers, blame themselves. They think, did I really want a girl, rather than a boy? Since my son was not aggressive enough, was I being too punitive? Did I demonstrate too much Mom and not enough Dad?

The same applies to those born a girl label. Did I really want a boy? Was there not enough Mom?

It is amazing how a mother can come up with an abundance of reasons and the most imaginative reasons why she is responsible. She can always come up with more reasons to blame herself than seems possible. Fathers are not immune from self-blame.

You can be sure none of those things cause a gender variance in your child. Neither did anything else you or your spouse did or did not do. The evidence is a variation in gender occurred before birth. The gestation period is so long and complex that it is an easy target for a variation.

It may be natural for you to feel remorse regarding what you hoped your child would grow up to be or the relationship you visualized you would have when she or he grew up. You must keep mindful your child needs your help and protection, not the life you wanted for your child.

When dealing with your child, especially a young child, special care is needed because children are fragile beings. The most important thing for you to know about transgenderism is your child will most likely not grow out of it. Some children grow out of it, but that rarely occurs. You can drive the transgenderism underground for a while, where it will adversely affect your child, and can result in depression and even suicide.

Your unconditional love is the most important contribution to your transgender child's happiness and well-being. Your rejection of that part of your child is very damaging.

Learning of your child's gender conflict presents a problem for you. You need to decide what is important and be completely secure in what you decide. You need to be secure in your support and love and not be concerned with what others think or say.

Your child's love and devotion toward you is the same as it ever was before telling you there is a gender conflict. In fact, telling you indicates the child's love for you and trust in you. This is important regardless of your child's age. Your understanding and acceptance is important. If you have any reservations, your child will sense there is a problem with your acceptance of her or his true gender. It is best to be honest and openly discuss any reservations you have.

If you read this far into this book, you probably already know more than your child, and most people, about transgenderism. Therefore, once you are convinced you definitely have a transgender child, she or he may need help in telling friends and relatives. For the young child, this is an important aid.

If you think you have a transgender child or may have a transgender child, you need to learn and practice permissiveness. You can inflict serious harm by not allowing her or him to express their inner gender—their core identity. It is better to have a transgender child with all the complications it introduces, than one who finds no other way than living in the streets and/or possibly committing suicide. This is no exaggeration or dramatization. The proneness to depression and suicide is a plain fact that statistics verify over and over.

If your child is not a transgender child, your permissiveness will not push her or him in that direction.

To reinforce what this book taught you, you learned it was nothing you did or didn't do to cause your child's transgenderism. In CHAPTER 4—Transgender Research, you saw this phenomenon occurred during congenital development and is not due to how you raised your child.

Problems that you anticipated after others found out your child is a transgender child may not be as the big problems as you felt they would be. You may wonder what you should say to relatives, friends and neighbors. It may be a major problem to you, but if you refer to Chapters 2 and 3 you will realize the transgenderism is most likely caused by a human in-utero variation. In Chapter 4, you learned more than enough information to explain what transgenderism is to others. If your child is old enough, encourage her or him to do the explaining.

You and your child need to get professional help from a therapist experienced in transgender issues. To locate an experienced therapist, check with an LGBTQ Center near you. The center may also offer or refer you to groups of parents with similar children (e.g., PFLAG or SOFFA). These groups are frequently the best way to find a referral to an experienced therapist.

Regardless of your child's age, it is an incredibly brave act to have told you he or she is a transgender person. Be assured, it was far more difficult to tell you than it will be to tell a neighbor, relative, or your friends. Together, you and your child can solve any perceived problem.

Knowing your child is a transgender child, dictates that you allow her or him some space. That is, let the young child decide the future, including whether and how to dress in public. Actually, you do not have a choice since some outlet for your child's true gender will eventually find its place. To fight your child's inner sense of her or his gender is a battle you can't possibly win and shouldn't even try to win.

You may feel wanting to be a different gender is just a stage your child is going through. You hope she or he will eventually grow out of it. Your wish may come true, but I can assure you that, just as your actions or inactions didn't cause it, you won't play any part in making it go away. You can only have a temporary effect, regardless of any action you take. That temporary effect will not be helpful to your child. It is alright to tell your child her or his declaration of being a transgender person may be changed at any time, but staying that way is okay also.

The help of the clergy, a psychologist, a social worker, or anyone else to change your child will not have a permanent affect if the transgender brain says otherwise. Such counseling can be beneficial, but it won't change a person's true gender. If you seek professional counseling, be certain you use someone experienced with transgender people.

The offering of punishment, a reward, or anything else will not have a permanent effect if the transgender brain says otherwise. If your child is not a transgender child, this gender stuff is an experiment and will go away by itself. Time has proven your child is the only one qualified to ultimately make that decision.

You have previously seen (in CHAPTER 1—The Meaning of Sex, Gender, and Transgender, Comparison of Gender and Sex) how transgender children reacted to the expression of negativism. Older transgender people reacted similarly. The same thing applies to a daughter's desire to be a man as a son's desire to be a woman.

Negativism will merely drive your child underground—into the closet. Mental health professionals tell us how destructive that is. It leads to guilt, shame, fear, and self-hate. In the extreme, it leads to self-destruction. Even suicide is common.

Suicide is a real danger. In 1981, it was estimated 50% of transgender children less than 30 years old died, mostly from suicide. Your acceptance will help keep your daughter or son alive. The fact is, you are not losing a daughter/son and you did not do, or fail to do, anything that caused your child's transgenderism.

The situation may need your intervention. Your guidance is helpful, especially for young children. They need to be alerted to expect a negative reaction from others, if they exhibit behavior usually associated with the other gender. Alert her or him to the possible reaction of others and then let your child make the decision whether to go ahead or appear to be more conventional. If at some point she or he decides to keep "it" a secret from outsiders, make all other times open and free so the undesirable "closet affect" is minimized.

Of course, if you feel serious harm will come to your child, you may properly limit your young child's actions. You must understand you can only drive the desire to be the other sex underground, temporarily. Regardless of your child's age, your unconditional love and protection is your prime duty. Your love and acceptance is desperately needed by your child. Your acceptance and guidance is the best way to deal with your child's gender conflict or perceived conflict.

School is a place where your child may need your help and intervention. Her or his gender conflict may not be understood or taken "seriously" by teachers and school administrators. They may need to be educated. Your child may be told her or his gender identity is invalid. It is psychologically very destructive for your child to be told her or his gender identity is bad, invalid, or not real.

In addition, your child may have special needs regarding gym classes, the use of restrooms, and the use of locker rooms. In some cases and some locations, special arrangements may be necessary. Such things as arrangements for single occupancy toilets and dressing facilities may be necessary to retain the comfort of your child and the other students. A suitable restroom is something you must be sure to check into, since many transgender children injure their bladders and kidneys, when they avoid using what they see as the wrong toilet because they are denied their correct one.

You are the only one who can insure the special care your child needs is provided. One mother of a transgender child said,

> Because I will be with [name withheld] every step of the way just like I would be if he had cancer or any other devastating illness. I will not rest until I see my sweet . . . transformed into the girl that she so desires.

For more detailed help and information, you should consult the web site http://www.Transgenderlaw.org/resources/tlcschools.htm. It will lead to other web sites that may be helpful.

Susan Coates,[1] is a clinical psychologist who ran the Childhood Gender Identity Project at Roosevelt Hospital in New York, which is the largest gender treatment center for children in the U.S. She was asked what can happen in the offices of psychiatrists and psychologists all over the world to children who refuse to behave "like a girl" or "like a boy." She replied,

> You'd be shocked! You would be shocked, at what goes on even at this age level.

The evidence indicates Dr. Coates is not exaggerating. She fears these children will be referred to therapists who use intense behavior modification and/or electroshock and drug therapy. WPATH has declared those reparative therapy treatments are unethical. Thank God lobotomy, used in the past, is not practiced anymore. A recently published book, *Gender Shock*[2] exposes the abuses of those with gender identity dysphoria.

Adults can argue about the "labels" used to justify the abuse, but that does not alter the fact that youths are being abused. In recent years, the medical abuse of youths has actually become more prevalent. You are therefore, alerted to protect your child from such abuse.

President Obama called for an end to conversion therapies for Gay and Transgender Youths in a statement on April 8, 2015.

Spouses of a Transgender Person

The ultimate reaction of wives and husbands to the news their partner is a transgender person varies anywhere from total rejection to total acceptance. The two extremes exist in substantial numbers. However, as would be expected, observations indicate the typical reaction is somewhere between those two extremes for almost everyone.

For sure, you did not bargain for this when you married and have every right to feel betrayed and deceived. It would be nice for it to go away, but it won't. You were wronged, regardless of the reason, and this section will not dwell on the point, but will try to provide some information to help you make a wise decision regarding your marriage.

The fact that she or he told you is a sure sign your spouse can't contain his or her transgenderism any longer and is tired of hiding from you and deceiving you. Almost all transgender people fight their gender conflict and eventually lose. You may pressure her or him to put it away, but it will only be put underground again.

If you cannot accept your spouse's transgenderism or your spouse can't moderate it to some sort of compromise, you need to seek an amicable separation and/or divorce. This is unfortunate, but inevitable, in some cases. Don't fight it! It is a no win situation.

On the other hand, and most of the time, you love each other and would prefer to remain living together and maintain your relationship. This is possible and motivated by several reasons: you love each other, you both want to live with your children in a two parent home, either of you have a financial need to live together, and you both have an emotional dependence and a sociological reason for the marriage. Sometimes maintaining employment, family relations, friendships, some other factor, or a combination of these reason are enough to stay together.

Assuming you both would prefer to stay together, you need to arrive at a mutually acceptable arrangement. That is, you both must agree on some amount of transgender expression and your mutual tolerance of that amount of expression.

When you agree it is best to try to stay together, you need some facts. You need to understand what you are dealing with, so you can either get the result you want or at least tolerate it.

Some insight into why you were deceived may help you calm any anger because anger may be a natural reaction but it could lead you to making poor decisions. Nearly every married transgender person believed that by marrying those transgender feelings will go away or that marriage will help control the need to express it. Unfortunately, that just doesn't happen. One transgender woman put it this way,

> Like everyone else I thought that if I got married the problem would go away and like everyone else I was wrong. Every time we went to the store, I would stop and look at dresses and just melt wanting to slip into one.

Another reason for the deception was your transgender spouse loved you and felt even if you were married and he or she wasn't cured, transgenderism could at least be controlled and kept buried. Your spouse truly believed a control of transgenderism is just as good as a cure. She or he felt somehow the problem would work out. There was no need to bare the shame to your intended spouse. Believe it or not, it is true! I believed that either I was cured or marriage made transgenderism unimportant. Furthermore, my love for my wife would surly overpower what society then made me believe was an antisocial and perverted feeling. That may have helped me resist dressing and not even think about it.

For many transgender people the "freedom" that marriage gave us continued for a few years. Yes, you feel free for a while; however, your impossible need sooner or later will returns. We don't understand it is a biological need—a Biological Imperative. The need seems to grow as the years go by.

Many transgender people rationalize marrying because they saw no other alternative. The only way to have any kind of decent life is to get married–there simply was no other choice available. In any case, we thought we were the only one with these unnatural, perverted, and shameful feelings.

It is probably difficult to believe your life together will be far better if you help her or him stay out of the closet. Shame is destructive for anyone and shame, like anxiety, can lead to mental and physical problems. Rather than transgenderism being a wedge between the two of you, you should try to reach a compromise you both can feel comfortable with. The best solution for everyone concerned is if you both can tolerate some accommodation.

It sounds a little weird, but you will have a much happier mate around if you make it possible for her/him to express her/his inner gender sometimes. It is rare the expression can be suppressed for a long time even though there is a strong social taboo. One transgender woman said she didn't dress when she was young because all transvestites were thought to be homosexual, and she was overpowered by the homophobia she had drummed into her:

Hopefully, as poor as your transgender spouse's reasons may seem to you and considering your mutual love, your anger has been quelled a bit. You have been wronged, but you need to be calm so you can make a decision that is best for you in the long run. It may be very difficult, but you need to look at this from an objective point of view. The basic information you need to know is the intensity of the Effective Transgenderism. That is, the strength of your spouse's transgender needs. There may be a compromise regarding how transgenderism needs to be manifested. Since no one is able to determine the Effective Transgenderism directly, you must learn from the resulting effect. What is the level of transition your spouse wants to achieve?

Calmly discuss what your spouse ultimately wants. Is a transition and ultimately having a genital/breast altering operation desired or will a course of hormone therapy be satisfactory? Sometimes occasionally dressing as the other sex is enough. There are many cases where being the other sex is expressed only at home. Others need to be in public once a week, once a month, or once in a while.

Sometimes your spouse may have an urgent need to alter her or his body parts or do hormones. You need to determine what this is leading to so you can make a decision regarding your tolerance of it. If a compromise you both can live with is possible, go for it! Most transgender spouses love you and will make sacrifices to remain living with you, especially if children are involved. However, most transgender people usually can't stop their transgender needs all the time and forever. If they could, there would have been no reason to tell you.

The best case would be for your spouse not to be a transgender person and instead be like everyone else. The next best case is if you can accept your mate as is and your mate can be happy with some restrictions on the transgender needs for expression. Most transgender spouses can. Your tolerance and the end of the shame, deception, sneaking, and lying will yield a happier mate. Your demonstrating understanding and acceptance will be returned by greater devotion and love.

There is a definite hazard for you as a spouse. You need to understand the desire to express one's gender identity frequently grows with time. I have heard the fact stated over and over that the more you dress, the more you want to dress. One transgender women said,

> One thing I have noticed in myself is that the older I get the stronger my femme feelings are getting. I can see it happening. It's amazing.

"It is not really amazing. As time elapses and the transgender person exposes his or her inner gender more and more and without consequences, the sociological barriers of shame, guilt, and fear are slowly peeled away. As our moderating forces (i.e., shame, guilt, and fear) decrease, our transgenderism's strength seems to increase.

The good news is there is no guarantee the need of your spouse will grow beyond your tolerance or will grow at all in the future. If it does grow, it may remain within acceptable limits and you will be able to accommodate the new terms. You need to be prepared in case the exact compromise does not last forever. However, there is a good chance your tolerance and your spouse's needs remain compatible even if they both grow in the years ahead.

Transgender women make good husbands because their nature is so much like their wife's. Their nurturing nature exceeds that of most men. They understand your needs and are devoted to their children to a greater degree than the average man. Transgender men make good wives because they are more like you and have similar likes and dislikes. After a compromise is reached, a greater bond will likely develop since your spouse's frustration will be minimized and your tolerance level will be respected. A compromise may be worth it and the positive qualities you admired will likely expand.

Children With a Transgender Parent

Your transgender parent still loves you and is still the same person you loved. This new knowledge will make you closer to each other, since the lying and deception are over. A new level of honesty became possible with the disclosure. Your parent will always be your parent and the same good characteristics you tried to emulate all your life are still valid and good characteristics. Furthermore, those characteristics you emulated are still part of your parent.

You do not need to change because your parent told you about her or his true self. You should remain the same and your relationship should also remain the same. Neither you nor anyone else caused it to happen and there doesn't seem to be anything that can change it. You need to understand this phenomenon is something that happened before your parent was born and therefore had no control over it. It is certainly not anything you did. In fact it wasn't easy to keep it a secret for so long; however, the desire to be the other gender, the one God intended, became stronger and stronger until it could not be kept a secret any longer.

Your mother or father is still the same steady, reliable, loving, and protective force she or he always was. Your parent is still

224

a source of stability and security, if you allow it and you should allow it. This phenomenon is not hereditary, so it is not likely it will happen to you. If you have no strong desire to be the other sex, or like the other sex by now, the same thing is unlikely to happen to you.

This is not something meant to hurt you or your mother/father. It may seem like that. It may be difficult to understand, but this is not something your parent ever wanted. Most transgender people always hoped it would go away, but it doesn't. Your parents should come to an understanding or work out an agreement that eases the pain for everyone.

You can help your parents in this difficult time. If one of your parents speaks badly about the other, try to ignore it. If you can, say you love both of them and nothing will change that, so please don't tell me someone I love is bad. You can also tell each of them you love them.

Siblings and Relatives of a Transgender Person and Others

Siblings and, in some families relatives, provide an important support group for each other. This applies to close friends also. We all need to understand the transgender individual is the same person and has the same attitude, character, and personality she or he always had. She or he can still fill the same role that was always filled and can still continue to enrich your life. Attempt to get some level of understanding before you make a final decision regarding the news. It will prove worthwhile. A valuable relationship will be lost if you reject someone close to you who expresses a need to be the other gender. All that is needed is your acceptance by demonstrating your willingness to understand and support her or him.

If there is still something about this sex versus gender thing you need help with, seek it on your own or ask for help. Chances are the transgender individual knows more about transgenderism than you do and may be able to help you understand all its implications. In any case, get the answers you need to help you continue the relationship.

If you liked your relationship before this knowledge came to light, there is no reason it can't continue the same way. Your approval, or at least your acceptance, of the new information is important. You don't have to like it but the transgender person needs your love and support. You can demonstrate this by using the new name and the proper pronouns. The only proper name and pronouns are the ones the transgender person prefers. If you don't know how to address the person now, ask what is preferred. My young grandnephew asked me what he should call me, indicating that in spite of his lack of specific knowledge his sensitivity and intelligence told him how to react—what to ask. I replied, Uncle Joanne, of course!

Employers of a Transgender Person

One of the problems an employer may think he or she has with employing a transgender person is the thought that it will cause a disruption to the business. Actual experience with transgender individuals has shown this does not happen. This only happens if the employer or supervisor indicates his disapproval.

It has been shown transgender individuals generally are intelligent, creative, and valuable employees. Due to discrimination against the transgender community, there is a very high rate of unemployment and underemployment. Employing transgender people can be beneficial to any enterprise, since you will have a smart, creative, and dedicated employee to do a good job. Due to discrimination elsewhere, you will have a loyal employee as well.

Could you find a more desirable employee than one who is intelligent, creative, dedicated, hardworking, and loyal all wrapped up in one person? Well, you have a far greater chance when you employ a transgender woman or man.

Your only extra trouble is to see that your other employees do not disrupt the normal course of business by make things difficult for the transgender person. Once you demonstrate you will not tolerate maltreatment of anyone, even that task is quickly terminated.

CHAPTER 13, On the Bright Side

Previous chapters described many of the hardships and frustrations transgender people experience. However, being a transgender person is not all bad. There is also a bright side to being a transgender person. Some positive characteristics transgender people have are described in subsequent chapters. Furthermore, those that express their transgenderism, experience an emotion that is difficult to describe. I feel when a transgender person expresses her or his (inner) gender he or she helps to validate their identity—a confirmation of their very existence—and the subsequent emotional response is intensely euphoric.

An example was when I had my feminine name approved for my automobile driver's license and was waiting to pay for and receive my new license. I sat patiently in the waiting area with tears making their way down my checks. I realized I was crying only by the tactile sensation of the tears moving down my cheeks. Having my name on my license obviously meant more than overcoming one obstacle in my transition! It was a deeply emotional experience! It validated the truth of my existence! I felt my name is Joanne and now the government of the State of New York agreed and said, yes, your name is Joanne!

Unfortunately, some transgender individuals deny their transgenderism or fear to express it even in private. Unfortunately, they never experience the bright side and take the negatives with them to their grave.

Some transgender individuals who believe circumstances prevent their expressing their true gender manifest their frustration in anger. A friend—a transgender woman—told me that after she came out as a crossdresser and was freer to express her true gender, her wife pointed out the change in her personality and attitude. She went from a bitter angry person to a more pleasant and likable person. I have had several people tell me how they were not a nice person before they came out and now feel they are a much nicer person.

A common thing divorced friends tell me was their divorce had nothing to do with their transgenderism. I believe the real reason for some of those divorces *was* transgenderism. Their frustration of not expressing their gender, or not expressing it enough, resulted in anger and the angry behavior was the only obvious reason for alienating their spouse.

The transgender people I know find a way to express their inner sex. The form, frequency, or duration of expressing their gender is immaterial to the euphoric feeling they have during the time of that expression. The taste of the bright side is so sweet—so wonderful—it has a high priority in their life. On the other hand, many transgender people cast off the negative aspects of transgenderism and enjoy the bright side from the time they start living as their true inner sex all the time.

Perhaps the most interesting transgender phenomenon involves how individual crossdressers use ingenuity and creativity to find ways to express their transgenderism, regardless of how short or long the time they experience it.

Talent

The developmental process, in the womb, that made us a transgender person seems to have given us at least 3 gifts. In her life story on the Internet, Jennifer Diane Reitz (see CHAPTER 1, Endnote 16) without referring to the source mentions transgender people are generally more intelligent and creative than the average person. She said transgender people score about 30 points higher on intelligence tests than the average person (transgender average IQ = 130 compared to an IQ of 100 for the average person). A disproportionate number of transgender people test at the genius level (i.e., IQ = over 140). From my observations, this seems to be generally true.

An investigation of intellectual capacity (Raven's test) was performed and reported in The Journal of Sex Research.[1] The study hypothesized that disorders in the supply of steroid hormones, acting in the formative period of hypothalamus and sexual development, have a tendency to increase the mental level of the subjects. This seems to lend some validity to the statement made by Ms. Reitz.

It is generally theorized that the alteration of the brain in the womb is responsible. Some researchers claim some benefit accrues at the time of brain development because a little is taken from the female and a little from the male. My feeling is that may sound good only when you are searching for a reason.

The theory continues with our brains and bodies gain from having been "bathed" in and altered by the hormones of both sexes. We appear to retain our visible youthfulness where others wrinkle years earlier. I believe that is true in my case.

There may be validity that we possess neural advantages "taken" from both sexes. For example, some of us have the language advantages of the stereotypical feminine brain and the spatial abilities of the stereotypical masculine brain, all at the same time.

As a group, transgender people are said to be more creative than the average person. There are a high proportion of transgender people employed in computer science, astronomy, physical science, biology, and other scientific fields than the general population. The arts also have a larger than average number of transgender people, (i.e., musicians, artists, and writers). In general, transgender people tend to follow complex and intellectual fields of work and play.

Am I rationalizing when I see nature trying to compensate somewhat for all the difficulties and hardships experienced by transgender people? Transgender persons' creativity is fortunate in any event because transgender people need those talents to help them exploit their needs, maintain their secret, and survive.

In addition, we frequently experience benefits in addition to generally being more intelligent and creative than the general population. Women suffer greatly from the pain of childbirth and return to give birth again, due to their pressing need for motherhood and the resultant joy a child brings to their life. Similarly, transgender women and men develop a high level of courage and determination to obtain their objective—womanhood or manhood—because it is so pressing a need within them. They instinctively know joy awaits them at the end of their journey.

Emotion

Transgender women also accrue some of the advantages women have over men. Women and open transgender women have the emotional freedom to cry at happiness, sadness, or for any reason they want, anytime they want (so there!). We have even been known to cry for no apparent reason at all, and that is also okay. As a woman, a transgender woman can express emotion and hug anyone, any time, and for any reason she decides is appropriate. The freedom to release one's emotion is a benefit to any individual's mental health.

On the other hand, transgender men shake away the male dominance that have plagued women since prehistoric times. People listen to their views attentively and take them more seriously. Older transgender men feel an extra measure of freedom because they were never comfortable playing the butch lesbian everyone believed they were.

In general, transgender people do not have to be silent in conversation because they might inadvertently reveal the dark secret of their transgenderism. Before becoming open, they created a lie by converting their experiences to sound gender "appropriate." In this sense, after a transgender person comes out, she or he can finally live honestly and without shame. Once shame is overcome, guilt evaporates, and there is also no need to feel embarrassed. Freedom accrues and results in happiness, which spills into mental health!

Furthermore, transgender people have the distinct advantage of experiencing actually being both a male and a female as they interface with general society. Some of these experiences occur in tandem and some simultaneously. The mix of the two genders seems to equal more than their sum in many ways. If nothing else, our lives are surely not mundane. Whether you want it or not, it is an adventurous life. It is adventurous in more ways than merely being overpowered by both male and female hormones. I was happy to learn Jennifer Reitz' story says it is not unusual to possess both male aptitudes (e.g., for mathematics) and the female aptitudes (e.g., for language).

Aptitudes are one of the factors that confused me regarding what I really am. Most transgender women and men have many aptitudes both typically feminine and masculine. I am good with numbers, mechanical things, carpentry, plumbing, electrical, tile work, mechanics, and generally fixing things. On the other hand, I also have some typically feminine attributes including a flair for colors, fashion, decorating, housekeeping, and makeup art. Most transgender men also have many aptitudes typically associated with both women and men. If some of these aptitudes are culturally based, the interest in them is associated with the other sex.

In addition to our visible youthfulness for years longer, makeup and hairstyle help transgender women more than they admit. The good grooming habits of women do not hurt either sex one bit. It is a big plus.

Achieving a Special Happiness

For some of us, transitioning is the result of discovering we were right. We knew all along something was different. We didn't always know what it was, but we simply were not like everyone else or even what anyone expected of us. It was ultraliberating to find out what that something was and we had a reason to be different than the other kids—different from the women or men, as the case may be.

I frequently hear there is a pot of gold at the end of the rainbow (i.e., there is happiness when you achieve your goal of being a woman or being a man). The pot of gold is a little different for each transgender person, but it is achievable in spite of the difficulties of life up to that point. The attainment of one's individual brand of womanhood or manhood is achieved by overcoming all odds. It is an uphill battle with frequent feelings of guilt, shame, frustration, hardship, disappointment, fear, and embarrassment, and when one achieves what was thought to be possible only in a fantasy, a level of joy is experienced that also was believed to not exist. These negative feelings were generated by sexism!

The trip is difficult and often a sad one, but the joy at the end of the journey is intense in some important aspects. You can finally be open about yourself. The lying and hiding are over! You are liberated! You feel a new level of confidence, are happy, and free of shame, fear, guilt, and embarrassment. You feel an unexplainable contentment, and wonder why you ever thought your transgenderism was a curse.

Some transgender individuals have the clear goal of transitioning to include sex reassignment. They say they feel they will never be happy until they have the operation. They closely fit into the above paragraph. Their actual happiness will not be totally realized until a time after they achieve their ultimate goal.

Unfortunately, not all transgender individuals are happy after they have an operation (i.e., bottom or top). A small percentage of transsexual women, an estimate is about one percent, are unhappy after reaching their goal. My observations are their unhappiness involves discrimination that caused the loss of relationships and a feeling of isolation, rather than unhappiness regarding a change caused by an operation.

I talk to many transgender women and they do not feel joy. Most seem to express contentment and happiness. Many are happy with themselves, but unhappy because their loved ones became alienated during the transition process. I can honestly say I am happier than I have ever been and that is saying a lot because I was always generally a happy person. I previously didn't imagine there could be a higher level of happiness, but I was wrong.

Many transgender women arrived at their brand of womanhood the way I did—one step at a time. Personally, that was because I did not believe another step was possible, so each step was an ultimate goal. Therefore, I was happy in the sense that I was closer to something every woman experiences. I know I am not alone in this. This one step attitude resulted in us being better off than those with a far reaching ultimate goal because we experience a high level of happiness several times, whereas those reaching for their ultimate goal are dissatisfied until their last step is achieved. In our one-step-at-a-time approach, we continue to seek another "woman thing" until we feel satisfied with our womanhood and have no need to go further. We seek our own brand and not someone else's concept of being a woman.

As stated, a plan to this point in my life did not exist. I was driven to take the next step deeper into the waters of womanhood after each preceding step was completed. For example, my first step was when I started to dress as a woman in public. My next step was to have my ears pierced. Once that was accomplished, in spite of what I said about hormones, I started to take them. There were several other steps, taken one at a time, until the final one when I said I wouldn't tell anyone about being a transgender woman unless they had a need to know. Those needing to know included my doctor and my therapist, of course. I finally realized my children, friends, and relatives needed to know, simply because I needed them to know! I needed to share my secret and stop hiding. It was as simple as that! Therefore, I eventually told everyone. I now understand my ultimate preconscious goal was to put deception and hiding away for good. Most important to my health, I eradicated guilt and shame by substituting honesty and pride.

My step-by-step "method" of transitioning is probably the most satisfying approach. I experienced joy after each step. I was happy when my ears were pierced, when I had long nails, and every other step along the way. Those who knew what their ultimate goal was from the beginning did not see the level of joy I experienced many times until their transition was completed. There may have been a sense of accomplishment after each step, but the rush to the next step didn't leave much time to feel the joy of happiness between steps.

It is true, I now have a level of joy that comes from simply being who I really am. You feel good being able to be yourself. The general population does not experience this kind of joy because they don't know what it's like to have a core secret—a gender identity that is different from their physical sex. They never experienced the shame and subsequent need to conceal a large part of their life. They never had the need to sneak, hide, and lie to express their femininity or masculinity because their gender and sex were aligned. They never felt different from their facade and never felt obligated to hide their core feelings. They never felt the need to avoid expressing their true nature. The nature that was different from what they were supposed to be. The behavior of transgender individuals stem from trying to find the congruency between their sex label and their gender, and to be as close to whole as possible. That is the only real way to possibly live a "normal" life.

CHAPTER 14, A Personal Theory of Transgenderism

After 4 years of thinking seriously about and intensely researching the transgender phenomenon on a full time basis, I have a somewhat educated view of the subject; however, since many "facts" in this field are simply clues, probability, and not known as fact, a great deal is based on theory. By its very nature, every theory has an element of subjectivity because it boils down to a degree of speculation. It is the speculation element that definitely qualifies me to expound on a personal theory just as much as all the distinguished professors and researchers.

I am not claiming anything very radical in explaining my beliefs regarding transgenderism. I build on what has been learned and previously stated, fill in some cracks, and expand on some areas that are a bit neglected. Simply put, I believe my interpretation of what is known and theorized, my observation of how so many transgender women and transgender men behave, and my independent research and analysis of what transgender people say when expressing their personal feelings and experiences provides a novel way of putting the entire story together.

Thus, this chapter begins with a summary of previously stated knowledge and theories as seen through my eyes. The chapter explains my view of transgender research and what it means up to this point from the womb to adult behavior. All this leads up to a personal theory that comes to a somewhat radical conclusion that evolved in my mind mostly from observation.

How Transgender Babies Happen

How a transgender baby happens is quite ordinary and the same as any other baby. All babies develop in the mother's womb following a precise process. They follow what one of my physiology teachers quoted that became burned in my memory, "Ontogeny recapitulates phylogeny" (i.e., fetal development follows the evolutionary development of the species). The interest in the relationship between ontogeny and phylogeny extends back to the nineteenth century. Since then, Darwin's "Evolutionary Developmental Biology" and the contemporary field of Evo-Devo (i.e., a branch of biology investigating the links between evolution and the development of different organisms) have gained impetus from the discovery that genes regulate embryonic development.

Many subsequent supporting ideas, altering ideas, and opposing ideas exist. Regardless of the label, much more is known today about the development of the embryo and fetus.

In a sense, all babies are at the "mercy" of, and subject to, the actions and interactions of inherited genes, DNA, and chromosomes. They engage in a complex and predetermined process in which they are programmed to communicate with each other and within themselves. For example, a gene (i.e., SRY gene = Sex-determining region Y gene) signals the release of testosterone in a boy baby and R-Spondin 1 is thought to play a part in signaling the release of estrogen in a girl baby.

The action and interaction of genes frequently depends on chemicals as a communicating medium. The variability of the chemicals' quantity, potency, and the timing of their release provide ample opportunity to cause a variation in the baby's developmental process and thus influence the expression of one or a combination of genes in the baby. Add to this other processes and many chains of processes plus environmental influences on the fetus and mother and you begin to understand the resulting variations in a gene's action or variations in the gene itself, at any point in the fetus' development. Variations in the baby not only can occur, but are likely to occur.

Embryonic development during the gestation period is so lengthy, so involved, and so complex that it is actually an easy target for producing variations from the intended outcome. That is, no variation from exactly what the genes, DNA, and chromosomes originally intended rarely, if ever, happens in a baby. In fact, all babies have some variation(s) from the prescribed outcome. Variations from the usual is what evolutionists attribute to evolution. Some of these novel features that are a manifestation of one or a combination of genetic variations "survive" and can continue through many generations and become the basis for establishing a new feature or characteristic in our species.

Dr. Milton Diamond stated this with other words when discussing the birth variation in transgenderism specifically as follows:

> Differences from the usual course of development are not seen as "things gone wrong" or errors of development but as to-be-expected occasional variations due to chance interaction of all the variables involved.

Many kinds of genetic variations may occur. Most of them result in a physical and socially acceptable characteristic. The major difference of the variation we call transgenderism from most other variations is that transgenderism does not result in a socially acceptable deviation.

Categories of In Utero Variations

I have defined each of these mental and physical variations into one of three broad categories:

Category 1—Includes variations that involve an unusual appearance, an illness, and/or an abnormal formation of a body part(s). They are often, but not always, detected early. However, they are dealt with medically when they are discovered or when the timing is right for corrective action.

Category 2—Comprises of variations that occur frequently. Most, if not all, babies have one or more of them. Most of these variations are not very important to the functioning, health, or appearance of the baby and are either ignored or go unnoticed at birth. Even in later life they are not noticeable or considered to be of little consequence by the parents or the child. Thus, they rarely are subject to corrective action of any kind.

Category 3—Contains variations that are not apparent at birth, but are manifested or noticed only later in life. They involve systemic problems that may lead to a "condition" or illness later in life (e.g., heart disease); as well as psychological, social, and behavioral problems. Some of them are significant and some are not. Where a corrective remedy is known, it may be taken or not taken.

All, or nearly all, babies fit into one or more of the above categories. The transgender baby is no different. Regardless of fitting into other categories, the transgender baby fits into Category 3. That is, a variation occurs which leads the brain to deviate from the "intended" course during its development. The baby is born with the potential to feel that it is a different gender than the sex the doctor observed and wrote on the birth certificate. Of course, the infant has no concept of female and male until it grows older. The parents and doctors have no idea there is a gender conflict issue, since at birth and early in life there isn't any visible or other means of detecting it.

Total Transgender Variations

It is likely that the occurrence of transgenderism is the result of a misreading of a gene's signal or an untimely signal, which prevents an exposure to a needed hormone or allows an exposure to an amount of the hormone of the other sex, when the correct one should be doing its job (i.e., estrogen when testosterone is usually called for or testosterone when estrogen is needed). This "wrong" hormone, or inappropriate hormone, needs to be present at a precise moment and only in minute quantities to impact the result. Considering that some of both male and female hormones are produced in organs other than the ovaries and testes of the baby and the mother, the "wrong" hormone influence seems a bit more likely. Also, it is possible the required hormone does not appear at the precise moment it is needed or in the quantity and/or strength required for the usual development of the baby. Another possibility is the baby does not absorb the required hormone or enough of the required hormone for its usual development. This issue remains to be settled by research in the future.

Regardless of how gender is implanted in the brain, all babies are born with an intuitive sense of their gender. At some point in their development they observe other children are not all alike. They see 2 kinds of children—boys and girls. Of the 2 choices they identify with either the boys or the girls. Each baby knows its gender intuitively. It is not a decision or a choice—it's automatic! Some baby's genitals match their gender and some do not. Those whose sense of their gender does not match their genitals are called transgender babies.

All transgender babies, regardless of their sex, are born with a varying intensity of transgenderism; however, all transgender babies feel and/or believe they are the sex their brain says they are—the one with which they identify when they see and distinguish between children's sex.. Of course, initially babies have no concept of gender or what sex organs their body has. For the baby, it is an unimportant detail she or he will discover later in life.

Perhaps all babies have an element of transgenderism; however, in most babies, if an element of transgenderism exists, the transgender intensity is so low that they accept the gender they are told they are or the gender to which they hear they are referred.

Although all transgender girl and boy babies initially think they are, in fact, the other sex, at some later point in their lives, they find out their bodies do not resemble the sex they know they are. This startling fact is greeted with one of two basic reactions. Some think, "Why did I get the wrong body?" However, the majority accept the fact they are actually not what they identified with, but are what their body and everyone says they are. These "realists" feel they want to be the sex they originally thought they were, but accept they are what their body, parents, and everyone they come in contact with say they are.

The intensity of transgenderism at birth depends on the variability of the inborn transgenderism itself and may be impacted by other inborn characteristics. These other characteristics modify the implanted transgenderism. They can intensify or dampen the inherent transgenderism prior to birth.

There are post birth factors that affect the effective intensity of transgenderism. In addition to the inborn transgenderism (the nature part of transgenderism), nurture (the socialization factors) also adds to or subtract from the transgender intensity that was present at birth.

Soon after birth, the child receives signals from the parents that reinforce or moderate the way the child reacts to the in-utero implanted transgenderism. The parents' facial expressions and tone of voice are some of the communications that take place even before the child is verbal. When the child becomes verbal, the words themselves have an added effect.

Most parents rarely directly tell a child it is a boy or a girl. They take the child's sex for granted and see no reason to go out of their way to tell them what sex they are. Surely, the child already knows that. It seems so obvious!

The animal kingdom reinforces the fact that the child automatically knows its gender. Animals are not told their gender, they automatically assume the role of their gender. No one tells a bull it is a male. Even castrated bulls (steers) prove gender is inborn, when they mount cows in a vain attempt to fulfill their male role. No one tells your cat or dog its gender. They know it from somewhere inside like all mammals do.

Parents frequently give indirect signals to their child. Just the other day I heard parents, in a form of praise or approval, say to a pretoddler, "That's a good girl!" When I was tiny did I heard, "That's a good boy!" over and over?

Sometimes when the child's and the parent's gender concept differs, the parent may try to resolve the conflict by informing the child of its sex. Sometimes the child first learns its gender is different from what others say it is doesn't happen until the child dresses as the other sex, expresses a desire to dress as the other sex, wants to play house assuming the role of the other sex, or wants a Barbie or G.I. Joe doll that is sex inappropriate. Sometimes the transgenderism is not noticeable until there is a conflict outside the home. The outside conflict can occur when there is interaction with other children or an incident in school, when the child lines up with the "wrong" sex or uses the "wrong" toilet.

There are two groups of transgender kids that develop early in life. The children who feel they have the wrong body and insist they be treated as the gender they feel they really are. The rest of the transgender children, those who accept the fact that their gender is what their body and society insists they are. This second group simply want to be the other gender.

The inborn implanting of transgenderism, regarding both the desire to be the other sex and the belief they are the other sex, stems from the same phenomenon. Which group you belong to usually depends on how far back your memory goes (see Appendix V, Category Versus Age of Transgender Realization). The difference between the two groups may also involve the Effective Transgenderism or other imposing facts.

Both nature, the strength of inborn transgenderism with the experiences that modify it, influence a transgender child's future action to reconcile the gender conflict. It is incorrect to believe it is nature versus nurture. Clearly, it is nurture applied to the inborn transgenderism (nature), that governs the individual's reaction. He or she will either do nothing, at one extreme, or rush to the operating table for a genital operation, facial surgery, breast augmentation or removal, and liposuction to rearrange body fat without delay and at the other extreme. It is no surprise that nearly all transgender individuals react somewhere between the two extremes. Exactly where one lands depends on your personal desire/need, financial ability, or other circumstance (e.g., married or single).

The modifying effect of the nurture variable mixed with the nature variable accounts for the difference between what we call crossdressers and transsexuals. Transgenderism accounts for everyone in between the extremes and everything lateral.

To verify this, simply ask transsexuals if they ever could have been considered by others as a crossdresser and most say yes. I have noted a majority of married men who are self-identified as crossdressers frequently become transsexuals after a divorce or separation.

Although some researchers feel there are as many female-to-male transgender individuals as male-to-female, I believe transgender women have a slight edge in number over transgender men. The imbalance of MtF verses the fewer FtM babies is the result of either one or both of two factors present as the fetus develops. The first factor is polluting chemicals. In CHAPTER 4—Transgender Research, The Effect of Foreign Substances, it was indicated there are far more polluting chemicals that feminize the male brain than there are ones that masculinize the female brain. The second factor is the fact that the mother carries the fetus through its development and the mother herself has both testosterone and estrogen in her body; however, estrogen predominates. Thus, there is more likely an unplanned influence of estrogen, which can feminize parts of the brain, and less likely the influence of testosterone, which causes a more masculine brain in the "female.".

I feel there is an imbalance between MtF and FtM, but not as great as previously believed. A factor that gives the perception of a far greater number of MtFs than FtMs is that FtMs pass and assimilate far better than MtFs. I was at an advocate training conference where I thought I recognized an FtM which he voluntarily confirmed. On the last day, I learned of three more FtM attendees whom I thought were born male, based on their appearance, voice, and behavior.

Dressing Compulsion

The imperative need to dress as the other sex applies equally to transgender girls and boys. However, transgender boys do not have as difficult a time with dressing because it is far more socially acceptable for a female to be seen buying and wearing male type clothes (e.g., jeans) than it is for a male to be seen wearing typically female clothes (e.g., a skirt). Social acceptance of the attire transgender boys/men wear minimizes the difficulty of a transgender boy/man dressing as a boy/man. I once heard a young girl proudly say to another young girl she bought her jeans in the men's department. She said, "They fit so much better." I will never hear boys talk that way about girls' clothes. The perceived low numbers of transgender boys/men is due to their more natural blending into society.

I am not trivializing the torment, difficulties, and agony a transgender man faces because it is difficult; however, dressing like the gender you are or want to be is definitely less of an issue— definitely a considerably lower level of shame. However, it is far more difficult to hide breasts than it is to put on breast forms. It is also agonizing for a transgender man to be made to wear a dress. Never-the-less, a woman wearing jeans, a rugged flannel shirt, and heavy shoes attracts little or no attention. On the other hand, a man wearing heels and a dress will not make it 20 feet before hearing laughter.

The transgender girl learns early in life the feeling you are a girl or want to be a girl and especially dressing like one is not acceptable by others. Furthermore, they learn early in life that this desire needs to be kept a closely guarded secret. They learn this when they find society insists their sex is different from what they believe it is.

The most puzzling issue is why must transgender girls/women dress in feminine clothes even after they know it can lead to embarrassment and shame? Transgender boys/men must dress in masculine clothes even though it will eventually draw nasty remarks, snickering, giggles, and other forms of "flack." They all have a strong urge and an ever present need to "dress." Why? Why can't they feel like the gender they identify with without dressing that way? The answer seems basic, they want to be a girl or a boy, but their body and society dictates they can't be one, so they look for ways to be like their true gender. Since most clothes are identified with a sex and covers most of the body, clothes can transforms you to look like the other sex—to be as close as possible to the other sex.

Early on, transgender children are curious about how they would look if they really were allowed to be a girl or a boy. They want to wear the appropriate cloths because in their mind that is their only feasible path to being close to their true gender.

They wonder what they would look like if they put girl's clothes on and pretend they are a girl. How would it feel? Perhaps they got caught "dressing" a long time ago when they tried on a girl's garment. At that time, they were told boys don't do that, it was bad to do, and they should never do it again. So, some resorted to wrapping a towel around themselves after a shower to resemble a skirt. Even that was nice and felt better. They continually want to add more and more reality to their "being a girl." Wrapping a towel around after a shower and remaining that way for a while is nice, but not good enough for very long. They want the real thing, so they translate "never do it" to "never do it, if you might get caught."

They want to see how they would look as a girl. One girl wrote,

> I had some powerful experiences . . . that made me . . . wonder about this inner woman. What would she look like? Would she be beautiful? Finally, after a year or so of wondering, I ordered some pretty women's under things and breast forms and some makeup. Just to take a picture I told myself. Just to see. . . .

Many younger transgender girls don't have any girl clothes or the ability to buy any, so they turn to their only source, Mom's clothes (if they have an older sister, her clothes are even better). They find the right time and method to get something on just to see how it looks. They do this again and again and add a few more touches along the way to be more realistic. One girl wrote,

> The more I dress, the further I want to go with more femininity more often. . . .

Eventually, transgender people don't do it out of curiosity or even to want the feeling and the look any more. They now start dressing whenever there is an opportunity of not getting caught. The desire grows from a curiosity to a conditioned response—the opportunity to dress "automatically" results in dressing. In the process, dressing advances to what approaches a complete outfit including makeup and long hair. The more they dress, the more they want to dress. It is a biological necessity that drives them. It is like an instinct. Like salmon swimming against strong currents to reach their spawning place up-stream.

Acquiring feminine clothes is a major problem transgender girls face that transgender boys find less difficult. Just imagine a boy walking into a store and declaring he wants to buy his sister a dress.

"Oh, she is about my size." How about, "My mother sent me to buy her a bra?" Who would ever believe that?

We think of present society as being very permissive; however, it is not permissive when it comes to a male wearing a feminine garment. Transgender girls/women are very careful. In fact, some are paranoid about hiding their true gender because the fear of exposure is so great it is frequently irrational. In the face of their fear, they dress anyhow, which reinforces the thought that dressing becomes an addiction—certainly at least a compulsion. They want to do it more and more. Emails I received illustrate how some transgender girls felt.

> You should go out dressed once you do you'll always want to go out.

> The first time is hard but once you go out there's no stopping you.

> Once I went out dressed I had to keep going out I couldn't get enough of it. The more I dress the more I want to dress.

They spend time planning and scheming on how to "dress" once again, without being exposed to all those who insist boys must not wear any feminine garment. Sometimes this is done at the expense of other important duties. It becomes like an addiction.

When they are young, they would like to be a girl when their parents, siblings, or friends are present until it becomes clear no one wants to see them that way. Then they must settle for seeing themselves (dressed) as a female in a mirror. When "dressed," they can't pass a mirror without at least glancing at themselves. Later, most of them want to be seen by others as a woman. They want to be seen in public because that will make them more like all the other women. In fact, many are driven to be seen in public.

Next, they want to do the different things women do. It is not a whim or anything other than a basic core need to be like all woman. In their efforts to be as much like a woman as possible, transgender women are continually faced with conflicts and frustration.

After venturing out in public, transgender girls want to have their ears pierced, but how will they explain that? If they grow their nails longer, what will people say? They need to take hormones to feel like and look more like other women, but how can they do that without someone noticing they're growing breasts and finding out? Transgender boys want to get rid of their breasts, but people will notice. They want to feel more like a boy and take hormones but how will they explain the beard they grow on them and the deeper voice it gives them.

At every step, they in effect ask themselves, "Will that out me, expose my secret?" They tend to become more and more frustrated, withdrawn, and paranoid because they are terrified they will be discovered and shamed or made to feel diminished.

Some transgender men, who can overcome the deep-rooted homosexual taboo, seek validation of their masculinity by dating a woman. They want more and more of what a man experiences because they still want to be like everyone else—like every other man. Transgender women are in a similar situation and they similarly seek validation of their femininity by dating a man. Both continually experience an increase of the shame, guilt, and anxiety, but they are stuck with the situation. They can't let anyone know their secret and yet they can't keep from being their true selves.

You either continue living a frustrated life with the necessary deception or you come out of the closet. Often, it is some of each because you can't seem to come out completely. Sometimes you keep your transgenderism from your parents, an employer, or others.

It is curious that after a transgender woman transitions, wearing a skirt frequently becomes less important. Two factors are involved in this change. Before transitioning, her need to look as feminine as possible dictated that she dress as the women she envied when she was young—a period when women always wore a skirt and heels. She no longer needs a skirt or a dress to feel like a woman, she is one! Another pertinent reason for a decreased interest in skirts is because today women wear pants most of the time. Now that she lives as a woman, she may still like skirts but pants make you more like other women. Younger transgender women do not seem to have the same need to wear a skirt because the women they envied and emulate wear pants most of the time. Therefore, their mode of dress looks more androgynous.

Transgender men have a different experience. The acquisition of pants and other masculine clothes is easy by comparison. There is no shame involved in obtaining boys clothes, avoiding makeup, doing boy things, and hanging out with the boys. At first there is no stigma. Society's attitude is "she" is a tomboy and tomboys will grow out of it when "she" meets "her" first boyfriend.

As "she" grows older, "she" experiences many difficulties similar to those of transgender women. People think "she" must be a lesbian. Even "she" may believe "she" is a lesbian, but even if "she" knows "she's" not a lesbian that is the only place "she" can fit. There is some tolerance due to less shame applied by society, but the large dose of isolation accrued is depressing. "She" needs to do guy things, but the boys don't want to hang around with a girl. Even the girls are uncomfortable with "her" around. Adopting a female persona would be a saving grace, but only some can adopt one successfully. "She" may be half way to adulthood before the realization hits. "She" is no she at all. Transgender man is the correct description. Becoming aware of that is liberating in itself, since he never really thought he was a lesbian. He had to fit in somewhere and lesbian was the closest and only thing he knew of at the time.

Moderating Forces

How the transgender phenomenon is dealt with varies widely by individual transgender people. Their needs are dealt with according to their individual mix of nature and nurture. Some people contain their desires completely and merely wish they could be the other sex. In spite of the frustrations, a great many transgender people take their secret gender issue to the grave. Others have a such a strong need to express their gender that they walk away from their past, consequences be damned, in pursuit of their true gender and seem to never look back. It seems like they do not care about anything or anyone outside of becoming who they are.

Callousness is not always the reason for walking away with little or no consideration of others. Sometime the separation from your past is so difficult that looking back would make transitioning impossible. However, separating from the past is so pressing a need that you don't dare look back! The only way to overcome the difficulty is to force the situation so you can get the transition ball rolling. It is like pushing a stalled car. It is very difficult to start it going but once you start it rolling, it's relatively easy to keep it moving.

The transgender "imprint" and the effect of other implanted factors add to and subtract from the basic inborn transgender feelings. This alone is a substantial reason for a highly variable reaction to one's transgender feeling—transgender strength or intensity, so to speak. However, the environmental influence, the socialization factor, is also a major influence. Your circumstances are such that it is sometimes difficult to give up for an unknown life..

The socialization factor plus the "transgender strength" yields the gender behavior of the transgender person. It is the classic nature and nurture combination seen in many aspects of our makeup. The need to be as much a woman or man as possible is tempered by several considerations that affect the transgender conflict. Transgenderism is not like much of the world thinks of it. It is not like an on/off switch—either you are or you aren't—with only two choices. It is more like the potentiometer (i.e., a volume control), which is completely variable. I call the final product of nature plus nurture, the Effective Transgenderism.

Of course, the inborn transgender strength fundamentally remains the same after birth; however, the nurture component is subject to change, resulting in a variable Effective Transgenderism.

Many transgender people have no idea they can have a life as the sex with which they identify. They live in the persona they adopted so they can appear to be like everyone else. They believe fitting in is the only choice. Many find a woman or a man they like and later love. They subsequently marry and have children. That frequently determines their future.

For those with a weak Effective Transgenderism and can control their transgender needs, that works well. Others, with a stronger Effective Transgenderism either live a double life or eventually "come out." Frequently, people in their past life isolates them from their past.

The distress caused by wanting to express their inner gender, and still maintain the present persona and life is frustrating. They do not want to jeopardize their marriage, possible contact with their children, employment, and simply put, they don't want to give up their lifetime investment in their present lifestyle. Women, who are usually favored in child custody cases, are at high risk of losing custody of them when their transgenderism is revealed to the court. Also, they do not want to give up their book club, bridge game, bowling, golf, or whatever. Their friends are an important part of their lives and social activities, and they fear losing them to the unknown life that would follow exposure.

Most Transgender people live in fear of discovery because they believe the discovery may jeopardize their relations with their marriage partner or are too ashamed to face their family, relatives, friends, and even casual acquaintances. The conflict grows and grows. The guilt gets stronger and stronger. The frustration grows into depression in some of us. Depression can and too often does lead to suicide. However, in spite of the frustrations, a great many transgender people take their secret gender issue to the grave because of the combination of both issues—commitments to their present life and/or the belief there is no good alternative.

What some transgender individuals value as a high cost seems to be of little consequence to others, but the present life is a factor, at some level and intensity, in everyone.

There are some who face their conflict and out themselves while trying to maintain their established relationships. They meet this with varying degrees of acceptance in their lives. Others go ahead with a transition with little thought of leaving their past life behind. In fact, some don't even want to remember any part of their past life.

Some reach a compromise with their family. They are allowed something that pacifies their need to express their inner gender, but within limits. In most cases, they lead a double life. That is, they keep their needed transgender expression strictly separate from their public life. Still others never get married and transitioning is more likely because they have fewer obligations and commitments.

The actual path taken is affected by a combination of the strength of the Effective Transgenderism, the people you interface with, the employment constraints, and the uncertain direction guilt and shame push you toward.

Another Transgender Theory

I believe everyone is born with an element of transgenderism. I feel we will eventually learn that transgenderism is highly variable and it occurs naturally in everyone. That is, everyone has transgenderism to some degree of intensity. The variable strength of transgenderism at birth, plus the later effect of socialization, results is an Effective Transgenderism varying anywhere from virtually zero (strong modifying influence) to virtually full strength (little or no modifying influence).

After birth, people begin to conform to either the female or male stereotype. I categorize the different strengths and resulting behaviors as follows:

Category 1, Very Low. This category has a strength varying from virtually zero to so weak that social taboos prevent any conscious thought of transgenderism.

Category 2, Low. People in this category have some transgender leanings, but never act on them. They may experiment once at Halloween or another occasion, but generally avoid any repeated expression of the other sex. Basically, their homophobia and/or transphobia far outweigh any foreseeable benefit.

Category 3, Medium. Those with a medium strength of Effective Transgenderism allow the social taboo to make them conform to their birth assigned sex publically. However, they dress in private and rarely venture in public. If on the rare occasions they venture in public, it is only for an "appropriate" occasion such as Halloween.

Category 4, Medium/High. These people are called crossdressers. They dress at home and some venture in public varying from occasionally to regularly.

Category 5, High. The members of this group dress as the other sex full time or nearly full time. Some appear as their birth sex only for their job and/or special people (e.g., parent(s), spouse or child). They are referred to as "no op" (i.e., they do not anticipate having a gender operation). Many of those in this group are on a hormone regimen. Transgender women may seek facial feminization, breast implants, and other feminizing operations. They may also seek feminine training such as voice training and deportment training. Transgender men may seek voice and deportment training. Some seek an operation including liposuction for hip minimization, and mastectomy for breast removal.

Category 6, Very High. Members of this group are gender reassignment surgery candidates. Operations include liposuction for hip minimization and mastectomy for breast removal. Their objective is to have the operation, usually the sooner the better. They also seek other physical changes and social training as they can afford them.

It should be noted we are dealing with individual differences and therefore there is no sharp dividing line between categories. Furthermore, these six categories are not static and may change as the individual's social factors change. It has been noted many Category 5 people may later become Category 6. Many Category 4 people may become Category 5 or even 6. I have observed several Category 4 transgender women who become Category 6 after a divorce. In my memory, I was never lower than Category 3. However, when my social status changed and I discovered it was possible, I went to a higher numbered category. This does not mean a higher category number is better than a low number. The numbers are just a convenient label aligned with transgender strength.

The Coming Evolution

Jennifer Diane Reitz referred to in Chapter 1, stated transgender individuals generally have a 30% higher intelligent quotient (i.e., IQ of 130%) and they are more creative than the average person (see CHAPTER 1, Endnote 16). Also, more transgender people have an intelligence score in the genius range than is found in the general population. Dr. Peter Ward,[1] paleontologist at the University of Washington said, "Evolution usually builds things that work really well." Is the transgender phenomenon another one of those tiny steps in evolution that improve our species. That is, "works really well" regarding the production of more intelligent and creative people? Is the transgender variation a sign of the future? Are transgender individuals the start of an evolutionary process to bring the female and male closer—more alike and at a generally higher intelligence level? Is it an evolutionary method of reacting to the highly technical society now evolving?

Transgender people who are "out," are not common, but transgenderism is distributed throughout the world in every culture and has been throughout history. This reinforces the belief transgenderism is a biological variation rather than acquired. We hear so many stories of transgenderism becoming evident at a very early age, when little or no exposure to transphobia is possible. Furthermore, it occurs at an early age when children experience a high level of permissiveness regarding gender expression. The absence of transphobia's influence leads me to the strong belief there is a biological cause aside from the scientific belief.

Recently there was a newspaper article describing an 18-month-old baby boy who refused to play with trucks and other boy toys and preferred to play with dolls. The evidence that gender is wired in the brain at birth has been shown time and again with intersex babies and babies with damaged genitals. The males among them were raised as girls because vaginas are possible to fabricate surgically and penises are not. Later, those who were originally boys, but never knew of their genital problem at birth and were raised as girls. Sooner or later most insist they are boys.

Perhaps strong transgender tendencies are an atavism. That is, a gene in the chain that produces a transgender tendency may remain dormant for many generations before it manifests, which may explain why transgenderism appears to not have a component of heredity. Eventually, a new efficiency in the form of a new "connection(s)" between genes may be made that makes the production of a transgender baby on a more regular basis, even on a predictable basis.

This or another process resulting in transgenderism may eventually find a way to circumvent the dormant state, find a more efficient way of combining to signal the development of transgender tendencies, and become the normal, usual, and expected result. Thus, transgenderism will seem to acquire a hereditary component. That is, the genetic variation(s) that now result in a transgender individual will appear more frequently. With more frequent occurrences, a more accepting environment will result and yield a common manifestation.

Once that takes place, it will only be a matter of several hundred thousand years before overt transgenderism is part of everyone worldwide. All we need is patience! As Dr. Ward also said, "There has been 500 million years of animals for evolution to play around to get where we are now." All we need is patience and the rest of humanity will eventually catch up with us girls and boys. That is, "us" transgender girls and transgender boys, of course.

CHAPTER 15, The Final Analyses

On a Personal Note

I believe my research did not answer all my original questions. Perhaps I will never know the answer to: what gender am I really, why transgenderism happened to me, how it happened to me, and other developmental questions? My personal theory in Chapter 14 addresses some of them and offers some possible answers. However, all I have are theories that seem logical, but I do not have proven facts.

I feel I am just as competitive and task oriented as when I had a good deal of testosterone as a man. I never lose sight of my objective, but my approach is definitely less aggressive. I like myself for that change. I also have a greater insight into what it means to be a transgender person and how all of us, women and men, react to our transgender status. We are all individuals, yet very alike in most things. My understanding of transgenderism and my ability to live as a woman provides a greater sense of peace, contentment, and happiness.

I believe I was always empathetic to others, but I am more so after living as a woman. Also, I gained greater understand of gay, lesbian, and, especially, bisexual people and others. The others, those that fit the binary concept of a man, a woman, or an in-between was the easy to understand. I have difficulty understanding people who do not relate at all to the binary concept but I have no problem accepting any person relating to whatever they want.

I find the most difficulty understanding the inflexibility of some people. People who are set in their way or have strict beliefs and can't seem to consider new information. The fact that many refuse to listen to information is the most difficult thing for me to accept.

I understand they have the right to not change their views, but the fact that they refuse to hear opposing thoughts is incomprehensible to me. This also applies to transgender people who were raised in a strict religious atmosphere and are very troubled with the Bible saying they are an abomination. They suffer unnecessarily because they seem to not be open to other parts of the Bible and Koran that contradict their belief and may be more pertinent.

Another mystery is why wearing the clothing of the other sex, while abhorrent to some people, is so comforting to transgender people. We derive satisfaction regardless of how completely we approach being a woman or man. Simply wearing a single garment or passing as the other sex seems joyful. I know more than one "man" who wears pantyhose hidden by "his" trousers and socks. It seems to make "him" and those like "him" happy. Regardless of what clothing pacifies our gender identity needs, why are we compelled to wear something at least some of the time? I call it a Biological Imperative, but I would like to understand the mechanism. The phrase sounds right to me. Biological stems from inside us where I feel all this originates. And it is imperative because it is difficult and near impossible to resist.

We cannot, not dress! At some point we quit dressing and discard our feminine garments (i.e., purge) because we recognize a social taboo has been breached. We are brainwashed with boys don't do that (or girls don't do the equivalent). Sooner or later we "do" it again. Why? In spite of the shame and guilt we "do" it again. We have an inner drive to look like our gender identity, even if it is only occasionally and to a mirror? I continue to search for answers, but I fear they will not be answered in my lifetime.

I always wonder what reaction I will get when someone knows me as a man sees me as a woman for the first time. So far, I have heard comments like "you look good." The first thing others say is they didn't expect me to look like a woman or as much like a woman. A common reaction is silence on the subject of how I look as a woman. They proceed as if nothing is different. That communicates that my appearance makes no difference to them.

A very complex and opposing situation exists in my mind. The present generation faces an ever increasing acceptance and permissiveness of transgenderism. If acceptance were a fact when I was born, I would have been allowed to grow up as any other girl. My dream in a different world would have been a fact! By this time in my life, I would have been a complete woman (i.e., sans ovaries and other female organs). Although growing up with female socialization was a great desire, I wonder, would that really have had a better outcome for me? If my growing up as a girl were the case, I would not have the male experience. I wouldn't have had the privilege of being partnered with my extraordinary spouse and I would have not had my children, my daughter-in-law and son-in-law or my grandchildren and grandchild-in-law. I don't think I would want to give that up. I feel good about my male experiences.

The opposing feeling is I would have had other experiences I would also most likely cherish. There is no answer regarding which would have been better for me.

It will be a different story with future generations. They may not have an investment in a life defined by their birth sex label because they would never experience that life. They can likely have a rich and fulfilling life as the female or male that matches the gender they feel inside. They would not experience the shame and guilt or the anxiety and frustration transgender people feel. They would definitely live a mentally healthier life.

I am confident growing up in one's inner gender is going to be a fact in future generations. Eventually, there will likely be an early diagnosis of transgenderism. Perhaps a newborn's reflexes to induced stimuli may be used to reveal if they react like the other sex, thus indicating the possibility they may be a transgender baby.

We see children come out at an earlier and earlier age and with parental understanding. More parents are willing to help their child rather than drive them underground. Many parents are now even willing to share their child's transition in an effort to help other parents with a transgender child.

I am happy, thrilled, and delighted that everyone I know and care about tells me they are happy for my newfound happiness. There may be reservations and even exceptions that I do not know about, but fortunately there has not been any outright rejection of me. In fact, as an indication of my good fortune, I have not heard any lack of understanding of my feelings and needs. I fully understand the difficulty in seeing someone you feel close to in a different "light." Regarding acceptance, I feel I have a good score. If there are those that knew my male persona have a degree of difficulty, they do not tell me, but everyone has said they are happy I am happy.

One of my doctors said the degree of acceptance has something to do with the kind of person I am. A few friends have said something similar. Although it is possible they welcome a change in me, I like to think people accept me because I was always a good person and therefore they like me regardless of my changing my gender's appearance. I am sure it is a great compliment and I am grateful for it. Generally, I am very lucky, very lucky indeed.

It is especially gratifying to hear others say "the kind of person I am," not the kind of person I used to be. That tells me they understand I am still the same person I always was.

Transgender women I know have had heartbreaking experiences of complete rejection from their job, neighbors, friends, and family. Between the extremes of complete acceptance and total rejection, there is every possible variation.

Unlike many other transgender women, I also have wonderful memories and I still derive great pleasure from some of my accomplishments as a man. I am proud of the success of my marriage, my children, the spouses my children chose, my friends, my professional accomplishments and, best of all, my wonderful grandchildren. Even my married grandchild picked a husband that is a winner!

My major fear in exposing my life-long secret was not rejection from my family. I knew our love is too strong for that. My fear was I would cause harm by declaring my male persona was an act, a lie, and it would destroy whatever role model I served.

One transgender man summed it up well and expressed some of my sentiments when he wrote,

> The reason it took me so long to come out was because I was always worried about my family thinking less of me, strangers thinking less of me, losing friends, and I was worried this facet of my life would negate every positive thing I did.

My life as a man was generally happier than most people experience. I somehow seemed to see the humorous side of situations even more so than others could. I was able to accept the inevitability of growing up to be a man. In fact, I was always a happy type of person. I was too serious about my responsibilities and still am, but that is only bad for me personally. However, in every endeavor, I always did my best to do my best. I am not an angel by any means, but I always did my best to be a good man and now I do my best to be a good woman.

I believe I am more helpful to others than when I was a man; however, I have more time, since I no longer have a need to support a family. Also, in my community, the transgender community, I meet more people who need help, since the closet most transgender women occupy is deep, dark, and overloaded with fear.

In the Transgender Community

It is my firm belief that sometime in the future we will find there is a significantly higher number of transgender individuals in the general population than we now recognize. Two factors will come into play: medical science's greater knowledge of how transgenderism happens and the greater number of transgender people that come out of hiding—out of the closet. These factors are explained below.

First, when the general population learns from medical science that transgenderism is a similar phenomenon to left-handedness, green eyes, and other birth variations, they will stop their erroneous thought that it is sexually motivated. At one time, a great deal of effort was expended to make left-handed children right handed. That practice was abandoned because the individual experienced psychological problems similar to the problems an individual experiences when trying to eradicate transgenderism. Eventually, people will pay hardly any notice to transgender people as they now do toward left handed people.

Secondly, as more and more transgender people emerge from the closet, the public will become accustomed to seeing us. The public will get to know us and learn we are just like them except our gender is different than our birth label.

The process of acceptance of transgenderism is now slowly occurring worldwide. It starts with tolerance and progresses to acceptance. The more transgender people come out, the more we will be accepted. The more we are accepted, the easier it will be for others to come out. However, the acceptance process will be accelerated when the cause(s) of transgenderism are no longer a theory, but are more definitely determined. At that time, transgenderism will be far less of a stigma, will induce less shame, and will generally result in a more accepting view of transgender people. These mutually reinforcing events will find our numbers are greater than anyone imagined. There are indications that over 10% of the population is driven to dress as the other sex to some extent (see Appendix IV), at least some of the time (see CHAPTER 4, Endnote 12).

The number of out-of-the-closet transgender people appears to be small outside of large cities because transgender individuals, when dressed, have no chance to avoid being recognized by employers, friends, and family. Furthermore, there are rarely any clubs, organizations, or support groups in rural areas, where expression of your inner self in public can begin.

In 1969, the police raided the Stonewall Inn, a bar in Greenwich Village, New York City. Plainclothes and uniformed police officers roughed up the transgender patrons. This was not the first time the police did such a thing. However, this time the mistreated transgender people fought back. It was later labeled a riot. Unfortunately, the transgender community did not follow up and we abandoned the assertion that we are people and deserve respect as citizens. We had our chance and blew it!

Conversely, look at what gay men have accomplished. They picked up the "Stonewall ball" and ran to a touchdown with it. They shouted "pride" long enough, loud enough, and in every place until pride in being gay became a fact. Gay pride smothered their self-imposed shame of being a gay person.

Unless the transgender community picks up the 'Stonewall ball," transgender women may never emerge from the closet and transgender men may never free themselves from hiding in stealth. It is not easy and there are real and imagined risks, but it can be done. It must be done! We must break the imaginary chains that keep us in bondage, link by link, and we must start now!

The bigotry in putting down transgender women is the invisible enemy of all women. The high level of shame imposed on transgender women is based on the belief women are inferior to men—sexism that started in ancient times! Transgender men also face the ancient enemy—sexism! In the eyes of heterosexual sexists, transgender men seek to discard their feminine inferiority for masculine superiority. So we are fighting a belief going back thousands of years.

Unfair discrimination against all women in employment is expressed as "The Glass Ceiling." A government sponsored Glass Ceiling Commission found over half of all Master's Degrees are awarded to women. However, 95% of senior level managers of the top 1,500 companies are men. If transgender women were to be accepted as full members of society, would the glass ceiling be applied to them as women, or would it not apply to them because they were declared men at birth?

Future Needs

The world of transgenderism is changing quickly. However, there are still many changes that are needed. I have enumerated many below to improve the world generally and the transgender world in particular.

1.   Several states and local governments have laws explicitly prohibiting harmful discrimination based on gender identity and expression. These laws should be passed at all levels of government and everywhere. They are necessary because the United States Constitution initiated discriminatory wording by mentioning a specific group that is granted civil rights (i.e., white male landowners). The practice of specifying who is included excludes those not mentioned. The Constitution should have an amendment that grants universal civil rights to all human beings. That is what Thomas Jefferson (See CHAPTER 9, Endnote 15) and other founding fathers believed.

2. Alan Alder, in a 1975 Ms. Magazine article,[1] stated that based on their behavior, men suffer from testosterone poisoning. Does this explain another phenomenon some transgender women experience? Several transgender women I know say they were nasty in their male persona and after a female hormone regimen they are much nicer. I am not convinced it is poisoning, since only a small number report the above. I feel it is frustration-induced anger regarding their gender conflict that drives some to be disagreeable men, but nice transgender women. Perhaps it may be advantageous for over aggressive and nasty men to take a small dose of an antiandrogen. This may result in a better world in the future.

3. It is my hope that some-day a transgender woman (or man) will be able to walk in public dressed as a woman (or as a man), but still obviously looking like their birth sex label. Those nearby will generally understand she or he is a transgender person and think nothing unusual, shameful, or amusing about it. For this to come about we need the passage of transgender equal rights and antidiscrimination legislation at all levels of government. We need everyone from local government to national government and every government level in-between, to show unity in believing all people are equal.

    We also need to fight for gender identity and expression antidiscrimination policies from our school boards, colleges, employers, and everywhere. Therefore, it is the duty and responsibility of everyone in the transgender community, those with a transgender person in their life, and all fair minded people to pursue these policies and legislation. This is difficult for such a closeted community; however, it is possible. Everyone can do what I did before I was out of the closet. We can all lobby legislators and administration officials under an assumed name.

The urgent need for our exercising this duty and honoring our responsibility is emphasized by a statement released in 2011 by the National Gay and Lesbian Task Force and the National Center for Transgender Equality (see CHAPTER 9, Endnote 6) that reported the abysmal economic conditions and lack of safety many transgender people experience. We need to have greater visibility. Those who can overcome their shame and fear, and those who disavowed their transgender past, should stop hiding their transgenderism. The more the transgender community adopts a public stance, the less of a curiosity, mystery, and oddity all of us will be and the greater will be our acceptance by society and favorable political action.

4. We need to educate the health care workers that treating transgender people is not a high HIV risk. Police officers need sensitivity training to learn transgender people are people. It is the police officers' job to treat all people courteously, respectfully, and fairly. Police officers need to recognize it is their duty and responsibility to correct bad apples among them and report uncorrectable ones for disciplinary action.

5. In 2011, the House of Delegates of the American Medical Society declared the practice of reparative therapy unethical (see CHAPTER 9, Endnote 9). On October 1, 2012, California became the first state to outlaw reparative therapy.[2] Since then other states have followed California's lead. A similar law should be adopted by all other states, since reparative therapy is just a modern name for torture. This "therapy" causes psychological harm. The claimed "successes" are some boys thought to be transgender boys live as gay men. My survey of the observation of boys desiring to be women in the Thailand school system, and other surveys that show the claimed "cure" is attributable to the passage of time and not the "therapy." (see CHAPTER 4—Transgender Sexual Characteristics, Homosexual Connection).

6. The scientific discovery of the cause of transgenderism and the method or physiological mechanism by which it occurs will help convince everyone transgenderism is a natural birth variation and not a whim, a life style, a sexual perversion, or a mental disorder.

7. The revised DSM issued in 2013[3] recognizes that transgenderism is not a mental disorder needs to be more widely known because it will improve acceptability of transgender people.

8. Hopefully, we will learn to diagnose transgenderism early in a child's life. There are several benefits to early diagnosis. The earlier the diagnosis, the more likely people will believe the phenomenon is congenital, resulting in greater acceptance of transgender individuals. Also, early diagnosis would provide the knowledge and opportunity to prevent the wrong secondary sex characteristics from developing until the child is old enough to make her or his own decision regarding gender.

9. Transgender individuals should not need a court order (permission of a judge) to change their given name to one more appropriate for their gender. The idea that we must prove we are innocent of intended fraud flies in the face of the American principle of being innocent until proven guilty. A transgender person's name change is frequently a safety issue because they appear as a specific gender and need an appropriate name on identification documents. Furthermore, transgender people should not need a doctor's note to change their sex on documents. This is not only demeaning but also a safety issue. Declaring your true gender and living that way should be sufficient for correcting the gender marker and one's name. Many transgender people live in poverty and do not have the money to obtain the safety of a name and gender change on documents.

10. The control of names and sex is a state function and right. All federal agencies should accept the state designation. At the very least, all federal agencies should be uniform. For example, the passport rules and Social Security Administration rules differ from each other and from many states.

11. Same-sex marriages were made legal and now protect the sanctity of the family. However, transgender people who marry must guard against having their marriage declared fraudulent regarding their partner' knowledge of their transgender status. There needs to be a document declaring their spouse knows of their transgenderism to avoid becoming easy prey for a relative, insurance company, or someone else who can benefit from having their marriage declared fraudulent, illegal, and thus void based on deception. Transgender people need the same equality in marriage, inheritance rights, and child custody as everyone else. Even with the legality of same sex marriage, transgender people still need health care, prison safety, and asylum for foreigners from their homeland's discrimination.

12. Transgender people and all people should have legal protection from all forms discrimination. This means we need a national universal bill of rights, rather continuing the practice of specifying who is included.

13. Children should not be restricted to colors, toys, clothes, or a fixed sexual assignment. From birth on they should be free to select their toys, clothes, and any other sex identifying inanimate object. They should have the freedom to express their gender without the social pressure to conform to current societal norms, when they reach the proper age for such a decision.

14. Transgender equality, including legal protection from harmful discrimination, depends heavily on women's equality. All LGBTQ people seeking protection from discrimination need to pursue, indeed work diligently toward, women's equality. It is white male heterosexual dominance—sexism—that is the foundation of harmful discrimination of gay, lesbian, bisexual, transgender, and queer people.

15. Most important, we must replace "boys don't do that" and "tomboys grow out of it" with "Boys and Girls *May* Do That!"

16. Hopefully, future generations will face a more knowledgeable, understanding, and accepting world so they will feel they can live according to their brain gender, openly, honestly, and without shame.

###

ENDNOTES

INTRODUCTION

1. Mike Penner (October 10, 1957-November 27, 2009) was a sports writer for the Los Angeles Times. Quotation from his obituary by Thursby, Keith, Los Angeles Times November 29, 2009 front page. Penner was an unhappy person. He was impelled to transition, soon reversed his transition, and eventually committed suicide.

2. Since most transgender individuals desire anonymity, credits for the quotations are not sited. Furthermore, I do not correct or alter these quotations. I copy them as received. I only add, in brackets or correct some grammar, when I feel something needs clarification. I feel I should not distract from the authenticity and power of the statements.

3. One well documented study was published by the American Association of Suicidology on the Internet at: http://www.TransformingFamily.org/pdfs/ Transgender Youth and Suicidal Behavior 37(5) October2007.

4. Lynn Conway (born January 10, 1938), Professor Emeritus of Engineering and Computer Science, University of Michigan, Ann Arbor, Michigan, is an advocate for transgender rights.

5. Joanne Herman, author, transitioned in 2002 to live as a female. She has since been active as spokeswoman for transgender awareness and understanding.

CHAPTER 1

1. Anne Fausto-Sterling, Ph. D. (born July 30, 1944) is Professor of Biology and Gender Studies in the Department of Molecular and Cell Biology and Biochemistry at Brown University.

2. Steven P. Rose (born July 4, 1938) is a Professor of Biology and Neurology at the Open University and University of London.

Rose studied biochemistry at Kings College and neurobiology at Cambridge and the Institute of Psychiatry, Kings College, London.

Richard Lewontin (born March 29, 1929) is an American evolutionary biologist, geneticist, and social commentator.

Leon J. Kamin (born December 29, 1927) is an American psychologist who chaired Princeton University's Department of Psychology in 1968.

3. Mujaderos: *Psychopathia Sexualis*, by Richard von Krafft-Ebing. Originally, Richard Freiherr von Krafft-Ebing (August 14, 1840-December 22, 1902) was an Austro-German sexologist and psychiatrist. He wrote *Psychopathia Sexualis* (1886), republished in New York, New York, 1998 by Arcade Publishing. It is a notable series of case studies of the varieties of human sexual behavior. Krafft-Ebing coined the terms sadism and masochism. He was born in Mannheim, Baden, Germany. He studied medicine at the University of Heidelberg.

4. Native Americans: "Two Spirits: A Third Gender," Cultural Anthropology by Nancy Bonvillian, Pearson Education, Inc. 2006. In other cultures, "Archeologists Unearth 5,000-Year-Old 'Third-Gender' Caveman," by Bryan Nelson. Mother Nature Network, 2006.

5. *Tritiya-Prakriti: People of the Third Sex* by Amara Das Wilhelm, first published in 2003 by Xlibris Corporation, Philadelphia, republished.

6. Louann Braizendine, M.D. (born in 1952) is at the University of California at San Francisco. She pursues active clinical, teaching, writing, and research activities. She wrote the book, *The Female Brain*, Three Rivers Press, New York, New York, 2006-2007.

7. John William Money (July 8, 1921-July 7, 2006) was a psychologist, sexologist, and author specializing in research into sexual identity and the biology of gender. He has been

the subject of controversy due to his work with the sex reassignment of David Reimer.

8. Relativism gained most prominence from Edward Sapir and his student Benjamin Lee Whorf. It is often called the Sapir-Whorf hypothesis or simply the "Whorf hypothesis."

   Edward Sapir (Jan. 26, 1884-Feb. 4, 1939) was a linguist born in Germany, emigrated to and died in the United States. He was prominent in American Structural Linguistics.

   Benjamin Lee Whorf (April 24, 1897-July 26, 1941) was an American linguist. He is best known for his relativist hypothesis that language influences the way we think.

9. Magnus Hirschfeld (May 14, 1868-May 14, 1935) was born in Germany. He studied philosophy (1887-1888), medicine (1888-1892), and, in 1892, he earned his doctoral degree. He started a naturopathic practice in Magdeburg; in 1896 he later moved his practice to Berlin-Charlottenburg. In 1933 he fled Hitler and settled in Southern France where he wrote *The Transvestites—An Erotic Drive to Cross Dress* by Magnus Hirschfeld, M.D., translated by Michael A. Lombardi-Nash, Ph.D., Amherst, New York, Prometheus Books, 1991.

10. Dr. Harry Benjamin (January 12, 1885-August 24, 1986). He was an endocrinologist. His 1966 book, *The Transsexual Phenomenon*, New York, New York: Julian Press, 1966, was based on a 17-year study of transvestites. The standards of care he developed were intended to determine who is eligible for hormone and surgical treatment and is still used worldwide. Although his work has been amended, it is carried out today by The World Professional Association for Transgender Health (WPATH) and was formerly known as the Harry Benjamin International Gender Dysphoria Association, HBIGDA.

11. John Colapinto (born in Toronto in 1958) is an award winning journalist, author, and novelist. He is best known for his popular book, *As Nature Made Him*, Scarborough Ontario, Harper Collins Canada Ltd., 2001.

12. Grace H. Dicks and A. T. Childers, M.D. coauthored "The Social Transformation of a Boy Who Had Lived His First Fourteen Years as a Girl: A Case History," American Orthopsychiatric Association, Volume 4, Issue 4, Pages 508-517, October 1934.

13. Lewis P. Lipsitt, Ph.D. and N. Levy, Stamford University coauthored "Tactile Sensitivity and Muscle Strength in Newborn Boys and Girls," Stanford University, 1959. Three samples of newborns were measured on tactile sensitivity (using an aesthesiometer) and two indices of muscle strength (prone head reaction and grip strength). There was no sex difference found in tactile sensitivity.

    When the probabilities of all 3 samples were combined, sex differences were found in prone head reaction and grip strength, with boys showing greater strength than girls. Chubbiness and weight were negatively related to tactile sensitivity for boys in one of the three samples. Weight did not account for the sex differences in strength.

14. Dr. Milton Diamond (born March 6, 1934), is a retired Professor of Anatomy and Reproductive Biology at the John A. Burns School of Medicine, University of Hawaii at Mānoa. He retired in December, 2009 after a long and productive career in the study of human sexuality.

15. Dr. William Reiner, Professor at the University of California at Irvine, College of Medicine, 1974. He is presently at the University of Oklahoma, Health Sciences Center, Department of Urology, Division of Pediatric Urology, Adolescent Psychiatry and Pediatric Psychiatry.

16. Jennifer Diane Reitz (born 1959) is a transgender woman. She is an American author, web designer, and computer programmer. She writes on transgender issues. Jennifer Reitz' claim of a higher intelligence quotient was reinforced by Money, J. & Lewis, V. (1966) in their article "IQ, Genetics and Accelerated Growth: Androgenital Syndrome," Bulletin Johns Hopkins Hospital, Volume 118: Pages 365-373. Money and Lewis explained that many human studies rely on statistics to justify their small sample size. Their conclusion was

challenged; however, they say their conclusions are statistically valid.

However, a bulletin by Collaer, M .L. & Hines, M. (1995) challenged Money & Lewis' conclusions in "Human Behavioral Sex Differences: a Role for Gonadal Hormones During Early Development?" Psychological Bulletin, Volume 118, Pages 55-107. They said, "High levels of hormones do not enhance intelligence, although a minimum level may be needed for optimal development of some cognitive processes." This study asserted that Money & Lewis' sample selection was biased and may explain the higher IQ.

17. Omitted

18. Dr. Carl W. Bushong established the Tampa Gender Identity Program, which allowed access to a variety of transition services from hormone therapy to guidance under one roof. He has helped hundreds to fully transition. Dr. Bushong continues to innovate. He is the author of "What is Gender and Who is Transsexual/Transgendered?" on the Internet.

CHAPTER 2

1. Peggy T. Cohen-Kettenis, Ph.D. is Professor of Gender Development and Psychopathology at the Department of Child and Adolescent Psychiatry, University Medical Center, Utrech, The Netherlands. She is now Professor of Medical Psychology at the Free University Medical Center in Amsterdam, where she is the head of a gender clinic for children, adolescents, and adults.

2. Catherine Tuerk, of the Children's National Medical Center in Washington, D.C., is an author and lecturer on the subject of gender variant children.

3. Gianna Israel (1963-2006) was a therapist who provided counseling services to the transgender community. She also published articles on transgender issues.

4. In 2011, WPATH declared reparative therapy unethical.

CHAPTER 3

1. Karl-Heinrich Ulrich (August 28, 1825-July 14, 1895) was a pioneer in the gay rights movement. He was a lawyer and the first person to publish a definition of homosexuality—a third sex. As a young child he wore girls' clothes, preferred playing with girls, and wanted to be a girl. He put forward the view that homosexuality was inborn and unchangeable. At that time transgenderism and homosexuality were thought to be the same. In about 1869, he proposed the first known statement by a scientist to remove the Anticrossdressing laws on that basis.

2. Karl-Maria Kertbeny, born Karl-Maria Benkert (February 28, 1824-January 23, 1882) known for coining the words homosexual and heterosexual. He invented the term Urning in Germany in the 1860s. An Urning is a male bodied person with a female psyche, who is sexually attracted to men and not women.

3. Sam Winter, Ph.D., is a Professor at the University of Hong Kong, Republic of China.

4. Lauren Hare is an Honors Student at Prince Henry's Institute, Melbourne, Australia. Home Department: Department of Genetics, Monash Medical Centre.

5. Vincent Harley, Professor, Prince Henry's Institute, Melbourne, Australia Group (Study) Leader and Senior Research Fellow.

6. Terry Read is well known to Britain's transgender community as a founding member of the Gender Identity Research and Education Society (GIRES).

7. R-Spondin 1 is an active ovarian determinant.

8. Cell biology—formerly cytology—is a scientific discipline of cells' physiological properties, structure, and their organelles, interactions with their environment, their life cycle, division, and death. Molecular biology chiefly concerns itself with the

interactions between the various systems of all types of cells and how their interactions are regulated.

9. Roger Gorski, Ph.D., (born 1935) is Distinguished Professor Emeritus, Professor of the Laboratory of Neuroendocrinology at the David Geffen School of Medicine, University of California at Los Angeles.

CHAPTER 4

1. Ray Milton Blanchard (born October 9, 1945) is an American-Canadian born in New Jersey. He is a sexologist, best known for his research studies on pedophilia, gender dysphoria, and sexual orientation.

2. Marshall Miller founded the BiHealth Program at Fenway Community Health, Massachusetts. He first funded bisexual specific programs targeting bisexual people and MSMW (men who have sex with men and women). BiNet, 4201 Wilson Boulevard, #110-311, Arlington, VA 22203-1859, Telephone:1-800-585-9368. BiNetUSA@BiNetUSA.Net.

3. Deleted.

4. Lisa M. Diamond, Ph.D., is at the Department of Psychology University of Utah, Lake City, Utah. She authored the book *Sexual Fluidity—Understanding Women's Love and Desires*, Harvard University Press, Boston, Massachusetts, 2008.

5. Krafft-Ebing: Richard von Krafft-Ebing (August 14, 1840-December 22, 1902) was an Austro–German sexologist and psychiatrist born in Mannheim, Baden, Germany. He studied medicine specializing in psychiatry at the University of Heidelberg.

6. Sigmund Freud (May 6, 1856-September 23, 1939) was an Austrian neurologist who originated the psychoanalytic procedures of Psychiatry.

7. Alfred Kinsey (June 23, 1894-August 26, 1956), born in Hoboken, New Jersey, was a Zoologist and Human Sexologist.

In 1948, he authored *The Kinsey Report on Sexual Behavior of the Human Male*, Bloomington, Indiana: Indiana University Press, 1998.

8. Marjorie B. Garber (born June 11, 1944) is a professor at Harvard University and the author of a wide variety of books.

9. Simon LeVey (born August 28, 1943) is a British-American neurologist. He studied brain structures and sexual orientation. He published "A Difference in Hypothalamic Structure between Heterosexual and Homosexual Men," Science: August 30, 1991, Volume 253, Number 5023, Pages 1034-1037.

10. Alicia Garcia-Falgueras Ph.D. and Dick F. Swaab, M.D., Ph.D., are scientists at the Netherlands Institute for Neuroscience in Amsterdam.

11. Dr. Richard Green (born June 6, 1936) is an American sexologist, psychiatrist, lawyer, and author who specializes in transsexualism, homosexuals , and concentrated on gender identity in children.

12. BBC News, Asian-Pacific, "Thai School Offers Transsexual Toilet," by Jonathan Head, July 29, 2008.

13. Group 1—Those in this group never felt they were or wanted to be a girl or a woman. Some seemed very macho, but most simply never had any thought of being or wanting to be in a feminine role. They never dressed in feminine clothes and never remember ever having a desire to dress as a girl. Even when wrapping a towel around their waist after a shower, it never occurred to them that the towel was like a skirt.

Group 2—This group is composed of those who did not definitely fit in Group 1 or Group 3. Some always gravitate toward feminine costumes at costume parties and sometimes dressed as a girl. They said they dressed as a woman, "For the fun of it." Others wanted to but gave excuses for not dressing (e.g., "I'm too big," "It's too much trouble," and "dressing as a man is simpler"). Some definitely liked dressing as a woman. Although many had some indication of transgender tendencies, it was not clear enough to definitely fit into Group 3.

Group 3—The self-description of those in this group clearly indicated a transgender component. This group did dress as a girl, really liked it, and still like it. One senior gay man said, "I wanted a Barbie doll and my father emphatically said, No! However, when G. I. Joe came out, he bought me one." Another gay man said, "I still have the dress, a wig, bra, falsies, and would still like to wear them. In fact, if the dress still fits, I'm going to go to a party in it."

14. Dr. Kenneth Zucker is an American residing in Toronto, Canada. He was associated with the former Clarke Institute in Toronto.

15. David Jay (born April 24, 1982) is an asexual activist. He established the Asexual Visibility and Education Network (AVEN) and the AVEN web site: http://www.asexuality.org/.

CHAPTER 5

1. Jiang-Ning Zhou, Michel A. Hofman, Louis J. G. Gooren and Dick F. Swaab (1997) in the Netherlands at the University of Amsterdam, investigated the BSTc area of the brain, "A sex difference in the human brain and its relation to transsexuality," Nature, November 2, 1995, Volume 378, Pages 68-70.

2. Frank P. M. Kruijver, Jiang-Ning Zhou, Chris W. Pool, Michel A. Hofman, Louis J. G. Gooren, and Dick F. Swaab, Graduate School of Neurosciences, Amsterdam University, The Netherlands. At the Institute for Brain Research, Department of Endocrinology, the authors studied male-to-female transsexuals and found their limbic nucleus has a neuron count similar to a female. "Male-to-Female Transsexuals Have Female Neuron Numbers in a Limbic Nucleus," The Journal of Clinical Endocrinology and Metabolism, 2000, Volume 85, Number 5, Pages 2034-2041.

3. W. J. Chung, G. J. De Vries, D. Swaab, "Sex differentiation of the bed nucleus of the stria terminalis central in humans may extend into adulthood," Journal of Neuroscience, 2007, Volume 22, Number 3, Pages 1027-1033.

4. H. Berglund, "Male-to-Female Transsexuals Show Sex-"Atypical Hypothalamus Activation When Smelling Odorous Steroids," Oxford Journals, Life Sciences and Medicine—Cerebral Cortex, Volume 18, Issue 8, Pages 1900-1908.

5. Hilleke E. Hulshoff-Pol, Hugo G. Schnack, et al, Department of Psychiatry, Utrecht, The Netherlands.

6. Frank P. M. Kruijver, Alonso Ferna´ Ndez-Guasti, Mariann Fodor, Elise M. Kraan, and Dick F. Swaab did this research work at the Graduate School of Neurosciences, Netherlands Institute for Brain Research, Amsterdam, The Netherlands.

7. "A Sex Difference in the Hypothalamic Uncinate Nucleus: Relationship to Gender Identity." Garcia-Falgueras and A, Swaab on the Internet at, http://www.BrainOxfordjournals/content/131/12/3132.

8. Dr. Eric Villian is a member of the Board of Medical Genetics who specializes in clinical biochemical genetics. He is at the Department of Pediatrics, Pediatric Genetics, University of California, Los Angeles.

CHAPTER 6

1. Merit Badge: a Boy Scout receives a merit badge symbolizing the accomplishment of a new skill.

2. Live 24/7 means living as a woman or a man all the time (24 hours a day and 7 days a week).

3. Stanislovsky was an acting coach famous for teaching actors to actually live the part before and during the time that they were performing the part.

4. http://www.sciencecentral.com/video/ 2009/10/girls-vs-boys-at-math.

5. http://www.earlhamsociologypages.co.uk/genddata.

CHAPTER 7

1. "Dressed:" transgender crossdresser people refer to being "dressed" when wearing the clothes of the other sex.

2. Binding is used to flatten the breasts so the chest will look masculine.

3. Miss Vera's Finishing School For Boys Who Want To Be Girls, 85 Eighth Avenue, New York, New York 10011. Telephone: 1-212-242-6449.

4. Femme Fever: http://www.FemmeFever.com. Wantagh, New York. Telephone 1-516-520-0380.

5. Transitions Binder, P. O. Box 3547, Conroe, TX, 77305.

6. http://www.colonialmedical.com/.

7. Christie Block, MA, MS, CCC-SLP at the New York Speech and Voice Lab in New York City: 65 Broadway, Suite 822, New York,
NY 10006, Tel: (347) 677-3619 email.

8. Tria Hair Removal Laser. Triabeauty.com/hairremovallaser-4x.

9. Melanie Speaks offers male to female voice tips on the internet.

10 Charles Lamb's "Ode to a Roast Pig" was the story he told of long ago, when people kept their farm animal in their living quarters. One day the building burned down. After the flames subsided, the man examined the damage and reached over to touch his favorite pig that was burned to death in the fire. The pig was still hot; he burned his finger, and brought them to his mouth to cool them. He found he liked the taste. It was so good he, followed by others nearby, burned a hut

down, with a pig inside, each time they wanted to taste that luscious morsel—a roast pig. Similarly, as a child, I thought I needed to take a bath to experience the pleasure of an orgasm.

11. Cross Dressers International: http://www.CDINYC.org. New York, New York. Telephone 1-212-564-4847.

12. Ina's is now closed and out of operation.

CHAPTER 8

1. Kate Winslet is a contributor.to *Becoming Myself, Reflections On Growing Up Female* edited by Willa Shalit, New York, New York, Hyperion Books, 2007.

2. Nada Stotland, M.D., is Professor of Psychiatry at Rush Medical College in Chicago. She was the 2008-2009 President of the American Psychiatric Association.

3. John Elliot Bradshaw June 29, 1933-May 8, 2016) was the American author of seven books and is an educator.

4. Callen-Lorde, Community Health Center, 356 West 38th Street, New York, New York 10011. Telephone 1-212-271-7200.

CHAPTER 9

1. In 342 A.D. Christian emperors Constantius II and Constans issued a law in the Theodosian Code (C. Th. 9.7.3) prohibiting same sex marriage in Rome and ordering execution for those so married. http://www.aliyaleighlive.libsyn.com/gay-marriage.

2. The Book of Leviticus, Chapter 18, Verse 22.

3. Persecution of gays, lesbians, bisexuals, and transgender people. http://www.WordIQ.com.

4. "Cross Dressing Case for Bathroom Equality" by Jennifer Levi, Western New England University School of Law.

5. American Psychological Association, Price Waterhouse v. Hopkins, 490 U.S. 288, brief filed: June, 1988, District Court of the United States, Year of Decision: 1989.

6. This extensive survey was funded by the National Gay and Lesbian Task Force and the National Center for Transgender Equality, 2011. The USTS 2016 study was conducted by the National Center for Transgender Equality (USTtranssurvey.org).

7. http://www.aclusd.org/LGBTQ-rights.html.

8. Schroer v. Billington, James H. Billington, Librarian of Congress, Defendant. March 31, 2006. http://www.aele.org/law/2008FPFEB/schroer-billington.html.

9. Declaration by The House of Delegates of the American Medical Association at a meeting in Chicago, June 16, 2008.

10. Robert Eads (December 18, 1945-January 17, 1999) in Toccoa, Georgia was a transsexual man who was the subject of the award winning documentary "Southern Comfort."

11. *A Life Remembered* by Yusef Najafi, Published by Metro Weekly, December 21, 2006.

12.
   .http://wwwcom/2010/07/an_interview_with_Eric_Vaught_about _experience.php.

13. Riki Wilchins (born 1952) is a transsexual woman. She is an activist focused on gender discrimination.

14. "Lesbian, Gay, Bisexual, and Transgender Concerns," Public Interest Directorate Booklet, American Psychological Association, 750 First Street, N.E., Washington, D.C., 20002-4242, 2008.

15. Thomas Jefferson said, "We cannot be complacent until two conditions are met. Every human being born on this continent has a right to equal, indeed identical, treatment in the machine of the law . . . . And secondly, every human being born on this continent has a right to roughly equal opportunity and modest prosperity. And until those conditions are met, we cannot rest."

16. On October 21, 2009 Health and Human Services Secretary Kathleen Sebelius announced the establishment of the first national resource center to assist communities across the country in their efforts to provide services and supports for older lesbian, gay, bisexual, and transgender (LGBTQ) individuals. The LGBTQ Resource Center helps community-based organizations understand the unique needs and concerns of older LGBTQ individuals and assists them in implementing programs for local service providers, including caregivers for older partners with health or other challenges. The Administration on Aging will award single Resource Center grants. For further information see::http://www.aoa.gov/AoARoot/Grants/Funding/index.aspx.

17. The World Professional Association for Transgender Health (WPATH), formerly known as the Harry Benjamin International Gender Dysphoria Association, is a professional organization devoted to the understanding and treatment of gender identity conflicts.

18. John Michael Bailey (born July 2, 1957) is an American psychologist and professor at Northwestern University. He is the author of *The Science of Gender-Bending, The Man Who Would Be Queen, and Transsexualism*, published by Joseph Henry Press, 2003.

19. Kelley Winters, Ph.D., is a writer on issues of transgender medical policy and founder of the GID Reform Advocates.

20. Attorney General "Pat" Edmund Brown, Sr. (April 21, 1905-February 16, 1996) was the governor of California from 1959-1967.

21. On December 23, 2009, transgender women from 10 Asia Pacific countries and areas met in Bangkok, Thailand to say no to discrimination and marginalization by forming the world's first Asia Pacific Transgender Network (APTN). After three days of intense meetings, it was decided that the APTN, composed entirely of transgender women across the region, will champion transgender women's health, legal, and social rights.

CHAPTER 10

1. Transgender People and Marriage: "The Importance of Legal Planning" booklet by Shannon Minter, Legal Director, National Center for Lesbian Rights, 870 Market Street, Suite 370, San Francisco, California 94102.

2. U.S. Supreme Court denies Littleton Writ of Certiorari on 10/2/2000. http://www.christielee.net/home1.htm.

3. "Kansas Supreme Court Says Transsexual Marriage Invalid." http://www.kscourts.org/cases-and-opinions/supreme-court-summaries/2002/20020315-85030.asp.

4. Dr. William Reiner, M.D. (born 1948) is a faculty member at the University of Oklahoma and Johns Hopkins. His practice includes urology and psychiatry, especially as applied to children.

5. In 1997 a trial court in Orange County, California affirmed the validity of a transsexual marriage. http://www.transgenderlaw.org/resources/translaw.htm.

6. "Federal Judge Rules Part of DOMA Unconstitutional," by Rachel Slajda, July 8, 2010.

7. Schipski v Flood, People of the State New York regarding Joel A. Schipski Et Al. v. Walter J. Flood, July 26, 1982.

8. U.S. Department of Justice, Federal Bureau of Prisons, OPI: SD/HPB Number: P6031.01, Program Date: January 15, 2005.

Subject: "Patient Care, Inmates with Gender Identity Disorder."

9. Court House News.
http://www.courthousenews.com/2012/09/05/49966.htm.

10. The British Broadcasting Company announcement, January 15, 2010.

11. Mildred "Babe" Didrikson mastered many sports in the 1930s and ended as a brilliant golfer. She was accomplished in just about every sport—basketball, track, golf, baseball, tennis, swimming, diving, boxing, volleyball, handball, bowling, billiards, skating, and cycling. She was an Olympic star and won medals in many events.

12. Dr. Richard Raskin (born August 19, 1934) is an American ophthalmologist, author, and former professional tennis player. She transitioned from male-to-female and competed in the 1977 U.S. Women's Open Tennis championship as Renée Richards.

13. Dora Ratjen was actually a man, Heinrich "Heinz" Ratjen, who had disguised himself as a woman while competing in athletics events. Germany has restored the 1936 high jump record to a 95-year-old Queens, New York woman who was kicked off the Nazi Olympic team because she was Jewish. Daily News, September 9, 2009.

14. National Institute of Health, :http://www.kidshealth.org. Marfan's Syndrome is a genetic disorder. It often affects the long bones of the body. This can lead to a tall, thin build, long arms, legs, fingers, and toes.

15. MedicinePlus Medical Encyclopedia: In congenital adrenal hyperplasia, an enzyme needed by the adrenal gland to make some hormones needed by the body is lacking. This causes the production of androgens (male hormones) in excess or inappropriate for the sufferer.

16. "Intersex and the Olympic Games" by Robert Ritchie, John Reynard, and Tom Lewis, J R Social Medicine, August 1, 2008, Volume 101, Number 8, Pages 395-399.

17. Helen Herring Stephens (February 3, 1918-January 17, 1994) was an American Olympic champion in 1936. She was so fast a runner that she was falsely accused of being male.

18. Stella Walsh, (1911-1980). Her Polish name was Stanislawa Walasiewicz. She emigrated to the U.S. and won a gold medal in the 1932 Olympics. Upon her death it was discovered she had male genitalia.

19. The WIAA issues a sport policy fair to transgender athletes. http://www.transgenderlaw.org/ resources/WIAA_Policy.pdf.

20. Women's Sport Foundation. http://www.womenssportfoundation.org.

21. Ladies European Tour. http://www.ladieseuropeantour.com.

22.
https://www.ncaa.org/sites/default/files/Transgender_Hand book_ 2011_Final.pdf.

23.. Caster Semenya (born January 7, 1991) from the Internet: http://www.cbsnews.com/news/caster-semenya-can-run-with-the-women-its-official/.

24. Doctor Jean Wilson's statement regarding transgender athletes. http://www.glbtq.com/arts/sports_transgender_issues,2.html .

25. American Immigration Lawyers Association. http://www.AILA.org.

26. Choosing an Attorney, http://www.Legallawhelp.com.

27. USCIS Student Visas. http://www.Travel.state.gov/visa/temp/types_1270.html.

28. William R. Yates, Associate Director, Operations. USCIS issued an August 4, 2003 memo to regional directors, service center directors, district directors, and officers in charge providing the guidance indicated.

29. Public policy can be defined as a general course of action or inaction taken by government decisions regarding an issue or issues. In this case it refers to the DOMA law regarding the definition of a legal marriage. www.musc.edu/vawprevention/policy/definition.shtml.

30. Internet: See United Nations Convention Against Torture.

CHAPTER 11

1. Some companies providing medical insurance coverage for gender operations include: American Express, American Telephone and Telegraph, Bank of America, Campbell Soup, Coca-Cola, Eastman Kodak, General Motors, Goldman Sacks, Kraft Foods, Microsoft, Morgan Stanley, Price Waterhouse, Sears, State Farm, Walt Disney, Wells Fargo, and Yahoo. There are over 80 other companies that have a similar policy.

CHAPTER 12

1. Susan Coates, Ph.D. (born 1980) is a Clinical Professor of Psychology in Psychiatry at the College of Physicians and Surgeons, Columbia University, New York City.

2. *Gender Shock*, by Phyllis Burke, Anchor Books, 1996, explores the many myths surrounding our rigid gender system of male and female.

CHAPTER 13

1. Journal of Sexual Research, May, 1974, Volume. 10, Number 2, Pages 156-161.

CHAPTER 14

1.   Dr. Peter Ward (born 1949) is Senior Councilor of the Paleontological Society and currently chairs an international panel on the Cretaceous-Tertiary extinction and served as editor for the recently published volume Global Catastrophes in Earth History (National Academy of Science and NASA). He was elected as a Fellow of the California Academy of Science in 1984, and has been honored by the Paleontological Society.

CHAPTER 15

1.   MS. Magazine, October 1975, Alan Alda Special Issue, and also cited in Kramarae and Treichler, editors, *A Feminist Dictionary*, Pandora Press, 1985.

2.   Eckholm, Erik, "California Is First State to Ban Gay 'Cure' for Minors," New York Times, September 30, 2012.

3.   http://www.glaad.org/. /apa-removes-gender-identity-disorder-updated-mental_healthguide.

APPENDIX I, Dictionary and Abbreviations

APA = American Psychiatric Association.

APTN = Asia Pacific Transgender Network.

AILA = American Immigration Lawyers Association.

Bi = Bisexual.

BIA = Board of Immigration Appeals.

Boi = boy.

BSTc = Bed Nucleus of the Stria Terminalis, central region of the brain.

CD = crossdresser.

Cis woman = nontransgender straight woman.

CIS = Citizenship and Immigration Service.

DDT = dichloro diphenyl trichloroethane, an insecticide.

DEC = Dept. of Environmental Conservation.

DES = diethylstilbestrol.

DNA = deoxyribonucleic acid.

DOMA = Defense of Marriage Act.

Drab = men's clothes.

Drag = women's clothes.

DSM = Diagnostic and Statistical Manual, APA.

Et al. = and others.

Fem = feminine.

FtM = female-to-male.

Galz = girls.

GID = Gender Identity Disorder.

GLBTQ = Gay, Lesbian, Bisexual, Transgender and Queer.

GIRES = Gender Identity Research and Education Society.

GRC = Gender Recognition Certificate.

Gurl = girl.

GG/gg = genetic girl.

G/W = genetic woman.

HUD = Department of Housing and Urban Development.

ICD = International Classification Of Diseases (World Health Organization).

IOC = International Olympic Committee.

INAH = Interstitial Nucleus of the Anterior Hypothalamus.

LGBTQ = Lesbian, Gay, Bisexual, Transgender and Queer.

lol = lots of luck and lots of laughs.

LPR = legal permanent resident.

MtF = male-to-female.

MSM = men who have sex with men.

MSMW = men who have sex with men and women.

NIEHS = National Institute of Environmental Health Sciences.

NIH = National Institute of Health.

Op = operation.

Pansexual = attracted to all genders.

PCB = Polychlorinated biphenyls.

PFLAG = Parents and Friends of Lesbians and Gays Organization.

Pic = picture.

Purging = discarding all objects associated with the other sex.

R-Spondin 1 = female sex determining gene.

RNA = Ribonucleic acid.

SAGE = Services and advocacy for GLBT elders.

SOFFA = Significant Other, Family, Friends and Allies.

T = testosterone.

TG/tg = transgender.

T-Girls = transgender girls.

Tranny = derogatory slang for transgender.

Trans = transgender.

TS/ts = transsexual.

TV = transvestite.

UK = United Kingdom.

UN = United Nations.

USCIS = U. S. Citizenship and Immigration Services.

WIAA = Washington Interscholastic Athletic Association.

Wikipedia = on-line encyclopedia.

Womyn = woman.

WPATH = World Professional Association for Transgender Health.

WSW = women who have sex with women.

SRS = sexual reassignment surgery.

SRY = Sex-determining region Y gene (male).

APPENDIX II, Transgender Legal Assistance Organizations

The Transgender Legal Defense and Education Fund (TLDEF), 151 West 19th Street, New York City. Telephone: 1-646-862-9396.

LGBTQ Center, 34 Park Avenue, Bay Shore, Long Island, New York will help with miscellaneous legal issues including legal cases of discrimination in employment, housing and public accommodations. The Center provides other services such as medical and psychological counseling. http://LGBTQnetwork.org/the-center. Telephone: 1-631-665-2300.

LGBTQ Center, 20 Crossways Park Drive, North, Suite 110, Woodbury, New York 11797. Services are the same as its sister center in Bay Shore, Long Island, New York Center. http://LGBTQnetwork.org/the-center. Telephone 1-516-323-0011.

LGBTQ Center East End, 44 Union Street, Sag Harbor, New York 11963. Services are the same as its sister center in Bay Shore, Long Island, New York Center. http://LGBTQnetwork.org/the-center. Telephone: 1-631-899-4950.

The Lambda Legal Defense and Education Fund is a national organization that has a Help Desk staff located near you that responds directly to LGBT and HIV individuals. They also provide leads to other organizations and practical information that might be helpful. They have many ways to serve you at http://www.Lambdalegal.org/help.

The Transgender Law and Policy Institute will provide legal advice at Query@transgenderlaw.org./ Transgender Law Center, 160 14th Street, San Francisco, California 94103. Help is offered at info@TransgenderLawCenter.org.

The ACLU LGBTQ/HIV Project, 125 Broad Street, New York, New York 10004 has a toll free telephone number 1-888-567-ACLU or http://www.aclu.org.

APPENDIX III, Homeless Youth Services in Some Major Cities

Below is a list of youth oriented homes and services for LGBTQ youths in some major cities. Another source for many youth services is Covenant House with facilities in many locations in the United States and Latin America (www.covenanthouse.org click on *Get Help* and scroll down for many other. For other sources of assistance, contact your state or local social services department.

California
LA Gay and Lesbian Homeless Youth Services
Kruks/Tilsner Transitional Housing
1625 N. Schrader Boulevard
Los Angeles, CA 90028
1-888-255-2429

Gay and Lesbian Adolescent Social Services
650 North Robertson Boulevard
West Hollywood, CA 90069
1-310-358-8727

Larkin Street Youth Services
Eliza Gibson, Chief of Programs
Administrative Offices
1138 Sutter Street
San Francisco, CA 94109
1-415-673-0911

Colorado
Urban Peak Denver
Craig Archibald, CEO
730 21st Street
Denver, CO 80205
1-303-295-9198

Florida
SunServe Center, LGBTQ Youth
1480 SW Ninth Avenue

Fort Lauderdale, FL
1-954-764-5557

Florida continued
Florida Keys Children's Shelter,
Administrative Office
73 High Point Road
Tavernier, FL 33070
1-305-852-6903

Key West Satellite Office
5503 College Road, Suite 2085,
Key West, FL
1-305-852-4246

Illinois
Melissa McGuire, director
Youth Shelter Network
4711 N. Ravenswood Avenue, Chicago, IL 60640-4407
Toll free number for youths
1-877-286-2423

Open Door Youth Shelter (West Town)
The Night Ministry
4711 N. Ravenswood Ave.,
Chicago, IL 60640-4407
1-773-784-9000
Toll free number for youths
1-877-286-2523

Massachusetts
Cloby Berger, Ed.M.
GLBT Training Manager
The Home for Little Wanderers
780 American Legion Highway
Roslindale, MA 02131
1-617-469-8581
cberger@thehome.org

Michigan
Ruth Ellis Center
Grace A. McClelland, Executive Director
77 Victor Street
Highland Park, MI 48203
1-313-252-1950

New York
Sylvia's Place
Kate Barnhart, Program Manager
446 West 36th Street
New York, NY 10018
1-718-300-0133

NYC Chimneys Children's Services
Bill Chong
156 William Street
New York, NY 10038
1-800-246-4646

APPENDIX IV, Transgender Population

There is no way of determining the exact number of transgender children, women, and men. There must be a large number of closeted crossdressers who keep their transgenderism a deep secret, never buy transgender literature, look at transgender web sites, or engage in anything other than crossdressing in private. Also, a large number of transgender people are in denial and never dress due to society's intense transphobia.

Many population reports refer to 1:30,000. This was based on a count of old hospital records indicating a gender operation was performed. More recent studies show the number of transsexual operations is greater. The transgender population appears to be increasing commensurate with better understanding and subsequent acceptance. Also, transgender women's numbers seem to indicate a larger population of transgender people than previously believed.

My personal feeling is transgenderism occurs far more often than the current belief. I feel transgenderism will involve roughly 10% or more of the population based on the Thailand High School experience. However, the Bangkok estimate is too high for current thinking.

Estimates of Transgender Population - Various Sources (in millions)

ESTIMATED BY	RANGE USED	U.S. TG POPUL[1]	WORLD TG POPUL[2]
TransEquality	1/4 to 1% 1/2%	1.7	34.9
GRIS	1%	3.1	69.7
Transgender Law	2 to 5% 3.5%	11.0	244.1
Williams Institute	3%	0.9	20.1
MA Behavioral Risk Factor Surveillance Survey	.5%	1.6	34.9
China Yu (2009)	.5 to .6% .55%	1.7	34.9
Thailand High School[3]	--	58.1[4]	1290.1[4]
United Kingdom	.8%	2.5	55.8

Population Calculation:

Eliminating the Thailand estimate, the highest estimate (Transgender Law) and lowest estimate (Williams Institute):(1.7+3.1+1.6+1.7+2.5 = 10.6 million. total of 5 locations
10.6 million divided by 5 locations) =
2.1 MILLION Estimated Transgender People Now in the United States.

Notes To Chart

1   314 million—population in the U.S. per U.S. Census Bureau.
2   6,974 million—population in the world per World Bank.
3   BBC, July 8, 2008 reported: The Head teacher, Sitisak Sumontha, said in his 35 years of working in the Thailand education system, he has consistently seen between 10% and 20% of the boys who want to grow to be women. "Many go on to have sex change surgery, while others will live as gay men." I have used the median of 15% (10% to 20%) less 5% to account for those that will live as gay men (roughly based on the study in Chapter 4, the Homosexual Connection, Figure B). To account for transgender men, I used 8.5%. A smaller number of transgender men is used to approximate to effect of polluting chemicals and the effect of the predominantly female hormones in the mother's womb, which tend to feminize. This yields a total of 18.5%.
4   Society is not ready for such a high number (18.5%); however, we know that the number of known transgender people grows as transgenderism is better understood and more closeted people come out. Thailand is an example of the number of transgender people when society is more permissive.

APPENDIX V, Category Versus Age of Transgender
Realization

CONCLUSION

Age and Category: There appears to be a correlation between a person's age when first realizing they are or when first realizing they want to be a different gender from the label assigned at birth. They have what is classified as a moderate correlation, which is meaningful for psychological studies. Furthermore, their P Score indicates the results are highly significant. That is, there is less than 1/10 of 1% probability that results are due to chance $(r(43) = .49, p < .001)$.

Generally, people whose memory recalls an incident between ages 3 and 6 believed they ARE or once believed they were female. People whose first memory of transgenderism is around puberty, "WANTed" to be a woman. The 6 respondents whose first memory indicated they LIKE to dress as a woman (i.e., like to be a woman sometimes?) reported an age 2 to 3 times the puberty ages. They were considered out-of-range and not included in the study. This considers a person's first memory and is separate from how they react to being a transgender person. How they react depends a good deal on their nurturing. The intent of this study was to not consider behavior.

Secrecy: Regardless of any other factor, all participants always knew it was a secret from their earliest memory or immediately after the experience of their earliest memory.

Birth Order: There does not seem to be a correlation with any other data.

Marital Status: There does not seem to be a correlation with any other data.

COMMENTS:

The group participating in the survey is becoming more open about their feelings. Two years ago I received a little more than half the 49 responses to this survey (6 respondents were in their late 30s and

40s) out of the range of this study resulting in a consideration of 43 in the sample. It should be noted that the survey depended on memory, self-appraisal, and individual differences. Therefore, it is expected that the sample will be quite scattered. In fact, the results indicates the participants were quite objective in their self-appraisal.

QUESTIONS ASKED

QUESTION 1: In which Category would you fit best at your earliest memory of being different?
Category 1. You actually ARE a women, similar to being in the wrong body.
Category 2. You feel you are not a woman, but WANT to be a woman.
Category 3. You never wanted to be a woman and don't want to be one now, but LIKE to dress as a woman.

QUESTION 2: At what age do you remember first discovering you are a woman, want to be a woman, or liked to dress as a woman?

QUESTION 3: When you first remembered Question 2 above, did you know it needed to be a secret?

QUESTION 4: What is the order number of child in your family (e.g., only child, oldest of 3, oldest of 2, middle of 3, etc.).

QUESTION 5: Your "marital" status (e.g., single, married, separated or divorced).

Scatter Diagram—Category Verses Age

The slanted line is line of best fit and excludes those whose first memory occurred over the ages listed.

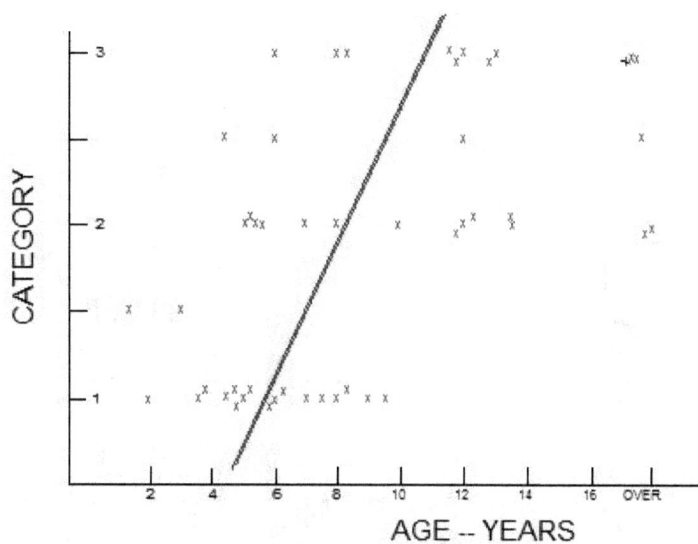

$r(43) = .49, p < .001$

APPENDIX VI, Survey-No Assaults Due To Transgender Non-discrimination Laws 12/10/2017

THE FACTS - SEXUAL ASSAULT RESULTING FROM TRANSGENDER NON-DISCRIMINATION LAWS

LAW DATE	LOCATION	STATEMENT BY & STATEMENT
1993	Minnesota	Minneapolis Police Dept. : Fears About Sexual Assault "Not Even Remotely" A Problem.
1997	Cambridge MA	Police Superintendent : "No Incidents" Of Transgender Protections Being Abused
2001	Rhode Island	State Commission for Human Rights Spokesman Charlie Burr : No Increase In Sex Crimes Due To Non-Discrimination Law
2003	New Mexico	Albuquerque Police Department : Unaware Of Any Cases Of Assault Due To Non-Discrimination Law.
2005	Maine	State Human Rights Commission: "No Factual Basis" For Sexual Assault Fears
2006	Hawaii	William Hoshijo, Executive Director, Civil Rights Comm : Non-Discrimination Law "Has Not Resulted In Increase[d] Sexual Assault Or Rape.
2007	Vermont	State Human Rights Commission: "We Are Not Aware" Of Any Problems From Non-Discrimination Law.
2007	Oregon	Bureau of Labor and Industries spokesman : "Zero Allegations" Of Assault Due To 2007 Law.
2007	Iowa	Des Moines Police Department : Hadn't seen cases of sexual assault related to the state's non-discrimination ordinance
2008	Colorado	Colorado Coalition Against Sexual Assault : Reported no problems as a result of her state's non-discrimination law.
2011	Nevada	Las Vegas Police Department : The department had not "had any incidents involving transgender suspects."
2011	Connecticut	State Commission On Human Rights : "Unaware Of Any Sexual Assault."

BIBLIOGRAPHY

"Adolescence," Committee on Normal Adolescence, Group for the Advancement of Psychiatry, New York, New York, Charles Scribner's Sons, 1968.

Bailey, J. Michael, *The Man Who Would Be Queen: The Science of Gender Bending and Transsexualism*, Washington, D.C., Joseph Henry Press, 2003.

Bandura, Albert and Walters, Richard H., *Social Learning and Personality Development*, New York, New York, Holt, Rinehart, and Winston, 1963.

Benjamin, Harry, M.D., *The Transsexual Phenomenon*, New York, New York, Julian Press, 1966.

Berglund, H., "Male-to-Female Transsexuals Show Sex-Atypical Hypothalamus Activation When Smelling Odorous Steroids." Life Sciences and Medicine—Cerebral Cortex. December 3, 2007, Volume 18, Issue 8, Pages 1900-1908.

Berkowitz, Leonard, *the Development of Motives and Values in the Child*, New York, New York, Basic Books, Inc., 1964.

Boyd, Helen, *My Husband Betty*, New York, New York, Thunders Mouth Press, 2003.

Bradshaw, John, *Healing the Shame That Binds You*, Deerfield Beach, Florida, Health Communications, Inc., 1988.

Brill, Stephanie and Pepper, Rachel, *The Transgender Child, A Handbook for Families and Professionals*, San Francisco, California, Cleis Press, Inc. 2008.

Brizendine, Louann, M.D., *The Female Brain*, New York, New York, Three Rivers Press, 2006-2007.

Burke, Phyllis, *Gender Shock* New York, New York, Anchor Books, 1996.

Chung, W.J., De Vries, G.J., and Swaab, Dick, (2007) "Sex Differentiation of the Bed Nucleus of the Stria Terminalis in Humans May Extend Into Adulthood," Journal of Neuroscience, Volume.22, Number 3, Pages 1027-1033.

Colapinto, John, *As Nature Made Him*, Scarborough, Ontario, Canada, Harper Collins Canada Ltd., 2001.

Cromwell, Jason, *Trans men and FTMs*, Urbana and Chicago, Illinois, University of Illinois Press, 1999.

Diamond, Lisa, Ph.D., *Sexual Fluidity—Understanding Women's Love And Desires*, Boston, Massachusetts, Harvard University Press, 2008.

Diamond, Milton, "Biased-Interaction Theory of Psychosexual Development: How Does One Know if One is Male or Female?" Sex Roles (2006). Volume 55, Pages: 589-600.

Eagerly, Alice H., Beall, A.E., Sternberg, R.J., editors, *The Psychology of Gender, Second Edition*, New York, New York, The Guilford Press, 2004.

Ford, Clallan S. and Beach, Frank A., *Patterns of Sexual Behavior, New York*, New York, Harper and Row, 1951.

Forisha, Barbara Lusk, *Sex Roles and Personal Awareness*, Morristown, New Jersey, Silver Burdett Co., General Learning Press, 1978.

Falgueras, Garcia A., Swaab, D.F., "A Sex Difference in the Hypothalamic Uncinate Nucleus: Relationship to Gender Identity." Brain, November 2, 2008, Pages 3132-3146.

Hagner, Drake, "Fighting for Our Lives: The D.C. Trans Coalition's Campaign for Humane Treatment of Transgender Inmates in District Of Columbia Correctional Facilities." The Georgetown Journal of Gender and the Law, 2010, Volume XI, Pages 837-867.

Hendricks, Melissa, "Into the Hands of Babes—Decline of the Male," Johns Hopkins Magazine, Health and Medicine, September, 2000.

Herman, Joanne, *Transgender Explained For Those Who Are Not*, Bloomington, Indiana, Author House, 2009.

Hirschfeld, Magnus, M.D., "*The Transvestites—An Erotic Drive To Cross Dress* translated by Lombardi-Nash, Michael A., Ph.D., Amherst, New York, Reissued by Prometheus Books, 1991.

Hutt, Corinne, *Males and Females*, Baltimore, Maryland, Penguin Books, Inc. 1972.

Kailey, Matt, *Just Add Hormones—An Insider's Guide to the Transsexual Experience*, Boston, Massachusetts, Beacon Press, 2005.

Kinsey, Alfred C., Pomeroy, Wardell B. and Martin, Clyde E. *Sexual Behavior in the Human Male*, Bloomington, Indiana, The University of Indiana Press, 1948.

Krafft-Ebing, Richard von (1886) *Psychopathia Sexualis*, Republished New York, New York, Arcade Publishing, 1998.

Kruijver, Frank P.M., Zhou, Jiang-Ning, Pool, Chris W., Hofman Michel A., Gooren, Louis J.G. and Swaab, Dick F. (2000), "Male-to-female Transsexuals Have Female Neuron Numbers in a Limbic Nucleus," The Journal of Clinical Endocrinology and Metabolism, Volume 85, Number 5, Pages 2034-2041.

LeVey, Simon, "A Difference in Hypothalamic Structure Between Heterosexual and Homosexual Men," Science, Volume 253, Number 5023, Pages 1034-1037.

Levi, Jennifer and Redman, Daniel, "The Cross Dressing Case for Bathroom Equality."_ Seattle University Law Review, 2010, Volume 34, Pages 68-70.

Lipsitt, Lewis P., and Levy, N., "Electrotactal Threshold Neonate," Child Development, ' 1959, Volume 30, Pages 547-534.

294

Meyerowitz, Joanne, *How Sex Changed: A History of Transsexuality in the United States*, Boston, Massachusetts, Harvard University Press, 2002.

Minter, Shannon "Transgender People and Marriage: The Importance of Legal Planning" booklet, National Center for Lesbian Rights, 870 Market Street, Suite 370, San Francisco, California, 2002.

Money, J., and Lewis, V., "IQ, Genetics and Accelerated Growth: Androgenital Syndrome," Department of Psychiatry and Behavioral Sciences and Department of Pediatrics Bulletin, Johns Hopkins Hospital, 1966, Volume 118, Pages: 365-373.

Pharr, Suzanne, *Homophobia, a Weapon of Sexism*, Inverness, CA, Chardon Press, 1988.

Morrison, Eleanor S. and Borosage, Vera, *Human Sexuality, Contemporary Perspectives*, Palo Alto, California, Mayfield Publishing Company, 1977.

Robinson, Gene, *God Believes in Love*, New York, Alfred A. Knoff, 2012.

Schaffer, Kay F., *Sex Role Issues in Mental Health*, Reading, Pennsylvania, Addison Wesley Publishing Company, 1980.

Serano, Julia, *Whipping Girl, A Transsexual Woman on Sexism and the Scapegoating of Femininity*, Berkeley, California, Seal Press, 2007.

Shalit, Willa, editor, *Becoming Myself, Reflections On Growing Up Female*, New York, New York Hyperion Books, 2006.

Werner, Heinz, *Comparative Psychology of Mental Development*, New York, New York, Editions, Inc., 1948.

Wilhelm, Amara Das, *Tritiya-Prakriti: People of the Third Sex*, Philadelphia, Pennsylvania, Xlibris Corporation, 2008.

Zhou: Jiang-Ning, Hofman, Michel A., Gooren, Louis J.G., and Swaab, Dick F., "A Sex Difference in the Human Brain and Its Relation to Transsexuality," Nature, 1997, Volume 378, Pages 68-70.

<u>OTHER eBOOKS BY JOANNE BORDEN</u>

The Transgender Monologues, Gender, Sexuality, and LGBTQ Life.

>A compilation of 58 essays and short stories concerning various aspects of the lives of transgender people, all LGBTQ people, and some issues that all people must deal with. One reader said, "The monologues are enlightening, entertaining, and always provocative."

and

Identical Treatment In The Machine Of The Law, The Quest For Transgender Civil Rights.

>A simple explanation of transgenderism, the need for laws that protect transgender people from harmful discrimination, the opposition to transgender civil rights, and over 50 speeches that may contain ideas for advocates to use in furthering civil rights.

###

www.ingramcontent.com/pod-product-compliance
Lightning Source LLC
Chambersburg PA
CBHW062201270326
41930CB00009B/1603